Unruly Penelopes and the Ghosts

Unruly Penelopes and the Ghosts

Narratives of English Canada

EVA DARIAS-BEAUTELL
editor

WILFRID LAURIER
UNIVERSITY PRESS

This publication has been generously funded by the Spanish Ministry of Education (Research Project Reference HUM2006-09288FIL) with the collaboration of the TransCanada Institute (University of Guelph). Wilfrid Laurier University Press acknowledges the financial support of the Government of Canada through the Canada Book Fund for our publishing activities.

trañsCanâðа
— INSTITUTE —

Library and Archives Canada Cataloguing in Publication

Unruly Penelopes and the ghosts : narratives of English Canada / Eva Darias-Beautell, editor.

Includes bibliographical references and index.
Issued also in electronic format.
ISBN 978-1-55458-363-8

1. Canadian literature (English)—20th century—History and criticism. 2. National characteristics, Canadian, in literature. I. Darias-Beautell, Eva

PS8071.4.U57 2012   C810.9'0054   C2011-907620-9

Electronic monograph in PDF format.
Issued also in print format.
ISBN 978-1-55458-638-7 (PDF)

1. Canadian literature (English)—20th century—History and criticism. 2. National characteristics, Canadian, in literature. I. Darias-Beautell, Eva

PS8071.4.U57 2012   C810.9'0054   C2011-907620-9

© 2012 Wilfrid Laurier University Press
Waterloo, Ontario, Canada
www.wlupress.ca

Cover design and front-cover image by David Drummond. Text design by Daiva Villa, Chris Rowat Design.

This book is printed on FSC recycled paper and is certified Ecologo. It is made from 100% post-consumer fibre, processed chlorine free, and manufactured using biogas energy.

Printed in Canada

Every reasonable effort has been made to acquire permission for copyright material used in this text, and to acknowledge all such indebtedness accurately. Any errors and omissions called to the publisher's attention will be corrected in future printings.

No part of this publication may be reproduced, stored in a retrieval system, or transmitted, in any form or by any means, without the prior written consent of the publisher or a licence from the Canadian Copyright Licensing Agency (Access Copyright). For an Access Copyright licence, visit http://www.accesscopyright.ca or call toll free to 1-800-893-5777.

Contents

Acknowledgements
vii

INTRODUCTION
Why Penelopes? How Unruly? Which Ghosts?
Narratives of English Canada
Eva Darias-Beautell
1

ONE
Rewriting Tradition: Literature,
History, and Changing Narratives in English
Canada since the 1970s
Coral Ann Howells
19

TWO
(Reading Closely) Calling for the Formation
of Asian Canadian Studies
Smaro Kamboureli
43

THREE
When Race Does Not Matter, "except to everyone else":
Mixed Race Subjectivity and the Fantasy of a Post-Racial Canada in
Lawrence Hill and Kim Barry Brunhuber
Ana María Fraile
77

FOUR
Of Aliens, Monsters, and Vampires: Speculative Fantasy's Strategies of Dissent (Transnational Feminist Fiction)
Belén Martín-Lucas
107

FIVE
The Production of Vancouver: Termination Views in the City of Glass
Eva Darias-Beautell
131

SIX
Jane Rule and the Memory of Canada
Richard Cavell
157

SEVEN
Confession as Antidote to Historical Truth in *River Thieves*
María Jesús Hernáez Lerena
183

EIGHT
Indigenous Criticism and Indigenous Literature in the 1990s: Critical Intimacy
Michèle Lacombe
199

Contributors
225

Index
229

Acknowledgements

This work is the result of a three-year international research project on contemporary Canadian fiction funded by the Spanish Ministry of Education with the participation of Canadian literature specialists from Spain, Canada, and the UK. The project's title was "Penelope's Embroidery: Literary Tradition, Cultural Identities, and Theoretical Discourses in the Anglo-Canadian Fiction of the Late 20th Century" (Code: HUM2006-09288FIL, 2007–2010: http://penelopewebproject.googlepages.com/penelopeproject).

I wish to thank all the contributors to this collection for their work and their patience with the revision process. Special thanks go to Coral Ann Howells, for her creative energy and helpful suggestions, and to Smaro Kamboureli, for her constant support and generosity, in particular for hosting one of this project's workshops at the TransCanada Institute, which she directs, and for funding, through her Canada Research Chair, the index of this book. I am also very grateful to Brian McMorrow for letting me use his photographic work and for his love.

INTRODUCTION

Why Penelopes? How Unruly? Which Ghosts? Narratives of English Canada

Eva Darias-Beautell

In "Notes from the Cultural Field: Canadian Literature from Identity to Commodity," Barbara Godard interrogates the changing paradigms in Canadian literary discourses between the 1950s and the 1990s, a period of immense transformation not only in the spatial composition of the social imaginary of the nation (extending its territory within and beyond Canada), but also in the conditions of possibility for articulating a consensual notion of communal identity. Probing Northrop Frye's famous diagnosis of the national culture as a paradox and a riddle, in the question "Where is here?" ("Conclusion" 338), Godard sets out to analyze the differences between "here" and "there," "now" and "then," with the intention of elucidating the extent and impact of the transformations that the second half of the twentieth century has introduced into the literary and cultural fields. "To a certain extent, nothing has changed," she writes, alluding to the continuity of the nation as the major narrative frame for thinking the literary and of identity as the centre of critical practice, "though literature serves to mobilize the claims of many groups for inclusion in a more broadly imagined community reconfiguring the nation" (248). From a different, larger perspective, however, Godard continues, "everything has changed under the material conditions produced by the rise of a distinctively transnational capitalism" (248). It is to the complex logic of relations produced by these diverse signifying systems that critical attention should turn, "rather than parse the allegories through which the nation's culture is expressed and its identity discerned" (270). Writing in 2000, and providing a shrewd commentary on the material, political, historical, and institutional conditions of production of Canadian literature at that time, Godard advances the constituents of an effective critical discourse for the twenty-first century.

This collection of essays is the result of a three-year international research project on contemporary Canadian fiction and criticism, with the participation of scholars from Spain, Canada, and the UK. Under the title "Penelope's Embroidery: Literary Tradition, Cultural Identities and Theoretical Discourses in the Anglo-Canadian Fiction of the Late 20th Century," the project proposed to explore the possibilities of innovative approaches to the cultural and literary contexts of English Canada over the last forty years. We took the nationalist movement of the 1960s and '70s as a starting point, when the supposed absence or weakness of a national sense became the touchstone for official discourses about cultural identity. In those years, I believed, that metaphor of *lack* provided the nation, somehow paradoxically, with the distinctive elements it was looking for and contributed to the creation of an oxymoronic sense of tradition that had, to some extent, survived to the end of the century. "The difficulty of celebrating the nation as a function of dismissing it," writes Robert Lecker in this context, "creates a potent paradox that is eminently Canadian" (10). In the following decades, however, critics, artists, and writers repeatedly questioned such a fragile and centralizing model of national identity by reading the nation from the new perspectives that had thrived within the discourses of alternative social and theoretical paradigms such as multiculturalism, environmentalism, cultural studies, queer theory, feminism, or post-colonialism.[1] I could, in fact, suggest that the artistic and cultural flowering which Canada is experiencing at the beginning of the twenty-first century is, to a great extent, based on the dismantling, from the above perspectives, of the few images constructed only forty years ago to represent the nation. Moreover, an immense and promising field of literary creativity is taking place as a result of a constant process of questioning of, and resistance to, official modes of national belonging.

The project's starting point was thus a questioning of the rhetoric of absence mentioned above as well as the current validity of certain tropes of supposed national identification. I argued for the existence of a plural and fluid Canadian narrative tradition, created ironically through a process of deconstruction of those official discourses and from the new perspectives opened by the literary and cultural theories of the 1980s and '90s. The chronological frame was tentatively and only implicitly located between 1972, when Margaret Atwood's *Survival* was published, and the mid-2000s, when the idea of *The Cambridge History of Canadian Literature,* edited by Coral Ann Howells and Eva-Marie Kröller, was conceived.[2] Atwood's seminal text was representative of the ideology of cultural nationalism, with its Ontario-centred construction of a national identity around wilderness tropes, and in a direct relation of opposition to much more powerful British and American traditions. That the book soon became a landmark of Canadian literature, Northrop Frye remarked in 1977, was partly due to its title: "the word 'survival' in itself implies a discontinuous series of crises, each to be met on its own terms, each having to face the imminent threat of not surviving" (Frye, "Haunted" 474).

The second text, *The Cambridge History of Canadian Literature,* was the product of international collaboration and was still in the making when the Penelope project was designed. Those circumstances provided us with an outer framework of analysis in process that ran somehow parallel to, and at times intersected with, our own research.[3] As Coral Ann Howells explains in the first essay of this book, the most difficult task was not only to decide what to include in the new literary history and why, but to work within the intensely self-conscious and highly self-deconstructive literary and cultural contexts of contemporary CanLit. The very project of a literary history threatened to undermine itself, sometimes working against the editors' initial plans and changing their directions and strategies to accommodate new issues and previously excluded information. I thought that the complications attending the process of making this history could act as a paradigm of the current decentralization of the idea of national identity as well as of the displacement, literal (spatial) and metaphorical, of the parameters that constituted such a Canadian literary project. In methodological terms, the distance between Atwood's structuralist, thematic approach and Howells's and Kröller's literary history, written at a moment in which post-structuralist theories of literature are being rethought and rearticulated in a new light, also seems rich and relevant. The physical, temporal, thematic, and methodological spaces between those two moments (the *here* and the *there,* the *then* and the *now*) define, in my opinion, the process of maturation of Canadian literary tradition and may contain, I believe, the *essence* and the basis of its contemporary fiction and criticism.

Through their readings of representative primary and critical texts, their contextual analyses, and their selected methodological tools, the essays in this collection offer a tapestry of approaches to that *Penelopian* process of simultaneous dismantling and reconstruction of the Canadian tradition. Despite the growing number of studies dedicated to the analysis of contemporary Canadian texts from a variety of theoretical viewpoints, I believe there still is a critical need to analyze recent Canadian production as both self-deconstructive and creative of a solid literary tradition. This book pursues such a double objective. It is born from the hypothesis that the literature written and published in the past few decades often aims at deconstructing the national myths that, created in the 1960s, have somehow haunted literary and cultural production in Canada since. A parallel focus is placed on the processes of producing and supporting an incipient literary tradition that is potentially more inclusive and plural, and that, despite its self-promoting fluidity, is providing the nation with sound literary grounds. On the larger cultural and social planes, the essays that follow trace lines of connection and interaction between contemporary Canadian narrative and transnational discourses of culture, as well as between such literary production and current sociopolitical movements that have preceded it and that now go hand in hand with it, such as feminism, (post-)colonial and diaspora studies, queer studies, theories of hybridity, and environmentalism. On the theoretical and methodological planes, they implicitly address the role of Canadian literature in the current revision of post-structuralist paradigms, evaluating their influence as well as their limits, articulating new relationships, and retrieving and reclaiming a meaningful corpus of texts. In so doing, the collection as a whole attests to the fact that CanLit cannot be taken for granted, for the discipline "resonates with the same ambiguities characterizing literature at large, but also with the complexities—even nervousness—associated with its own history and location," writes Smaro Kamboureli in this context (in uncanny reverberation with Frye's words on *Survival* above). "The specific trajectories of CanLit bespeak a continuing anxiety over intent and purpose, its ends always threatening to dissolve" (Kamboureli, Preface viii).

The reference to Greek mythology is thus not frivolous or casual. It draws our attention to the continuous process of unmooring dominant literary paradigms both in criticism and in the very fictions that make CanLit. It is also designed to highlight the multiple threads of connection between Canadian literatures and the world outside, where many writers have been fascinated by the possibilities contained in the mythological act of (un)weaving as a linguistic, feminist, or post-colonial trope. Literary critics in the twentieth century have produced numerous seminal interpretations of the enigmatic mythical weavers and their post-structuralist potential as a critical methodology. From Walter Benjamin's "The Image of Proust" to J. Hillis Miller's *Ariadne's Thread*, from Nancy Miller's "Arachnologies: The Woman, the Text, and the Critic" to Susan Stanford Friedman's *Penelope's Web* to Barbara Clayton's *A Penelopean Poetics*, readings of the (un)weaving act abound that put forward the intertwining of remembrance and forgetting, writing and reading, presence and absence.

Yet the approaches have not always been resolutely affirmative. In the mid-1990s, and signalling what could be called a post-structuralist fatigue, David Hirsch would use the powerful Penelopian metaphor with a tone of frustration to describe what he then saw as the trivialization of literary practices: "What one critic (or 'school' of critics) weaves by day, another unravels at night. Nor can we console ourselves with the notion that this weaving and unweaving constitutes a dialectic, since no forward movement takes place. Nevertheless, the theory industry prospers, never completing the robe, never even progressing toward completion, just laboring assiduously till the eyes grow dim and the fingers falter" (Hirsch 23).

Elsewhere, from the perspective of feminist theory, the validity of the mythical trope also seems highly contested today. For some critics, rather than providing a liberating possibility, Penelope's role in the *Odyssey* has come to represent what feminism should fight against: passivity, stasis, and the representation of women as objects of male desire. For others, the ambiguity of Penelope's actions invites a deconstructive reading of the character as both central to the work's meaning (through Penelope's web) and undermining, at the same time, its desire for closure (through the strategy of postponement thereby contained). After all, as Barbara Clayton suggests, "the web itself is a coded language which contains the major themes of the *Odyssey*: memory and forgetting, marriage and death and trickery" (Clayton 18).[4]

In Canada, as we have suggested, the metaphor could figure as paradigm of the contradictory processes of formation of cultural memory, identity, canon, and literary traditions, constantly unmooring familiar tropes. Most interestingly, however, the elements of ambiguity, dissonance, and contradiction revealed by a meta-critical history of the Penelopian trope seem to fit well with those processes, akin perhaps to the formation of many contemporary literary traditions, but especially *unruly,* or so it seems, in the Canadian case. In a literal sense, Atwood's *The Penelopiad* appears to be an obvious instance of this unruliness, a retelling of Homer's story from a multiplicity of viewpoints, including Penelope's (the story's leading voice) and her maids' (in the way of a chorus). In this version of Homer's myth, the ambiguity of Penelope's actions (her work of [un]weaving, her supposed faithfulness, and, especially, her complicity in the killing of the maids), remain side by side with the introduction of perspective and polyphony—an interesting combination of complicity with, and critique of, master narratives that has been said to also characterize CanLit today (see Hutcheon).

Yet (arguably) one of the most unruly characters in Canadian fiction to this day is the protagonist of Aritha van Herk's novel *No Fixed Address*

(1987), a daring character who, implicitly signalling the limitations of Penelope as a feminist model, is instead called Arachne, after the mortal weaver in Ovid's *Metamorphoses*. "I want to trouble the reader, to upset, annoy, confuse; to make the reader react to the unexpected, the unpredictable, the amoral, the political," van Herk writes. "I want to explode writing as prescription, as a code for the proper behaviour of good little girls" (*In Visible* 131). In the novel, Arachne is a (un)weaver of words and roads, doing and undoing the specific narrative and physical maps of Canada. The text's labyrinthine rewriting of generic and thematic conventions, as well as its web-like spatial structure, certainly indicate alternative ways of dealing with reading, writing, and literary tradition, as well as with female subjectivity. In so doing, it constitutes a brave and daring attempt to break the circles of customary knowledge and enter the uncertain web of alternative fields. The elements of these fields are not, to be sure, spelled out by the novel. Yet, written in the mid-1980s, the text definitely envisions the need for new directions and fresh beginnings.[5] At the same time, as is usually the case in much Canadian criticism and fiction, the strategy of postponement contained in the event of Penelope's web figures prominently in van Herk's text: the making and unmaking of national myths, the mapping and unmapping of new territories, and the permanent inconclusiveness of the discourses that have attempted to liberate CanLit from Fryegian articulations of the national culture. As Diana Brydon puts it (in response to Kertzer's nostalgia-ridden argument in *Worrying the Nation*):

> How hard is it really to conceive of a nation as "a viable cultural form" without this nostalgic evocation of a lost authenticity that never, in truth, existed? The desire for authenticity is certainly part of dominant Canadian literary traditions and is perhaps both celebrated and lamented in Frye's question, but that desire never needed fulfilment to serve its nation-forming function. Indeed, that particular conceptual basis for national identity depends on loss and deferral for its force. (Brydon, "It's Time" 17)

The type of deconstructive approach to tradition we are suggesting does in fact depend on a constant process of loss and deferral. It also relies on a powerful interrelation between the present and the past, memory and forgetting, presence and absence, and can therefore be discussed as a Derridean *hauntology*.[6] In implicitly addressing the function of individual and collective memory in the shaping of national cultures, this form of hauntology asks, as Pamela McCallum would put it (in a different context), "How does the emotion circulating in cultural memory inscribe itself in the present?" (McCallum). This kind of question, in turn, promotes an ontological shift, since as Colin Davis asserts:

Hauntology supplants its near-homonym ontology, replacing the priority of being and presence with the figure of the ghost as that which is neither present nor absent, neither dead nor alive. Attending to the ghost is an ethical injunction insofar as it occupies the place of the Levinasian Other: a wholly irrecuperable intrusion in our world, which is not comprehensible within our available intellectual frameworks, but whose otherness we are responsible for preserving. Hauntology is thus related to, and represents a new aspect of, the ethical turn of deconstruction which has been palpable for at least two decades. (Davis 373)

Associating that kind of spectral dynamics to literature in general, Derrida sees the *spectre's essential secret* as "a productive opening of meaning rather than a determinate content to be uncovered" (Davis 376; see also Derrida, *Papier* 398). According to Davis, "the attraction of hauntology for deconstructive-minded critics arises from the link between a theme (haunting, ghosts, the supernatural) and the processes of literature and textuality in general" (376).

Those links have been explored by Marlene Goldman and Joanne Saul, who, probing the literary possibilities of the notion, argue that "[Derrida's] injunction, tied to a politics of memory and a conception of justice, seems, at least on the surface, vexed and difficult to heed in a settler-nation such as Canada which, for many years, was renowned for its supposed lack of ghosts.... Nonetheless, despite or perhaps because of Birney's suggestion that Canadians are haunted by a lack of spectres, contemporary Canadian authors, artists, and filmmakers are obsessed with ghosts and haunting" (645).[7]

From a very different perspective, yet striking a similar chord, Cynthia Sugars highlights the immense imaginative potential implied in the notion of cultural haunting. In her review of Sherrill Grace's *Inventing Tom Thomson*, a book-length investigation of the role of the figure of the famous painter as part of Canada's collective memory, Sugars comments that Grace's book contradicts Earle Birney's much-quoted assertion that "it's only by our lack of ghosts we're haunted":

And yet, there is something very resonant about the idea of a haunting that both is and is not one. Admittedly, this was Birney's way of nudging his 1960s contemporaries out of their cultural and intellectual somnambulance. It also points to the notorious Canadian identity crisis which persists in dogging cultural debate in Canada today. Notwithstanding the fact that Canada has proven to be haunted by a plethora of national ghosts, from John Franklin to Louis Riel to Thomas D'Arcy McGee to the infamous Donnellys, it may be true that Canadians have long been searching for a nationally resonant (and resident) phantom who would satisfy two needs: the gratifyingly frisson effect that we demand of a ghost, the sort of thing that makes the hair stand up on the back of your neck; and a link with those things that have become fixed in Canadian iconography, namely images of the wilderness and northern landscape, which in turn give Canadians a vicarious sense of history and belonging. Paradoxically, being haunted may be what makes one feel most at home. (Sugars, "Review")

The fact that the role of what Sugars identifies here as nationally resonant images has been highly contested in the past forty years does not seem to lessen the strength of the argument, but rather it contributes to underlining the existence in Canada of a self-erasing hauntological process of the type described above. In that context, while also arguing that the notion of haunting is key to a contemporary understanding of CanLit, Teresa Gibert takes the 1967 centennial of Canadian Confederation as a turning point in the promotion of social and cultural cohesion within an increasingly debated nationalist project. The period following this celebration marked the beginning of a new cultural era where a critical revisiting of Canada's collective memory replaced nostalgia, and the project of constructing a unified sense of tradition was proved impossible. "The 'ghost history' that haunts Canadian literature in the post-1960s is the symbolic representation of those elements of the country's society that were previously barred from consciousness," Gibert writes. These ghosts include the histories of Canadian subjects and parts of the country "whose unfulfilled aspirations illustrate the strains within the Canadian body politic" (478).

In their implicit emphasis on the need to rearticulate Canadian culture's relationship to otherness in more positive ways, these critics hint at the mechanisms of hauntology and delineate a process for the construction of literary tradition as "a productive opening of meaning rather than a determinate content to be uncovered" (Davis 376). Following Gayatri Spivak's arguments in *Death of a Discipline,* where she calls for the necessary interdisciplinarity of the literary field and presents a new intellectual project that she calls *planetary vision*, we could think of the very discipline of CanLit as a ghost in that its nature has notably shifted from the cosy utopian *nationscape* of cultural nationalism to a restless, borderless *globalscape* (see Appadurai). By this, we do not necessarily imply the death of the nationalist project. Rather, the nation persists as haunting force of a tradition that acknowledges its imaginative energy, at the same time as it questions its ideology and power, a double move that has the effect of making the nation's borders more permeable to previously antagonistic notions such as globalization (see Dobson).

Significantly, that is the common argument in Smaro Kamboureli's and Roy Miki's groundbreaking *Trans.Can.Lit: Resituating the Study of Canadian Literature*. Diana Brydon's essay in that collection talks about "the need to rethink Canadian literature beyond older forms of nationalism and internationalism, and towards multiscaled visions of place—local, regional, national, and global—each imbricated within the other" ("Metamorphoses" 14), while Richard Cavell borrows Kwame Anthony Appiah's notion of "rooted cosmopolitanism" to argue for a dynamic engagement with the local and the cosmopolitan, moving away from polarizing debates about Canadian literatures (91). That collection (as well as the Vancouver Conference in which the papers were first presented) has marked a firm step forward, suggesting the beginning of what Kamboureli has called "an elsewhereness," or "an alternative cognitive space" producing "epistemic breaks that require new tools to comprehend its materiality.... This elsewhereness inscribed in CanLit intimates that Canada is an unimaginable community, that is, a community constituted in excess of the knowledge of itself, always transitioning" (Preface x).[8] The essays that follow investigate, from a wide range of perspectives and methodologies, some of the constituents of that community in excess of knowledge as well as the process of its constant transitioning.

* * *

Each essay in this collection addresses a different set of questions. Each seems haunted by a particular ghost and thus explores a particular *spectrum* of methodological, historical, cultural, and literary paradigms. Framed by Howells's and Lacombe's contributions around the significant transformations of normative and indigenous literary histories respectively, the different essays offer relevant critical insights as well as close readings of specific texts, drawing various points of intersection with one another at key discursive moments, such as literary history and the literary institution, race, gender, sexuality, cultural memory, locality, and the body.

Coral Ann Howells's "Rewriting Tradition: Literature, History, and Changing Narratives in English Canada since the 1970s" offers a panoramic inquiry into the processes of production of literary histories in Canada in the past forty years, including a look at key meta-critical texts and anthologies whose institutionalizing drive has intersected with the former historical projects. Howells's focus is on the processes of reshaping the category of Canadianness, and her analysis addresses the ideological, institutional, and historical implications of texts as encoders of particular national images. Both her essay in this book and the much larger and ambitious project of a literary history she undertakes elsewhere (Howells and Kröller, *The Cambridge History*) are examples of the need of what Robert Lecker has called "an effective critique—aesthetic, political, material, social—as a kind of narrative that allows one to see the way things are constructed without necessarily calling for a demolition of what is standing" (8–9). Hence the self-conscious framing of her argument within the parameters of the white Anglo-Canadian literary establishment (namely, around a quotation on historiography from Margaret Atwood's *The Robber Bride*), which Howells turns to the advantage of her argument by demonstrating the capacity of master narratives to provide the elements of their own dismantling. In so doing, this essay resonates with critical strategies and questions structuring the present collection as a whole.

"(Reading Closely): Calling for the Formation of Asian Canadian Studies," by Smaro Kamboureli, affords a shrewd analysis of the power of institutional practices to enforce particular processes of canon formation, connecting thus in fundamental ways with the discussion supplied by Howells about the ideological and methodological conditions of production of CanLit. Kamboureli's essay explores one important aspect of those conditions under the effects of multiculturalism that have resulted in the current racialization and minoritization of certain sectors of the national culture. Specifically, she offers an investigation of the sign *Asian Canadian* in the context of canon formation and literary tradition and vis-à-vis similar developments in the US, where the field has been created as Area Studies. Through an intricate, close reading of key meta-critical texts (namely, Donald Goellnicht's "A Long Labor: The Protracted Birth of Asian Canadian Literature" and "Asian Kanadian, eh?" and Guy Beauregard's "Asian Canadian Studies: Unfinished Projects"), she demonstrates the ambiguity produced by, as well as the paradigm shifts through which, the call for institutionalization of Asian Canadian literature has taken place. This call, Kamboureli reflects, has ultimately failed to unsettle the systemic historical and cultural conditions of normativity that structure the relationship between Asian Canadian literature and CanLit as a national formation. The call for difference and its legitimizing will often transmute into a strategy for the commodification of such difference and the very means of its containment.

The following two essays, by Ana María Fraile and Belén Martín-Lucas, deal, from two very different perspectives, with the material, symbolic, and institutional issues attending diasporic writers/texts and their resistance to the identitary commodification implicitly proposed and implemented by official policies of multiculturalism. In their detailed analyses of the systemic structures that have produced racialized subjects within the national imaginary, these two essays unveil the mechanisms of what Daniel Coleman has called "white civility," a form of "Canadian trance" that operates as an insulation from reality, "a mantra that asserts that Canadians are more civilized than others on all levels" (25). At the same time, these essays work within a double frame of reference, simultaneously within and beyond the national paradigm. The ambiguities that their critical readings of diasporic or transnational subjectivities expose seem proof that, as Diana Brydon has argued, "the contemporary fascination with diaspora is an element of current conjunctions across globalization, community, and culture that requires further investigation. Why is this term attaining such prominence now? How can it help us to rethink and re-enact local and global belongings? What kinds of thinking and acting might it repress?" ("It's Time" 23).

Ana María Fraile's "When Race Does Not Matter, 'except to everyone else': Mixed Race Subjectivity and the Fantasy of a Post-Racial Canada in Lawrence Hill and Kim Barry Brunhuber" analyzes Hill's *Any Known Blood* and Brunhuber's *Kameleon Man* from the perspective of mixed race aesthetics and in the light of recent criticism about the role of African Canadian literature in the current reconfiguration of CanLit. Fraile sets out to prove how a common strategy of unsettling normative notions of Canadian identity is at work in the writing of African Canadian writers of mixed racial origins that exposes the pitfalls of institutional multiculturalism while denouncing the fallacy of post-racial discourses. Furthermore, Fraile argues, the in-betweenness of these mixed race texts dismantles the discourses of both Canadian cultural nationalism and black nationalism: on the one hand, they often look at *African Canadian* not as a supplementary sign of the nation but as a foundational culture in its own right; on the other, the identitary approach they propose is inextricably enmeshed in the globalized context of diasporic hybridity, and thus essentially transnational. If, as Kamboureli suggests in the previous essay, Asian Canadian has recently emerged as a powerful cultural field that is gradually reshaping CanLit, so is African Canadian literature increasingly occupying a position within the institution that forces us to rethink the relationships between the national and the transnational. Interestingly, both Fraile and Kamboureli look at the history of these shifting paradigms vis-à-vis similar developments in the US, but whereas Fraile promotes a reading of African Canadian culture in connection with its African American counterpart, Kamboureli is very suspicious of such a move.

In "Of Aliens, Monsters, and Vampires: Speculative Fantasy's Strategies of Dissent (Transnational Feminist Fiction)," Belén Martín-Lucas interprets the current recourse, in speculative fiction by transnational feminist Canadian writers, to metamorphic strategies as an effective response to dominant assumptions about the racialized and sexualized body. Such strategies are seen as signs of political import that allegorize the "flexible citizen" theorized by Aiwha Ong, a fluid subject both in dearth and in excess of the nation. This essay seems a direct response to Jonathan Kertzer's assertion that for "ethnic, feminist, and Native writers, the bourgeois nation is a monster" (133). Martín-Lucas reads selected texts by Hiromi Goto, Larissa Lai, Nalo Hopkinson, and Suzette Mayr against the context of institutional multiculturalism with the intention of theorizing the possibilities of speculative fiction, in particular, its use of body metamorphoses (cyborg, mutant, post-human bodies), as a critique of the neo-liberal nation-state, upon whose ideology official multicultural policies are currently implemented. Writing through what Kamboureli has elsewhere called the "scandalous body," a figure of excess that escapes official inscription (*Scandalous*), becomes thus a key form of cultural and political dissent.

Shifting the focus towards the interaction between the local and the global, together with the significant challenges to land-based approaches to the nation that have proliferated in recent years, "The Production of Vancouver: Termination Views in the City of Glass," investigates the function of literature and art in both producing and contesting spatial modes of urban belonging in contemporary Canada. This essay could be framed within the current turn in critical discourse towards the recognition of Canada's always already urban nature (see Edwards and Ivison). It offers a reading of the representation of Vancouver in a selection of contemporary texts and artworks vis-à-vis one another. The aim is to disclose the labyrinthine structures within the social construction of place as well as to investigate how these works may function as "termination views," a notion put forward by Cliff Eyland in relation to Bernie Miller's and Alan Tregebov's deconstructive techniques and implying a particular work's capacity to block or cancel a certain spatial perspective. From a national perspective, the growth of Vancouver as an emblematic "world city" has had important debilitating effects on the city's identity as an extension of the national project; from an urban studies point of view, these transformations may have also implied a drastic loss of the city's social cohesiveness. My essay engages with the ideological implications of those changes by looking at works as sites for the manufacture of discordant images of the city and as effective tools to block idealized views of Vancouver.

In his introductory essay to the special issue of *Essays on Canadian Writing* which addresses the state of CanLit as a discipline at the threshold of the new millennium, Robert Lecker complains about the lack of historical perspective in Canadian criticism. "Contemporary literary nationalism needs memory to survive," he writes, "and memory is in short order these days" (10). Cultural memory in its multiform manifestations is the subject, more or less explicit, of the three remaining essays. The notion is central to "Jane Rule and the Memory of Canada," by Richard Cavell, which rewrites the context of Canadian national identity from the perspective of queer cultural memory. By that, Cavell means *embodied memory*, referring to the belief that sexuality is crucial to our understanding of citizenship and of nationhood. In the first part of this essay, Cavell lays out the basis of a theory of queer cultural memory based on the individual and collective performance of embodied identity. He then applies those questions to the analysis of the work of Jane Rule, emphasizing this writer's interest in the possibility of building communities outside the nation-state ideology of the family. In that sense, Cavell argues, *queer* is not exclusively a sexual denotation, but rather proposes a form of cultural memory that, by introducing an ethics of alterity, denies the completion of identity, national or otherwise. To remember is to forget, and cultural memory is necessarily a never-ending process, as much about including as it is about excluding.

The tensions between remembering and forgetting, speaking and silence, history and experience, also inform "Confession as Antidote to Historical Truth in *River Thieves*," by María Jesús Hernáez Lerena. This essay undertakes a reading of Michael Crummey's *River Thieves*, a Canadian bestseller and award-winning novel about the collective sense of loss and guilt that the extinction of the Beothuk has brought to the narratives of Newfoundland, in the light of confession narratives that, in their own nature, provoke a rupture of the very notion of historical meaning. By choosing to analyze this particular text about a trauma of national dimensions (the demise of the Aboriginal), Hernáez Lerena addresses and revisits the notions of colonial guilt and ambivalence at the heart of Canada's foundational narratives, which Diana Brydon has identified as typical of CanLit and in need of further investigation: "This colonial guilt," Brydon argues, "requires reading beyond thematic or apparent content to explore instead the whole realm of what cannot be told or what can only be told indirectly, through slippages, contradictions, or apparent ungrammaticalities.... Such readings," she continues, "identify symptoms of unease in apparently seamless stories" ("It's Time" 20–21). Accordingly, Hernáez Lerena avoids the most obvious historical interpretation of Crummey's novel and rather aims at investigating the rhetorical strategies that are used to represent the unrepresentable, to figure the meaning of silence and of a sense of permanent loss.

Michèle Lacombe's "Indigenous Criticism and Indigenous Literature in the 1990s: Critical Intimacy" closes the volume with a panoramic discussion of indigenous literary histories, criticism, and fiction. This final essay is designed to talk back to the first, by Howells, acting as a Derridean supplement to it: it adds something that was missing and it is something *else*, transforming received knowledges about both the genre of literary history and the conditions of production, distribution, and reception of the national literature. Lacombe's contribution thus figures the destabilization that post-colonial theories have brought to official definitions of national identity, be they thought in terms of the Fryegian land-based metaphors of the 1960s and '70s or the result of the multicultural policies of the 1980s and '90s. On the one hand, it is now clear that Frye's "here" implicitly excluded an indigenous view of the nation (Hulan 63). On the other, multiculturalism's approaches to aboriginality have continued to be figured within colonial frameworks of otherness (see Mathur). The work of indigenous theoreticians, critics, historians, sociologists, and writers, Lacombe demonstrates, is modifying these preconceptions not only of indigenous literature in Canada, but equally important, of CanLit as a body of national identification, pushing it in directions it may not have otherwise gone.

As Barbara Godard would have it in the quotation which opens this introductory essay, *nothing has changed and everything has changed* in CanLit throughout the past forty years. Dissonance has definitely increased in recent creative, critical, and theoretical writing, drawing attention to "new forms of cultural listening" (Heble 28). There has also been a clear turn in focus from a land-based national identity to the ideological, material, political, and cultural constituents of national identity. And this has implied an important epistemological shift towards what we have called a Penelopian mode of criticism. As Renée Hulan puts it, writing in 2000: "Over the past two decades, criticism has been characterized by readings that debunk, expose, reread, or revise, as critics attempt to show representation at work by analysing language for unstated assumptions and to make transparent the relationship between representational practices and meaning" (64). Hulan's argument here hints at the nature of a self-consciousness that has historically characterized Canadian culture and that, I would further argue, seems to be associated with what Imre Szeman has referred to as "a sense of *belatedness*," or of having arrived "too late for it to be organically distinctive or authentically representative of the national space in which it originates" (189). According to Szeman, this sense of belatedness, which he describes as "a historical-metaphysical problem of cultural inauthenticity," can disappear in the new transnational scenario, in which spatial and temporal differences are flattened out by technology, with its privileging of an *isochronic* image of the world, or "the creation of a single global time in which it is no longer possible to position oneself as out of sync with the main currents of modernity" (190). However, the rampant neo-liberalization of the global paradigm today introduces crucial doubts about the desirability of entering that isochronic order of culture in which the possibility of ideological dissent as well as the ability to think the literary through the cultural, the social, and the political specificities of the nation are also omitted. The essays that follow explore the complexities of this contemporary predicament in unexpected and inviting ways. Together, they seem to read as an unruly *Penelopiad*, weaving and unweaving significant threads of connection within and between national and global cultures, their unravelling arguments self-consciously interrogating Canada's sense of belatedness.

Notes
I wish to thank the anonymous readers of the manuscript for suggesting the need of a longer and more explanatory introduction to this collection of essays. The Introduction above is a response to most of their queries in that respect.

1 The following are just a few important works in the different fields that have modified the way in which Canadian culture is perceived: Daniel Francis's *National Dreams* (history), Cynthia Sugars's *Home-work* and *Unhomely States* (post-colonial theory and practice), Justin Edwards and Douglas Ivison's *Downtown Canada* (urban studies and Canadian fiction), John O'Brian and Peter White's *Beyond the Wilderness* (art history), William H. New's *Land Sliding* (landscape approaches to CanLit), Ian Angus's *A Border Within* (cultural studies), Peter Dickinson's *Here is Queer* (queer studies and CanLit), Smaro Kamboureli and Roy Miki's *Trans.Can.Lit* (literary methodologies), and Julia Emberley's *Defamiliarizing the Aboriginal* (indigenous cultural studies).
2 I am slightly adapting the temporal framework used by Howells and Kröller in their joint keynote lecture delivered at the International Council for Canadian Studies Conference in Ottawa, 2008. This paper was later published as "Switching the Plot: From *Survival* to *The Cambridge History of Canadian Literature*."
3 The fact that one of the editors of *The Cambridge History of Canadian Literature*, Coral Ann Howells, was part of our research team made this close connection possible and also facilitated the articulation of a tentative temporal framework that would include this important work.
4 Clayton is here paraphrasing Ioanna Papadopoulou-Belmehdi's *Le chant de Penelope* (20).
5 For a thorough analysis of the innovative possibilities offered by van Herk's novel, see Howells's "Aritha van Herk's *No Fixed Address*: An Exploration of Prairie Space as Fictional Space" and Darias-Beautell's *Graphies and Grafts*.
6 Although coined by Jacques Derrida in *Spectres de Marx*, there is a second, chronologically prior, source of hauntology in the work of psychoanalysts Nicolas Abraham and Maria Torok, which Derrida had read. These two forms of hauntology may conflict with each other (see Davis).

7 Birney was echoing Catharine Parr Traill, who in 1833 had written: "As to ghosts or spirits they appear totally banished from Canada" (qtd. in Goldman and Saul 645).
8 Kamboureli is implicitly referencing Benedict Anderson's *Imagined Communities: Reflections on the Origin and Spread of Nationalism*.

Works Cited

Anderson, Benedict. *Imagined Communities: Reflections on the Origin and Spread of Nationalism*. New York: Verso, 1996.
Angus, Ian. *A Border Within: National Identity, Cultural Plurality, and Wilderness*. Montreal: McGill-Queen's UP, 1997.
Appadurai, Arjun. *Modernity at Large: Cultural Dimensions of Globalization*. Minneapolis: U of Minnesota P, 1996.
Atwood, Margaret. *The Penelopiad*. Toronto: Knopf, 2005.
Atwood, Margaret. *Survival: A Thematic Guide to Canadian Literature*. Toronto: Anansi, 1972.
Benjamin, Walter. "The Image of Proust." *Illuminations*. Trans. Harry Zohn. New York: Schocken Books, 1969. 201–15.
Brydon, Diana. "It's Time for a New Set of Questions." *Essays on Canadian Writing* 71 (2000): 14–25.
Brydon, Diana. "Metamorphoses of a Discipline: Rethinking Canadian Literature within Institutional Contexts." *Trans.Can.Lit: Resituating the Study of Canadian Literature*. Ed. Smaro Kamboureli and Roy Miki. Waterloo, ON: Wilfrid Laurier UP, 2007. 1–16.
Cavell, Richard. "World Famous across Canada, or TransNational Localities." *Trans.Can.Lit: Resituating the Study of Canadian Literature*. Ed. Smaro Kamboureli and Roy Miki. Waterloo, ON: Wilfrid Laurier UP, 2007. 85–92.
Clayton, Barbara. *A Penelopean Poetics: Reweaving the Feminine in Homer's Odyssey*. Oxford: Lexington, 2004.
Coleman, Daniel. "From Canadian Trance to TransCanada: White Civility to Wry Civility in the CanLit Project." *Trans.Can.Lit: Resituating the Study of Canadian Literature*. Ed. Smaro Kamboureli and Roy Miki. Waterloo, ON: Wilfrid Laurier UP, 2007. 25–44.
Darias-Beautell, Eva. *Graphies and Grafts: (Con)Texts and (Inter)Texts in the Fiction of Four Contemporary Canadian Women*. Brussels: Peter Lang, 2001.
Davis, Colin. "Hauntology, Spectres and Phantoms." *French Studies* 59.3 (2005): 373–79.
Derrida, Jacques. *Papier machine*. Paris: Galilée, 2001.
Derrida, Jacques. *Spectres de Marx*. Paris: Galilée, 1993.
Dickinson, Peter. *Here Is Queer: Nationalisms, Sexualities, and the Literatures of Canada*. Toronto: U of Toronto P, 1999.
Dobson, Kit. *Transnational Canadas: Anglo-Canadian Literature and Globalization*. Waterloo, ON: Wilfrid Laurier UP, 2009.
Edwards, Justin D., and Douglas Ivison, eds. *Downtown Canada: Writing Canadian Cities*. Toronto: U of Toronto P, 2005.

Emberley, Julia. *Defamiliarizing the Aboriginal: Cultural Practices and Decolonization in Canada.* Toronto: U of Toronto P, 2007.

Francis, Daniel. *National Dreams: Myths, Memory, and Canadian History.* Vancouver: Arsenal Pulp, 1997.

Friedman, Susan Stanford. *Penelope's Web: Gender, Modernity, H.D.'s Fiction.* Cambridge: Cambridge UP, 1990.

Frye, Northrop. "Conclusion." (1965). *Literary History of Canada.* 2nd ed. Vol. 2 and 3. Ed. Carl F. Klinck. Toronto: U of Toronto P, 1976. 333–61.

Frye, Northrop. "Haunted by Lack of Ghosts." *Northrop Frye on Canada: Collected Works of Northrop Frye.* Ed. Jean O'Grady and David Staines. Toronto: U of Toronto P, 2003. 472–92.

Gibert, Teresa. "'Ghost Stories': Fictions of History and Myth." *The Cambridge History of Canadian Literature.* Ed. Coral Ann Howells and Eva-Marie Kröller. Cambridge: Cambridge UP, 2009. 478–98.

Godard, Barbara. "Notes from the Cultural Field: Canadian Literature from Identity to Commodity." (2000). *Canadian Literature at the Crossroads of Language and Culture.* Ed. Smaro Kamboureli. Edmonton: NeWest Press, 2008. 235–72.

Goldman, Marlene, and Joanne Saul. "Talking with Ghosts: Haunting in Canadian Cultural Production." *University of Toronto Quarterly* 75.2 (2006): 645–55.

Grace, Sherrill. *Inventing Tom Thomson: From Biographical Fictions to Fictional Autobiographies and Reproductions.* Montreal: McGill-Queen's UP, 2004.

Heble, Ajay. "Sounds of Change: Dissonance, History, and Cultural Listening." *Essays on Canadian Writing* 71 (2000): 26–36.

Hirsch, David. *The Deconstruction of Literature: Criticism after Auschwitz.* Providence: Brown UP, 1991.

Howells, Coral. "Aritha van Herk's *No Fixed Address*: An Exploration of Prairie Space as Fictional Space." *The London Journal of Canadian Studies* 12 (1996): 6–19.

Howells, Coral Ann, and Eva-Marie Kröller, eds. *The Cambridge History of Canadian Literature.* Cambridge: Cambridge UP, 2009.

Howells, Coral Ann, and Eva-Marie Kröller. "Switching the Plot: From *Survival* to *The Cambridge History of Canadian Literature.*" *Canada Exposed / Le Canada a découvert.* Ed. Pierre Anctil, André Loiselle, and Christopher Rolfe. Brussels: Peter Lang, 2009. 45–60.

Hulan, Renée. "Who's There?" *Essays on Canadian Writing* 71 (2000): 61–70.

Hutcheon, Linda. *The Canadian Postmodern: A Study of Contemporary English-Canadian Fiction.* Toronto: Oxford UP, 1988.

Kamboureli, Smaro. Preface. *Trans.Can.Lit: Resituating the Study of Canadian Literature.* Ed. Smaro Kamboureli and Roy Miki. Waterloo, ON: Wilfrid Laurier UP, 2007. vii–xvi.

Kamboureli, Smaro. *Scandalous Bodies: Diasporic Literature in English Canada.* 2nd ed. Waterloo, ON: Wilfrid Laurier UP, 2009.

Kamboureli, Smaro, and Roy Miki, eds. *Trans.Can.Lit: Resituating the Study of Canadian Literature.* Waterloo, ON: Wilfrid Laurier UP, 2007.

Kertzer, Jonathan. *Worrying the Nation: Imagining a National Literature in English Canada.* Toronto: U of Toronto P, 1998.

Lecker, Robert. "Where Is Here Now?" *Essays on Canadian Writing* 71 (2000): 5–13.
Mathur, Ashok. "Cultivations, Land, and a Politics of Becoming." *Cultivating Canada: Reconciliation through the Lens of Cultural Diversity*. Ed. Ashok Mathur, Jonathan Dewar, and Mike DeGagné. Ottawa: Aboriginal Healing Foundation, 2011. 1–10.
McCallum, Pamela. "Questions of Haunting: Jacques Derrida's Specters of Marx and Raymond Williams's Modern Tragedy." *Mosaic* 40.2 (2007). http://www.umanitoba.ca/publications/mosaic.
Miller, J. Hillis. *Ariadne's Thread: Story Lines*. New Haven: Yale UP, 1992.
Miller, Nancy K. "Arachnologies: The Woman, the Text, and the Critic." *The Poetics of Gender*. Ed. Nancy Miller. New York: Columbia UP, 1986. 270–95.
New, William H. *Land Sliding: Imagining Space, Presence, and Power in Canadian Writing*. Toronto: U of Toronto P, 1997.
O'Brian, John, and Peter White. *Beyond the Wilderness: The Group of Seven, Canadian Identity and Contemporary Art*. Montreal: McGill-Queen's UP, 2007.
Papadopoulou-Belmehdi, Ioanna. *Le chant de Penelope: Poetique du tissage feminin dans l'Odyssee (L'Antiquite au present)*. Paris: Belin, 1994.
Spivak, Gayatri Chakravorty. *Death of a Discipline*. New York: Columbia UP, 2003.
Sugars, Cynthia. *Home-work: Postcolonialism, Pedagogy, and Canadian Literature*. Ottawa: U of Ottawa P, 2004.
Sugars, Cynthia. Review of *Inventing Tom Thomson: From Biographical Fictions to Fictional Autobiographies and Reproductions*, by Sherrill Grace. Books in Canada (April 2005). http://www.booksincanada.com/article_view.asp?id=4066.
Sugars, Cynthia, ed. *Unhomely States: Theorizing English-Canadian Postcolonialism*. Toronto: Broadview, 2004.
Szeman, Imre. "Belated or Isochronic? Canadian Writing, Time, and Globalization." *Essays on Canadian Writing* 71 (2000): 186–94.
van Herk, Aritha. *In Visible Ink: Crypto-Frictions*. Edmonton: NeWest Press, 1991.
van Herk, Aritha. *No Fixed Address*. Toronto: Bantam-Seal Books, 1987.

ONE

Rewriting Tradition: Literature, History, and Changing Narratives in English Canada since the 1970s

Coral Ann Howells

> Nothing begins when it begins and nothing's over when it's over, and everything needs a preface: a preface, a postscript, a chart of simultaneous events. History is a construct.... Still, there are definitive moments...
> —Margaret Atwood, *The Robber Bride*

To establish a context for this historical analysis of changes in literary discourse in English Canada over the past forty years, what better place to begin than with Margaret Atwood's deconstruction of the traditional image of history as an authoritative and objective account of the past? This most representative writer of the Anglo-Canadian literary establishment is responding to debates over historiography and the implications of a postmodern distrust of the "grand narratives" of history, religion, and nation (Lyotard xxiv). At the same time, *The Robber Bride* addresses specific issues raised by the ideological shifts that have altered the terms of debate about Canadian identity and heritage. In what has become a contested terrain, the narrative dynamics of history have changed, thus opening the way for new formulations and a restructuring of tradition. However, this relativization of the absolute authority of history does not deny its value as a "construct" (a verbal artifact and explanatory device), for history does establish "definitive moments, moments we use as references"

(*Robber Bride* 4) in our attempts to articulate patterns of recurrence and change across time. Atwood's quotation provides the frame for my critical inquiry into reshaping the category of Canadianness since the 1970s, a period of immensely widened literary and cultural parameters and a new era of national self-consciousness. Arguably literary histories provide a series of such "definitive moments" in the nation's cultural history, representing both a story of heritage and a stock-taking in the present. At the same time, like any form of historiography, the stories they tell, as Hayden White observed, are inevitably shaped "in response to imperatives that are generally extrahistorical, ideological, aesthetic, or mythical in nature" (48). As Atwood's medieval military historian suggests with her talk of "a preface, a postscript, and a chart of simultaneous events," questions of context are crucial, for they determine not only the frame of reference for a particular history but also its theoretical assumptions and methodology, which in turn condition the choice of what materials are included as significant and what are marginalized or excluded. As every decade since the 1970s has been marked by changes in Canada's literary, cultural, and political contexts, my discussion, though it privileges literary histories as encoders of the nation's image, will offer a necessarily limited selection of these, while it will also include anthologies and seminal meta-critical texts about CanLit. Together these chart the changes over decades, as they offer new perspectives on nationalism, historiography, canon debates, gender and ethnicity, post-colonialism, multiculturalism, and globalization.

It may be noted that the most pressing challenge faced by literary historians and critics at the present time is how to situate the diversity of the contemporary Canadian literary scene (composed as it is of multiple narratives with different constructions of cultural memory, different affiliations and loyalties) in relation to four centuries of writing in Canada and to indigenous oral traditions before and after European contact. Clearly the elements of any historical narrative need to be realigned, as "emergent" discourses displace the formerly "dominant" discourse, provoking the need to take into account what is "residual" ("unsettled remains" as Sugars and Turcotte call them), using history itself to tell a different story about the relation between the present and the past.[1]

Thinking about the revisionist impulse in literary histories shown through their responses to shifts in national ideology and to new works produced over the past forty years, we find there is a certain correspondence between the trajectory of the Canadian texts discussed in this collection and the genre's own shape changes. This is no accident, for there are major questions to be addressed which resonate through this collection. These include such questions as: When did diasporic and Aboriginal writing become visible as distinctive components of Canadian literature, and why not earlier? When did Canadian and European critics start noticing "multicultural" writing? When did the new theoretical discourses around feminism, gender and sexuality, postmodernism, post-colonialism, multiculturalism, and environmentalism start to make a difference to the way that Canadian literary history was being written? When did terminology change (such as the replacement of "Indian" and "Eskimo" with "Aboriginal" or "Indigenous," or the first uses of "multicultural" and "diasporic" instead of "ethnic")? When did black Canadian writing and its historical legacies become a presence in the literary canon? How has the relationship between regionalism and nationalism been theorized and transformed in a globalized context? What happened to "Wilderness," the favourite Canadian identity marker for the cultural nationalists? And when did novels with urban settings displace dominant landscape tropes? These are historical issues at the centre of ongoing debates about nation and identity and about the reconstruction of heritage narratives and literary tradition. Charting a course of simultaneous events, we can trace a shift since the late 1970s as Canadian history has gradually been reinterpreted from diverse perspectives, so that the traditional Anglo-French model of a white settler history has been replaced by a more complex scenario of origins, with multiple "foundational moments," occluded histories, and forgotten stories— all "the complicated specific facts of our cultural past" (Hutcheon and Valdés 24) which stand behind or beneath the present contexts for reading and writing Canadianness for Canadians and the rest of the world.

Frame Narratives of CanLit and Signs of Change
The frame narrative of literary histories since the 1970s often begins with Margaret Atwood's *Survival: A Thematic Guide to Canadian Literature* (1972), on which much has been written. Though not a literary history proper, this book, addressed to a popular readership, represents a "definitive moment" when the concept of a distinctive national literature was made visible to Atwood's fellow Anglo-Canadians. Knowing one's literary heritage was represented as an important national survival strategy: "To know ourselves, we must know our own literature" (Atwood, *Survival* 17). Emblematic of cultural nationalist views of Canadian literary tradition, the focus of *Survival* was on establishing Canadian difference from Britain and the US, through an emphasis on literary tropes related to the country's white settler history—wilderness, map-making, colonial victimhood, and staying alive. Adopting a structuralist methodology, Atwood identified "key patterns" which "function like the field markings in bird-books: they will help you to distinguish this species from all others, Canadian

literature from the other literatures with which it is often compared or confused" (13). Atwood made little claim for the originality of her thesis; instead she acknowledged her recent predecessors, Northrop Frye and Carl F. Klinck. (Indeed, Frye is one of the book's dedicatees.) It is to their work, then, that we must turn in order to explore the creation of a frame narrative of Canadian literature that has somehow implicitly survived until the present day.

Klinck's pioneering work, the multi-authored *Literary History of Canada: Canadian Literature in English*, was published in 1965, though the idea had originated in the mid-1950s in a conversation between Klinck and Frye—appropriately enough on an American college campus—with the aim of establishing Canadian literature as an academic discipline with its own scholarly and historical apparatus that would define the distinctiveness of Canada as a nation.[2] That enterprise was symptomatic of 1950s postwar Canadian cultural initiatives, typified by the Massey Report (1951), followed by the establishment of a National Library (1952), the Canada Council (1957), and the beginning of McClelland and Stewart's New Canadian Library series in 1958, which made Canadian fiction available in cheap paperbacks for the first time. Conceived as a project of national significance ("If we do not launch out from a studied knowledge of ourselves and of our own ways, no one else will," writes Klinck in his Introduction, ix), Klinck's *History* was by no means ideologically neutral. Like the Massey Report, it confirmed traditional structures of power and authority, while recognizing Canada's bilingual, bicultural Anglo-French traditions, and that Canada was "a land settled by people of many different origins" (Klinck ix).[3] Yet that recognition did not affect an ideological standpoint that was, as Richard Cavell has remarked, "implicitly white, British, and liberal...somehow never multicultural, but, rather, just cultural" (Cavell 87). Covering an impressive range of literary and para-literary materials produced between the seventeenth century and 1960, Klinck's *History* represents the beginnings of the institutionalization of Canadian literature, and his chronological divisions set up the periodization of Canadian literary history in English, which has remained substantially unchanged ever since, with breaks around 1870, 1920, and 1960 (see Hammill 184). But Klinck's assumptions of British dominance lead to some notable exclusions. He has very little to say about Aboriginal cultures, apart from brief mentions of Native storytelling in Edith Fowke's chapter on "Folk Tales and Folk Songs" and of the mixed race poet and performance artist Pauline (Tekahionwake) Johnson. Ethnic minority writing is practically invisible, and there is no vocabulary to interrogate ethnicity, though there is a reference to four novels by European immigrant writers in the chapter "Fiction 1940–1960."

These are described as novels with "Continental backgrounds" (Klinck 709). Klinck's immense work of writing the nation into existence ends with Frye's famous Conclusion, written in the context of the upcoming centennial of the Confederation of Canada (1967) and republished in *The Bush Garden* (1971). What Klinck and Frye wanted was to construct a unified cultural and historical framework defining the concept of a "Canadian consciousness" on the basis of a code aptly described by Daniel Coleman as "White Civility," the legacy of a white settler culture whose assumptions were Eurocentric, territorial and masculinist. Black Canadians remain invisible, and out of Klinck's forty contributors, only six are women.

Though Atwood revises that last point by writing her thematic guide, her view of Canadian literature is dominated by the combined authority of Klinck and Frye, and it may be argued that her classification of key patterns is basically Fryegian, reflecting Frye's emphasis in his Conclusion on landscape and wilderness ("deep terror in regard to Nature") and the "garrison mentality" (Frye 225). However, Atwood's book belongs not to the 1960s but to the early 1970s, when the cultural nationalist position with its vigorous promotion of Anglo-Canadian myths of a unified national identity was already being challenged, and *Survival* betrays anxieties that were invisible in Klinck's *History*.

As Eva-Marie Kröller has demonstrated, cracks in the paradigm of Canadian history and politics had appeared even during the 1967 centennial celebrations in Montreal ("The Centennial"). Atwood, as the winner of the Centennial Poetry Competition, would have heard the dissenting voices of the Quebec separatists represented in the Pavillon de Québec, of General de Gaulle's famous proclamation "Vivre le Québec libre!" delivered in Montreal's City Hall, of the indigenous voices from the Pavilion of Canada's Indians,[4] and of Scott Symons's alternative vision of a "shadow city" behind the glamorous media images of Montreal in his gay novel *Place d'Armes* (1967).[5] The influence of these new political cross-currents is apparent in *Survival* in several remarkable additions to Klinck's story, the most striking being the Appendix to the chapter "Early People: Indians and Eskimos as Symbols," where Atwood lists five books by Native writers, prefaced by the following comment: "All the books in this chapter are by white people. What the Indians themselves think is another story, and one that is just beginning to be written" (106). There is also a chapter on recent immigrant urban fictions, which includes the stories of black West Indians by Austin Clarke, though Atwood sees the Canadian experience for immigrants as "programmed for failure" (158). The chapter on Quebec literature in translation is Gothically titled "Burning Mansions," where, like Klinck, Atwood suggests that there ought to be a parallel book written in

French.[6] *Survival* is pervaded by an uneasy sense of failure and loss, which might be located not simply in the selection of texts discussed but in an incipient recognition of occluded histories of cultural and ethnic diversity that disturb the traditional narrative of the emergence of a white Canadian nation (WASP and "*pure laine*") in North America, defining itself against two founding European nations and the US. Tellingly, her study ends on a double note of interrogation and uncertainty:

Have we survived?
If so, what happens *after* Survival? (246)

A "chart of simultaneous events" provides some answers to Atwood's questions with its record of some of the factors influencing the transformation of that Eurocentric national narrative: the 1960s Royal Commission on Bilingualism and Biculturalism found that post-war Canada had a significant minority population who were neither English nor French; in 1971, Prime Minister Pierre Trudeau's first Multiculturalism Policy officially recognized Canada's changing demography, a factor that was amplified by revised immigration policies during the 1970s, which allowed for the entry of immigrants of Asian, Caribbean and southern European origin; Aboriginal protests over land claims and Indian status gave indigenous dissent a public profile for the first time; and Quebec's *Révolution tranquille* reasserted a separate francophone identity within Canada. These slippages within the socio-political system were paralleled in the literary politics and new kinds of creative writing that had begun to appear as the first signs of changing critical perceptions about Canada and its literary heritage. The 1970s saw the publication of the first Aboriginal and Métis autobiographies, and of the first anthologies of ethnic and Aboriginal writing; these collective statements from marginalized communities constitute what Smaro Kamboureli has described as "alternative sites of cultural production" or "symptoms of difference" and "signs of cultural excess" already circulating within the Canadian literary tradition (*Scandalous* 131–74).

Only two years after *Survival*, Frank Davey's "Surviving the Paraphrase" (delivered as a lecture in Montreal in 1974, and reprinted as the titular essay in *Surviving the Paraphrase* in 1983) launched a swingeing attack on the thematic criticism practised by Atwood, Klinck, and Frye as the expression of official policies of cultural nationalism, exposing the "repressed political stakes in the literary canon" and accusing such criticism of treating Canadian literature as "a signbook of national culture" (Davey, *Reading* 12). Davey's shift of emphasis away from a thematics of nationalism toward language and textuality was an early symptom of changing methodologies of literary criticism within the academy, though the influence of new theoretical approaches from Europe and the US really belongs to the 1980s, spearheaded by the efforts of individual scholars, often in tension with institutional structures.[7] Through that decade, traditional frameworks for reading Canadian literature and history were already being destabilized by feminist theory, post-structuralist theory, debates around historiography, and a nascent post-colonial discourse, as the following selection of publications from the decade demonstrates: Robert Kroetsch's "Disunity as Unity: A Canadian Strategy" (1985), *Gynocritics/Gynocritiques: Feminist Approaches to Canadian and Quebec Women's Writing*, edited by Barbara Godard (1987), *Future Indicative: Literary Theory and Canadian Literature*, edited by John Moss (1987), Frank Davey's *Reading Canadian Reading* (1988), and Linda Hutcheon's *The Canadian Postmodern: A Study of Contemporary English Canadian Fiction* (1988), with its key formulation of "Historiographic Metafiction," followed by her *The Politics of Postmodernism* (1990). W.J. Keith's history, *Canadian Literature in English* (1985), published in London for a non-Canadian readership, stood out against the influence of new theoretical perspectives with its espousal of Leavisite and Arnoldian principles together with its assertion of "a communal vision" (Keith 9), closely related to the ideology of the English-Canadian cultural nationalism. However, such a traditional approach to the narrative of Canada's literary history had little resonance in the late 1980s context with its diverse reappraisals of the nation, of history, and of literature as an academic discipline, a period when, as Kroetsch observed with his flair for postmodern paradox, "Canadians cannot agree on what their metanarrative is.... There is no centre. This disunity is our unity" (10).

By the end of the decade a confluence of factors was already contributing to the erosion of the cultural nationalist vision. Some of these were related to governmental policy, notably the 1988 Multiculturalism Act, which officially recognized ethnic, racial, and religious diversity as a fundamental characteristic of Canadian identity and heritage;[8] some were within academic institutions; and most, significantly, were in the field of publishing with the increasing visibility of writers from minoritized cultural communities such as: Joy Kogawa, Michael Ondaatje, Rohinton Mistry, M.G. Vassanji, Austin Clarke, Beatrice Culleton Mosionier, and Jeannette Armstrong, all of whom had published novels in the 1980s or earlier. However, it is also salutary to note the unsettled state of Canadian publishing in this decade and the divergences in representations of Canadian writing. While anthologies and novels by minority writers were already in circulation, those writers were still marginalized by the literary establishment. An example of this would be *The Oxford Book of*

Canadian Short Stories in English, edited by Atwood and Robert Weaver (1986), where diverse ethnicities make only a brief appearance and "one last sad statistic... none of the stories is by an Indian or Inuit. I hope that this situation will change, as Indian and Inuit writers begin to claim their own territory through writing, as they have in the visual arts" (Atwood, Introduction xv). The implied absence of Aboriginal writers in the mid-1980s would seem to reflect an editorial blind spot, given publications by Jeannette Armstrong, Beth Brant, Basil H. Johnston, Wayne Keon, and Thomas King at this time. Ten years later, shifts in attitudes towards canonicity may be measured by the additions and deletions in Atwood and Weaver's *The New Oxford Book of Canadian Short Stories in English* (1995), where Thomas King, Austin Clarke, Rohinton Mistry, Dionne Brand and Neil Bissoondath are included. Regarding these inclusions, Atwood wryly commented: "But to worry unduly over such matters as canons and classics is to make a fool of oneself eventually" (Introduction xii).

At a time of such instability the cultural work to be performed by any new national literary history was bound to be different from that of earlier literary histories; the criterion was no longer the establishment of a literary canon but its disestablishment. The "definitive moment" of change (strictly speaking, there were two "definitive moments") arrived with the publication in London of W.H. New's *A History of Canadian Literature* (1989), followed by his editorship of the multi-authored fourth volume of Klinck's *A Literary History of Canada* (1990). New shifted the whole construction of Canada's literary history with his radical reappraisal not only of the concept of canonicity but of the image of the nation, its history, and its culture. As the editor of the journal *Canadian Literature*, he had been a pioneer in changing preconceptions about Canadian writing throughout the 1980s, with issues on Caribbean-Canadian Connections (1982), Italian Connections (1985), Slavic and East European Connections (1989), a special double issue on Native Writers and Canadian Writing (1990), to be followed by South Asian Connections (1992), all evidence as he put it, "for the ongoing critical attack on received definitions of literary canon" (New, "Studies" 102).

Beginning with the single-authored *History*, which was a different project from the multi-authored Volume 4, though informed by the same revisionist agenda, New made a decisive break from traditional frames of reference. He shifted the concept of Canada's origins back thousands of years before European colonization, beginning his chronological table back in 13,000 BC, with the geological formation of Niagara Falls, and opening his literary history not with European contact and narratives of exploration and settlement but with Aboriginal Mythmakers, where he made the point that Canada was "French before it was British, Indian and

Inuit before that" (New, *A History* 1). By this significant temporal and ontological shift, New immensely widened the parameters of the nation, suddenly revealing new sets of competing narratives and redefining what could be included as literature. His *History* features images of Aboriginal graphic art juxtaposed with works by Québécois and Anglo-Canadian artists, and includes sections on Native and Inuit culture and mythology, as well as works by white ethnographers. In fact, this was the first inclusion of Aboriginal culture and oral traditions in an account of Canadian literary history. Always attentive to social and ideological contexts within which images of Canada have been constructed, New included reference to francophone writing as well, so marking a rapprochement between the two literatures, which has been followed in the 1990s and since by subsequent literary historians, both anglophone and francophone (i.e., Blodgett, Kröller, Nischik, Lemire and Biron, Howells and Kröller).[9] Postmodern debates about history and historiography influenced New's writing about history, just as they were influencing writers of historical novels; after all, *histoire* in French telescopes "history" and "story" into one word. In a further decisive shift from the cultural nationalist unitary vision of the nation, New stated his commitment to "cultural plurality" by including a large section on writing by ethnic minorities up to 1985, the end date of his volume. Subsequently, in his revised second edition (2003), which takes his narrative up to 2002, an additional chapter titled "Reconstructors" takes account of the multiplication of new literary voices and frames of historical reference since the mid-1980s. Here New has produced an expanded and nuanced representation of ethnic diversity and has added a section on black history in Canada, from the arrival of black United Empire Loyalists in the eighteenth century to contemporary Africadian, Caribbean and African-born writers. At the same time, one cannot help remarking that this effort to be up to date inevitably draws attention to the ways in which literary history as a genre always suffers from a kind of belatedness, constructing its account of the national narrative on the basis of creative writing that has already been published.

In parallel, as editor of the fourth volume of Klinck's *A Literary History of Canada* (1990), New continued to implement his innovative agenda to redefine the genre of literary history. Although the design (beginning with Poetry, Short Fiction, and The Novel) is not cast so radically as in his *History*, his editorial Introduction makes explicit the theoretical assumptions on which his own *History* was constructed, detailing the immensely diversified perspectives of which contemporary literary histories needed to take account, some specific to the academic discipline while others related to the wider socio-political context: "There were other genres to attend to, different priorities of subject, the immediacy of the literary experience, and the shifting character of the social framework" (New, *A Literary* xii). His reference to "other genres" and "different priorities" confronted the disturbances to old paradigms introduced by new critical theories, new kinds of writing, and publication trends; "the immediacy of literary experience" emphasizes language, textuality, and literary artifice, while the "shifting character of the social framework" is a reminder of the demographic and ideological context within which any literary history is produced. Throughout his Introduction, New skilfully avoids the conventional rhetoric of national identification through culture and literature by describing the volume as "a book about patterns of discourse" (xii). Significantly, his concluding paragraph positions Volume 4 in resistance to many of Klinck's premises, recording the radical changes in perspective since the 1970s shared by historians and literary critics alike: for historians "the whole [society] was inapprehensible," while critics had "edged away from seeing literature as foremost an expression of a single national character" (xxxii).

New's volume signalled the state of indeterminacy which characterized discourses around the category of Canadianness throughout the 1990s as cultural historians, together with literary critics and theorists, struggled to redefine the nation, its heritage, and its literature, in response to contemporary Canada's changing versions of multicultural post-colonial nationhood. It is symptomatic of the crisis that no new histories of English-Canadian literature were produced during the 1990s, though New's reconceptualization of the genre foregrounded the ways in which a literary history might relate to the context of shifting shapes of national and cultural formation. Those shifting forms with their challenges to traditional structures of power and authority constituted the basis of debates around Canadian identity and its representations, of questions of the relation between literature and national ideology, and of the search for an appropriate discourse that could articulate the multiple differences within the imagined communities of the nation.

That sense of a paradigm crisis was most skilfully anatomized by Barbara Godard in her 1992 essay "Canadian? Literary? Theory?", a flamboyant piece of deconstructive criticism which exposed the political interests underpinning Canadian literature as an academic discipline established in the 1960s and '70s. Godard takes into account both the canon debates of the early 1990s and the new complexities of gender, race, and ethnic difference, prompted by her recognition of challenges to nationalist ideology from writers and critics coming from a variety of different theoretical positions: "What 'Canadian' means in literary terms is a question that needs to be addressed, if only to rephrase it as a problem in the meaning of 'national' as it operates in literary discourse" (Godard 181). Her theoretical examination points with devastating clarity to the constructedness of a national literature: "The terms 'Canadian literature' or 'theory' are not embodied in the texts or authors themselves but are invested by institutionalized reading practices.... Without some form of nationalism (national difference, that is) the textual system of the Literary would not overlap with the textual system of the Canadian" (180). In other words, a political imperative overdetermines what constitutes a national literature, influencing what is included/excluded. Godard's questions continued to resonate in literary debates through the 1990s, from nationalists like W.H. New and Jonathan Kertzer (*Worrying the Nation*) to the post-nationalist position of Frank Davey (*Post-National Arguments*). The former sought to widen the parameters within which to reconstruct an English-Canadian literary tradition responsive to history and to contemporary social realities: "The nation is both a historical reality and a discursive need" (Kertzer 166); Davey, by contrast, argued that the signifier "Canadian" had been emptied of meaning in narratives since the late 1960s in favour of values that were local or global rather than national, and that Canadian cultural expression had become transnational. Oddly, however, Davey excluded many recent novels by immigrant writers like Nino Ricci, M.G. Vassanji, and Rohinton Mistry on the grounds that they "contain few if any significations of Canada or of Canadian polity," a comment whose political implications he noted but did not explore (Davey 7). This position would seem to restrict the signification of transnationalism as it has recently come to be understood.

The anxieties expressed by these white male critics need to be balanced against the dissatisfactions and dissent expressed by writers from minoritized cultures, whose reading often exposes what Godard called "the conflictual relations underlying the codes of nationalism, gender, race operative in the construction of a Canadian literary discourse" (195). To take just one example, Arun Mukherjee's *Postcolonialism: My Living* (1998) shifts the critical and pedagogical emphasis away from the English-Canadian literary canon and its mediatory efforts to accommodate the "Other" to a focus on ethnic minority and Aboriginal writing, arguing that "reading through race means to read against the dominant literary theories which are premised on whiteness" (90–91). She also reverses the lens through which to view multiculturalism, arguing that it may best be understood through direct encounters with minority writing: "Ethnic minority texts inform their readers, through the presence of other languages, as well as a whole repertoire of cultural signs, about the multicultural and multilingual nature of Canadian society" (102).

Those cultural debates intersect with the increasing visibility of fictions and poetry by writers from diverse ethnic and racial backgrounds, while anthologies of creative writing like *Making a Difference: Canadian Multicultural Literature*, edited by Smaro Kamboureli (1996), contribute to the critical mass of textual evidence for change in English Canada's literary profile. Interestingly, a record of such changes as viewed from the white Establishment may be read in Atwood's fictions published at the beginning, near the middle, and at the end of the decade. The title story of her collection *Wilderness Tips* (1991) signalled a point of crisis with its register of a "slippage in the bedrock" (221) of Anglo-Canadian myths of cultural dominance; *The Robber Bride* (1993) reappraised English-Canadian constructs of personal and national identity through women's hidden histories of immigrancy, ethnicity, and social class; while Atwood began the new century with her overtly elegiac historical novel *The Blind Assassin* (2000), where Iris Chase Griffen, her elderly representative of the old Anglo-Canadian hegemony, dies just as she finishes her memoir in the last year of the twentieth century. By the time we read Iris's story of family secrets and national scandals, it already belongs to the past.

However, though the traditional English-Canadian narratives of national identity and heritage had been destabilized, two important studies by female ethnic diasporic critics, published the same year as *The Blind Assassin*, argued that the old asymmetries of power between dominant white culture and minoritized identities had not been displaced but merely transformed through the rhetoric of multiculturalism. They are Smaro Kamboureli's *Scandalous Bodies: Diasporic Literature in English Canada* (2000) and Himani Bannerji's *The Dark Side of the Nation: Essays on Multiculturalism, Nationalism and Gender* (2000). While Kamboureli draws her evidence from a close study of the body (and bodies) of diasporic literature in relation to the body politic, Bannerji provides a political and cultural analysis of the representation of so-called visible minority women. Taken together, these studies illustrate the interdisciplinary context within which the issues raised by Godard have continued to be negotiated, while they also point to the cultural work still to be done in revisioning Canadian literary traditions.

A Chart of Simultaneous Events: Narratives of CanLit in the Twenty-First Century
The remarkable revival of interest in national literary histories in Canada during the first decade of the twenty-first century emerges from the contestations of the 1990s. Addressing the problems of historiography in a postmodern post-colonial context, critics recognize the need for narratives of

reappraisal that take into account official and non-official histories, with all their forgettings and suppressions, while bringing the present into sharper focus in relation to that past. Being "national" literary histories, none of them sets out to deconstruct the concept of nation but rather to try to redefine national distinctiveness in an era of globalization, though they vary in design, critical and theoretical emphases, and the readerships addressed. E.D. Blodgett's approach in his meta-critical study *Five-Part Invention: A History of Literary History in Canada* (2003) is explicitly retrospective, as he asserts in his final chapter: "The contemporary is largely significant for me in its relation with the past" (301). Blodgett argues for a redefinition of the context for Canadian literary history and indeed of the nation itself, based on the evidence of literary histories produced in Canada from 1864 to the mid-1990s. His comparative analysis of ideological disparities and salient points of difference across the wide spectrum of texts in English and French disperses any fixed idea of the nation: "The nation is never the same. The problem lies not so much in tensions that literary history possesses and cannot satisfactorily resolve, but rather in the fact that for the most part the image of the nation is so ethnically restricted" (18). This book might be read as Blodgett's answer to his own question in his 1993 essay "Is a History of the Literatures of Canada Possible?" As a comparativist, Blodgett addresses the questions of nation and literary tradition through the different perspectives of the five ethnic groups in Canada (his "Five-Part Invention"): English-Canadian, French-Canadian, First Nations, Inuit, and ethnic minority groups, arguing that Canada's meta-narrative of nation is still full of absences that need to be addressed "inasmuch as the Other is present from the beginning in the shape of one ghost or another" (303). His main focus is on the neglect of First Nations and Inuit people who "have always been part of the Canadian social contract, forgotten, neglected and abused as they may have been" (303–4), while he makes connections with analogous conditions of marginalization suffered by so-called ethnic minorities. At the beginning Blodgett declares that his aim is "to dismantle the essentializing tendencies of the two dominant cultural groups" (19), and in his conclusion he states the necessary conditions for a revised Canadian meta-narrative: "So long as the Other remains excluded from the contract, the realization of a 'Canadian identity' will always be thwarted" (304). However, it is his use of the term "Other" (under which he rather contentiously groups together Native and ethnic minority cultures) which reveals his own ethnocultural affinities and assumptions. His European framing of Canadian literary histories (from the British North America Act to Europeans' views of Canadian literature and to Canadian literary histories published in Britain and France) presents an argument from history which demonstrates "the limits of autonomous perspectives" (297), while at the same time he leaves in place the binary division between mainstream and minoritized writers. As a result, though Blodgett lays out the parameters which need to be renegotiated to achieve a more comprehensive analysis, his study lacks a resolution of the problems inherent in his narrative, which ends only with a renewed emphasis on "the matter of difference that these histories foreground" (19).

Blodgett's historical arguments concerning the largely unacknowledged role of Aboriginal peoples in Canada's social contract have recently been taken up and developed in the twenty-first-century politico-cultural context of multiculturalism, transculturalism, and transnationalism by John Ralston Saul in *A Fair Country: Telling Truths about Canada* (2008). Saul argues that diversity and *Métissage* should not be seen as recent phenomena related to present immigration patterns and globalization but that these characteristics have always represented "the undercurrent of Canadian civilization" (20). Within Canadian academic institutions, an extensive reappraisal of the disciplinary, pedagogical, and institutional frameworks for studying the country's literature is high on the agenda. W.H. New's massive *Encyclopedia of Literature in Canada* (2002) with over two thousand entries contributed by a team of three hundred international Canadianists is both a reprise and an amplification of his earlier pluralist constructions of literary history. This is a resource book that establishes a broad cultural and historical context for writers and writing in Canada (for New refuses to define "Canadian author"), where individual author entries are interspersed with survey articles on a wide variety of literary and paraliterary topics, as well as what New describes as "small courses of general education" (viii) ranging from entries on Film, Television and Literature, Historical Literature, and Historiography, to Nationalism, Regionalism, and Landscape. Taking full advantage of the miscellaneous narrative clusters of the encyclopedia form, New has constructed an extremely complex image of Canadianness and of the multiple literary identities within it. That revisionist approach to the whole framework of Canadian literary and cultural studies adopted by New has been variously amplified in the work of critics and anthologists like Cynthia Sugars and Laura Moss (2009) and the projects initiated by Smaro Kamboureli at the TransCanada Institute at the University of Guelph (see Kamboureli and Miki; Kamboureli, "Editorial" 6–13).The recent two-volume anthology, *Canadian Literature in English: Texts and Contexts*, edited by Sugars and Moss, deserves special mention as a pedagogical initiative. Though based on a chronological structure that looks quite traditional, its wide selection of texts from canonical and non-canonical sources includes the many conflictual discourses that have coexisted in every historical period, while patterns of connection are also established by selecting works that make intertextual reference to one another across periods. As a result, periodization ceases to be the major defining category, and the multiple narratives challenge what Hutcheon calls "the coherence of the concept of the nation-state" (Hutcheon and Valdés 25). Once again, as with anthologies of ethnic writing in the 1970s and '80s, anthologies provide the raw materials for a revisionary narrative of Canadian literary history.

One of the most striking features of the revival of interest in historiography is the enthusiasm outside Canada for Canadian literary history, with volumes published in Britain and the US that have been designed as collaborative projects between Canadian scholars and international Canadianists. This is all part of the process of continuous updating and rethinking of "Canadian literature" in the present context of increasingly politicized discourses around post-colonialism, diaspora, globalization and transnationalism. Significantly, these approaches have opened up the nation's history to recuperation and refiguring by a vanguard of creative writers, followed by cultural critics and indeed by literary historians.

The two major recent literary histories are both products of international collaboration: *History of Literature in Canada: English-Canadian and French-Canadian*, edited by Reingard M. Nischik (2008), and *The Cambridge History of Canadian Literature*, edited by Coral Ann Howells and Eva-Marie Kröller (2009). In both books, the editors face similar challenges in compiling a national literary history in an age of globalization. What is the function of a literary history? Is it a monument to national identity? Is it a stock-taking at a particular moment, and from whose perspective? Is it a statement of resistance to definitions of the nation and literature that are too restrictive? Is it an effort to realign the terms "nation," "literature," and "history" so as to alter the way we understand their shifting relationships over time by taking into account divergent concepts of nation and collective memory? Of course, these are problems faced by all contemporary literary historians, though the Canadian situation has some peculiar twists which constitute its distinctiveness. And finally, in practical terms of volume design, a pressing problem has been how to maintain a balance between the treatment of past literary production against the decades since the 1970s, during which literature in Canada has taken significant new directions. Does a transformed understanding of the recent period depend on its nuanced analysis, or on its historical contextualizing? Moreover, is "balance" the appropriate principle here, or is "unbalancing" a more accurate description of the contemporary literary historian's project to reflect the multiple competing narratives that make up the historical narrative of the nation?

Both these histories are multi-authored productions by Canadian scholars and international Canadianists and published outside Canada; both offer comprehensive accounts of writing in Canada within the expanded parameters introduced by W.H. New; both take account of the cultural and ideological shifts that have altered the terms of debate around the relation between the nation and its literature. Yet they have produced two very different narratives with different emphases and different designs, raising critical questions about methodology and the emplotment of literary histories. For those reasons I shall be dedicating the rest of my essay to a more detailed analysis of these two histories, as contrastive examples of the ways in which the radical changes that have occurred in Canadian literature and society may be conceptualized.

Nischik's volume is a substantially rewritten version of *Kanadische Literaturgeschichte* (2005), a multi-authored history by German-speaking Canadianists, which was co-edited by Konrad Gross, Wolfgang Kloos, and Nischik herself. In this more recent book, some of the original chapters are translated into English and new chapters by new contributors from Europe and Canada have been added, which poses serious organizational challenges for its editor. The editorial Introduction begins with the celebration of an already achieved cultural supremacy, suggesting a traditional teleological narrative of national development: "Literature in Canada...has arrived at the center stage of world literature" (1) individually and collectively, with "established writers" and "new talents" winning international literary prizes, while the institutionalized canon of "CanLit" is being taught in Canadian Studies programs worldwide and while French-Canadian literature has "found its own voice" in North America and in the global context of la Francophonie. It would be fair to say that Nischik's agenda emphasizes inclusiveness, "encompassing all major cultural traditions of literature written in Canada" (3) and that she welcomes the "increasing transcultural diversity [which] has become one of the strongest and most fascinating characteristics of contemporary literature in Canada" (19). She also acknowledges that the recent prominence of Aboriginal and diasporic writing has carried "the debate about what constitutes literature in Canada clearly beyond the traditions of the two founding nations" (3). Well aware of the problems of restaging Canada's literary narrative in the twenty-first century ("how to integrate Canada's ethnically diverse writing into a book largely structured according to the 'English-Canada' and 'French-Canada' dichotomy of its subtitle," 19), Nischik has opted for a modified version of the bicultural model designed to accommodate the transcultural realities of contemporary Canadian literature and society. Nevertheless, that model is put under severe strain by the scholarly evidence cited in many of the volume's thirty-five chapters, which tell a far more complex and divided story.

Indeed, the final words of the Introduction would seem to suggest a more transformative approach to explicating Canadian literature, with "the growing awareness of literature in Canada as a 'postnational' conglomerate of literatures with different cultural traditions—this being regarded as cultural wealth rather than lack of homogeneity or identity" (24).

The book's title and structure highlight its major innovation in an English-language literary history, for it offers a coverage of francophone literature as extensive as its treatment of literature in English. A comparative study of the two literatures at some future point had been envisaged by Klinck back in 1965, though as the editor notes, there are very few Canadian literary histories in either English or French that offer other than a limited treatment of writing in the other language.[10] But, while this volume presents the materials for a comparative study, it could not itself be called comparativist, for the abruptness of the transitions between anglophone and francophone sections reads like a textual reflection of the political and cultural divisions between the English and the French that have characterized Canada's history since the time of European contact. Inadvertently, the editorial policy of equal treatment throws into relief a divided narrative with different foundational moments, different crisis points, and divergent concepts of the nation, for the chronological arrangement depends substantially on traditional anglophone patterns of periodization at the expense of francophone ones. For example, it emphasizes 1763 and 1867 as "definitive moments" (as they were for the English), but at the same time it subsumes the significant dates in the francophone historical legacy of 1759 (the Conquest) and 1839 (Lord Durham's *Report*) within the British colonial period. It is significant that the chapters that come the closest to overcoming this binary are two near the end, "Canons of Diversity in Contemporary English-Canadian Literature" and "Transculturalism and *écritures émigrantes*," which are the very chapters where historical differences between anglophone and francophone Canada are transcended. As the editor acknowledges elsewhere, the organizing principle for a comprehensive Canadian literary history would seem to be not Unity but Disunity, a further endorsement of Robert Kroetsch's radical formulation of the 1980s.

Though to some extent the inherent limitations of the chosen model are managed by the use of introductory chapters focused on social, cultural, and political contexts for the particular historical periods treated in each of the six sections of the volume, this essential disunity becomes most evident in the final and by far the longest section, "Literature from 1967 to the Present," where the increasingly complex narrative of literary production as it is developed in individual chapters challenges the bicultural generic model to breaking point. Disruption is evident in the structure itself, where there are additional chapters on genres that were not previously included and for which no parallel chapter in the other language appears, such as chapters on "English-Canadian Literary Theory and Literary Criticism" and "Orality and the French-Canadian Chanson." The impact of diversity and the increasingly transcultural elements of writing in Canada are explored and theorized in the chapter on "Literature of the First Nations, Inuit and Métis," plus the two chapters on multicultural and transcultural writing in English and French previously mentioned. As a result, this volume offers a strangely fractured literary history that is continually obliged to rewrite its own premises relating to nation, canonicity and genre, biculturalism, multiculturalism, and transculturalism. The new theoretical perspectives and the new writing thrown into relief in this final section introduce discourses that are seriously at odds with the traditional teleological model at the basis of literary histories. However, they are not integrated into a critical narrative that would offer a revisionary reading of the literatures of Canada.

Turning to *The Cambridge History of Canadian Literature*, I shall write about it in the first person, acknowledging my own interest and involvement as its co-editor, with Professor Eva-Marie Kröller of the University of British Columbia.[11] When we were invited by Cambridge University Press to submit a proposal for their first-ever history of Canadian literature in their Cambridge Histories series, we had the real advantage that Professor Kröller had recently edited the *Cambridge Companion to Canadian Literature* (2004), a much shorter form than a history and addressed to a different readership, and that she had grappled with the question about what kind of story to tell in the early twenty-first century about Canadian literature. Yet we now had to think through different questions to do with the specific kind of cultural work that a national literary history is expected to perform, and what kind of methodology would best address the problem (to quote Godard again) of "the meaning of the 'national' as it operates in literary discourse" (181). How to find a form of historiography that would take into account the changing meanings of "Canada" and "Canadian" from the country's multiple beginnings and conflictual history through the diversified perspectives opened up since the 1960s and '70s, and which have shifted again since the 1990s with globalization and its coordinates of transculturalism and transnationalism?

We studied alternative models for telling the story of a restructured literary tradition in other countries, such as Bercovitch's multi-volume *The Cambridge History of American Literature* (2004), Hollier's *A New History of French Literature* (1989), and also the suggestions for comparativist models in Hutcheon and Valdés's *Rethinking Literary History: A Dialogue on Theory* (2002). Should we move beyond—and if so, how far beyond?— the traditional teleological nation narrative with its framework of periodization and generic categories? Bercovitch's methodology, described by Hutcheon as "a Bakhtinian dialogic approach" (30) and by himself as "critical decentralization," kept the concept of the nation (the US) as central while acknowledging that it had become a contested site: "'America' in these volumes is a shifting, many-sided focal point for exploring the historicity of the text and the textuality of history" (Bercovitch 3). Hollier, on the other hand, abandons both teleological narrative and periodization in favour of short essays covering "briefer time spans...focused on points, coincidences, returns, resurgences" (qtd. in Howells and Kröller, "Switching" 14). Neither of these models fits with Canada's history or its ideological and cultural patterns: Bercovitch is too imperialistic and Hollier too deconstructive. So, we decided to work subversively within the institutionalized framework. The volume thus is arranged for ease of reference in what looks at first glance like a traditional teleological model of a national literary history, though revisionist approaches within individual chapters and the emphasis on reassessment and cultural diversity throughout run counter to those first impressions to produce a new configuration of Canadian literary history.

Our basic premises are not unlike those spelled out by Moss and Sugars in their anthology, though historiography demands a different methodology and a degree of explicit emplotment which may be only implicit in a selection of texts and visual materials. Like them, a major element of our revisionist reading is to introduce such diversity of discourses within every historical period as to blur those chronological divisions, while the same element highlights the problematic relation between "nation" and "literature." We soon realized that any twenty-first century literary history was going to look unbalanced in the amount of space assigned to the present in relation to the past. Like Nischik's volume, more than half of *The Cambridge History* is devoted to writing since the 1960s, where our contributors pay detailed attention to a wide range of texts that mark the emergence of multicultural, Aboriginal, and black Canadian writing, and most recently to transnational dimensions of literary production. The significance of this recent period in terms of creative writing and critical theory cannot be overestimated, for the end of the story (at least for the present) has changed the way we think about its beginnings and middles and has also prompted a reimagining of the nation's history and its literature. In other words, the diversity of races, cultures, and languages that characterize contemporary Canada has resulted in a refiguring of literary traditions and heritage narratives, revealing that the supposedly recent phenomena of diversity, transcultural dialogue, and transnational affiliations were as much a distinctive feature of the country's colonial past as they are of its post-colonial present.

Unlike the US with its Founding Fathers, Canada has no single national myth of origin, but multiple foundational moments, occluded histories, and conflicting allegiances which still circulate in the subtext of any narrative of the nation.

That is why the first section of *The Cambridge History* is designed quite literally to lay out the groundwork, highlighting an interrogative approach to narratives of colonial history in English or French. Beginning with the first recorded contact between Europeans (French explorers and missionaries) and Natives in the sixteenth century, it ends not with Confederation in 1867, but with a chapter on "History in English and French, 1832–1898" which challenges conventional periodization while addressing contemporary theories around historiography. Questions of meta-history are again addressed in a later chapter on contemporary historical fiction entitled "Ghost stories: fictions of history and myth," uncovering repressed histories within the national narrative and their uncanny returns in post-colonial, postmodern fictive forms. There are similar pairings throughout, like those between Native oral traditions in the first chapter and two chapters in the post-1960s section on indigenous poetry and prose and contemporary Aboriginal theatre in English and French, and between literature of settlement (which includes narratives by fugitive slaves and black United Empire Loyalists) and analyses of contemporary black Canadian writing which recuperate those forgotten histories. Our aim here is to demonstrate interconnections across centuries. We adopt a similar differentiated approach to genre, where canonical genres are interspersed with many chapters on non-canonical genres like comic books and bestsellers, or writing by Victorian naturalists and transcultural life-writing, which includes the work of contemporary environmentalists. Other chapters challenge boundaries of genre and period in different ways, by implicit comparisons between experimentalism in women's genres at the turn of the nineteenth century and postmodern experiments in hybridized forms which combine fiction, poetry, and drama.

It is not my purpose here to offer a detailed analysis of the total design of *The Cambridge History*, but I have chosen the specific examples above to illustrate our revisionist methodology and the kinds of questions we set out to respond to, frequently writing against the chronological arrangement advertised in the table of contents and resisting the restrictions of conventional generic categories. Our aim was to rewrite Canadian literary history using many different scripts, incorporating both a historical narrative and the literary challenges to any single ideology of nation, while in the process offering a guide to Canada's evolving literary heritage.

Looking Back/Looking Forward
Looking back over the past forty years from the vantage point of the present, what may be observed in this historical analysis is a continual process of construction, interrogation, reappraisal, and reconstruction of English Canada's literary narrative. As any "chart of simultaneous events" would indicate, such dramatic changes in a relatively short time period are the result of a confluence of factors—political, social, ideological—to which literary narratives have both contributed and responded in a variety of ways. Not only has creative writing shifted perceptions and attitudes to CanLit within the country and internationally, but also theoretical and critical writing has transformed the contexts for thinking about literature, history, and the nation. If there is a common denominator in this wholesale rewriting of tradition, it lies in a determined recovery of formerly marginalized voices and suppressed histories, which resulted, first, in a destabilization of "what 'Canadian' means in literary terms" (to quote Godard) and, more recently, in acts of rebalancing the multiple competing perspectives within literary discourse, as we have seen with the latest literary histories. With the new emphasis on transnationalism, the boundaries of national literatures are shifting once again (and not only in Canada) with a repositioning of the national in a globalized context.

Yet in any reappraisal, successive changes need to be historicized in order to explain the reasons for their occurrence, the ways in which relations between present and past have been altered, and their possible consequences for the future. Like Atwood's postmodern historian, we too continue to believe in "the salutary power of explanations" (*Robber Bride* 3), while at the same time sharing a general skepticism about the legitimating narratives of history. A national literary history offers only one kind of account amid a proliferation of alternative narratives at any point in cultural history, though literary history nonetheless remains a significant dimension in the national literary construction. However, just as Atwood's quotation at the beginning of this essay registers a slippage in traditional structures of authority, so we may expect that future literary histories will continue to rewrite tradition, charting the multiple directions of English Canada's increasingly decentralized literary narrative.

Notes
1 This terminology is adapted from Raymond Williams's paradigm in *Marxism and Literature* (1977) to describe the dynamics of cultural change.
2 Carl F. Klinck's *A Literary History of Canada* (1965) was followed by a three-volume edition in 1976; Vol. 4 was edited by William H. New and published in 1990.

3 In fact, Klinck envisaged a comparative study of anglophone and francophone literatures, though that was not to happen for another twenty years. His *History* was translated into French in 1970.
4 Chief Dan George's poem "Lament for Confederation" was first performed in Vancouver at the time of the centennial.
5 Atwood discusses Symons's novel in *Survival* (189–90).
6 Pierre de Grandpré's *Histoire de la littérature française au Québec* had been published in four volumes between 1967 and 1969, though Atwood does not take note of that.
7 See Barbara Godard's exemplary account of her struggles to establish courses on Literary Theory and Women's Studies in Literature at York University in the late 1970s and early '80s in *Canadian Literature at the Crossroads of Language and Culture* (Kamboureli 28).
8 Aboriginals were not included in the 1988 Multiculturalism Act.
9 However, for a comparativist like Blodgett, New's history remains too focused on English Canada: "More significant, however, is the fact that francophone writing is clearly an adjunct to anglophone writing" (283).
10 William H. New's *History* and *Histoire de la littérature québécoise*, edited by Michel Biron, François Dumont, and Elisabeth Nardout-Lafarge (2007), are cited as exceptions here.
11 An earlier account of making the *CHCL* was presented in our joint keynote address at the International Council for Canadian Studies 2008 Conference in Ottawa, published as "Switching the Plot: From *Survival* to the *Cambridge History of Canadian Literature*" (Howells and Kröller). A small part of that material is repeated here.

Works Cited

Atwood, Margaret. *The Blind Assassin*. London: Virago, 2001 [2000].

Atwood, Margaret. *The Robber Bride*. London: Virago, 1994 [1993].

Atwood, Margaret. *Survival: A Thematic Guide to Canadian Literature*. Toronto: Anansi, 1972.

Atwood, Margaret. *Wilderness Tips*. Toronto: McClelland and Stewart, 1991.

Atwood, Margaret, and Robert Weaver, eds. *The New Oxford Book of Canadian Short Stories in English*. Toronto: Oxford UP, 1995.

Atwood, Margaret, and Robert Weaver, eds. *The Oxford Book of Canadian Short Stories in English*. Toronto: Oxford UP, 1986.

Bannerji, Himani. *The Dark Side of the Nation: Essays on Multiculturalism, Nationalism and Gender*. Toronto: Canadian Scholars' Press, 2000.

Bercovitch, Sacvan, ed. *The Cambridge History of American Literature*. Vol. 4. Cambridge: Cambridge UP, 2004.

Biron, Michel, François Dumont, and Elisabeth Nardout-Lafarge. *Histoire de la littérature québécoise*. Montreal: Boréal, 2007.

Blodgett, E.D. *Five-Part Invention: A History of Literary History in Canada*. Toronto: U of Toronto P, 2003.

Blodgett, E.D. "Is a History of the Literatures of Canada Possible?" *Essays on Canadian Writing* 50 (1993): 1–18.

Cavell, Richard. "World Famous across Canada, or Transnational Localities." *Trans.Can.Lit: Resituating the Study of Canadian Literature*. Ed. Smaro Kamboureli and Roy Miki. Waterloo, ON: Wilfrid Laurier UP, 2007. 85–92.

Coleman, Daniel. *White Civility: The Literary Project of English Canada*. Toronto: U of Toronto P, 2006.

Davey, Frank. *Post-National Arguments: The Politics of the Anglophone Canadian Novel since 1967*. Toronto: U of Toronto P, 1993.

Davey, Frank. *Reading Canadian Reading*. Winnipeg: Turnstone, 1988.

Davey, Frank. *Surviving the Paraphrase: Eleven Essays on Canadian Literature*. Winnipeg: Turnstone, 1983.

Frye, Northrop. *The Bush Garden: Essays on the Canadian Imagination*. Toronto: Anansi, 1971.

Godard, Barbara. "Canadian? Literary? Theory?" *Canadian Literature at the Crossroads of Language and Culture: Selected Essays by Barbara Godard, 1987–2005*. Ed. Smaro Kamboureli. Edmonton: NeWest, 2008.

Godard, Barbara, ed. *Gynocritics/Gynocritiques: Feminist Approaches to Canadian and Quebec Women's Writing*. Toronto: ECW Press, 1987.

Hammill, Faye. "'A nation's pride is a tangible thing': Canadian Literary Histories in the 21st Century." *International Journal of Canadian Studies* 29 (2004): 183–92.

Hollier, Denis. *A New History of French Literature*. Cambridge, MA: Harvard UP, 1989.

Howells, Coral Ann, and Eva-Marie Kröller, eds. *The Cambridge History of Canadian Literature*. Cambridge: Cambridge UP, 2009.

Howells, Coral Ann, and Eva-Marie Kröller. "Switching the Plot: From *Survival* to *The Cambridge History of Canadian Literature*." *Canada Exposed / Le Canada a découvert*. Ed. Pierre Anctil, André Loiselle, and Christopher Rolfe. Brussels: Peter Lang, 2009. 45–60.

Hutcheon, Linda. "Rethinking the National Model." *Rethinking Literary History: A Dialogue on Theory*. Ed. Linda Hutcheon and Mario J. Valdés. Oxford: Oxford UP, 2002. 3–34.

Hutcheon, Linda. *The Canadian Postmodern: A Study of Contemporary English-Canadian Fiction*. Toronto: U of Toronto P, 1989.

Hutcheon, Linda, and Mario J. Valdés, eds. *Rethinking Literary History: A Dialogue on Theory*. Oxford: Oxford UP, 2002.

Kamboureli, Smaro, ed. *Canadian Literature at the Crossroads of Language and Culture: Selected Essays by Barbara Godard, 1987–2005*. Edmonton: NeWest, 2008.

Kamboureli, Smaro. "Editorial: Disappearance and Mobility: A TransCanada Issue." *Canadian Literature* 201 (2009): 6–13.

Kamboureli, Smaro, ed. *Making a Difference: Canadian Multicultural Literature*. 2nd ed. Toronto: Oxford UP, 2007 [1996].

Kamboureli, Smaro. *Scandalous Bodies: Diasporic Literature in English Canada*. Toronto: Oxford UP, 2000.

Kamboureli, Smaro, and Roy Miki, eds. *Trans.Can.Lit: Resituating the Study of Canadian Literature*. Waterloo, ON: Wilfrid Laurier UP, 2007.

Keith, W.J. *Canadian Literature in English*. 2nd ed. 2 vols. Erin, ON: Porcupine's Quill, 2006 [1985].

Kertzer, Jonathan. *Worrying the Nation: Imagining a National Literature in English Canada*. Toronto: U of Toronto P, 1998.

Klinck, Carl F., ed. *A Literary History of Canada: Canadian Literature in English*. 2nd ed. 3 vols. Toronto: U of Toronto P, 1976 [1965]. Vol. 4. Ed. William H. New, 1990.

Kroetsch, Robert. "Disunity as Unity: A Canadian Strategy." *Canadian Story and History 1885–1895*. Ed. Colin Nicholson and Peter Easingwood. Edinburgh: Edinburgh UP, 1985. 1–11.

Kröller, Eva-Marie, ed. *Cambridge Companion to Canadian Literature*. Cambridge: Cambridge UP, 2004.

Kröller, Eva-Marie. "The Centennial." *The Cambridge History of Canadian Literature*. Ed. Coral Ann Howells and Eva-Marie Kröller. Cambridge: Cambridge UP, 2009. 312–34.

Lyotard, Jean-François. *The Postmodern Condition: A Report on Knowledge*. Trans. Geoff Bennington and Brian Massumi. Manchester: Manchester UP, 1984.

Moss, John, ed. *Future Indicative: Literary Theory and Canadian Literature*. Ottawa: U of Ottawa P, 1987.

Moss, Laura, and Cynthia Sugars, eds. *Canadian Literature in English: Texts and Contexts*. 2 vols. Toronto: Pearson Education Canada, 2009.

Mukherjee, Arun. *Postcolonialism: My Living*. Toronto: Tsar, 1998.

New, William H., ed. *Encyclopedia of Literature in Canada*. Toronto: U of Toronto P, 2002.

New, William H. *A History of Canadian Literature*. 2nd ed. Montreal: McGill-Queen's UP, 2003 [1989].

New, William H., ed. *A Literary History of Canada*. Vol. 4. Toronto: U of Toronto P, 1990.

New, William H. "Studies of English-Canadian Literature." *International Journal of Canadian Studies* 1–2 (1990): 97–114.

Nischik, Reingard M., ed. *History of Literature in Canada: English-Canadian and French-Canadian*. Rochester: Camden House, 2008.

Saul, John Ralston. *A Fair Country: Telling Truths about Canada*. Toronto: Viking Canada, 2008.

Sugars, Cynthia, ed. *Home-Work: Postcolonialism, Pedagogy and Canadian Literature*. Ottawa: U of Ottawa P, 2004.

Sugars, Cynthia, ed. *Unhomely States: Theorizing English-Canadian Postcolonialism*. Peterborough, ON: Broadview Press, 2004.

Sugars, Cynthia, and Gerry Turcotte, eds. *Unsettled Remains: Canadian Literature and the Postcolonial Gothic*. Waterloo, ON: Wilfrid Laurier UP, 2009.

Valdés, Mario J. "Rethinking the History of Literary History." *Rethinking Literary History: A Dialogue on Theory*. Ed. Linda Hutcheon and Mario J. Valdés. Oxford: Oxford UP, 2002. 63–115.

White, Hayden. "The Historical Text as Literary Artifact." *The Writing of History: Literary Form and Historical Understanding*. Ed. Robert H. Canary and Henry Kozicki. Madison, WI: U of Wisconsin P, 1978. 41–62.

TWO

(Reading Closely)
Calling for the Formation of Asian Canadian Studies

Smaro Kamboureli

Whither Asian Canadian Literature?
Since the late 1970s Asian Canadian culture has gradually begun to muster critical attention as a distinct field of cultural production that interrogates the representational politics of its historically minoritized communities, as well as the political and formal questions raised by these communities' cultural productions. From the large array of groundbreaking individual and group projects of the Asian Canadian art communities, such as *Yellow Peril* and *Racy Sexy*, to the Japanese Canadian Redress movement that began in the mid-1980s, from the appearance of the first Asian Canadian literary anthology, *Inalienable Rice: A Chinese and Japanese Canadian Anthology* (1979), to Joy Kogawa's *Obasan* (1981), from SKY Lee's *Disappearing Moon Cafe* (1990), Hiromi Goto's *Chorus of Mushrooms* (1994), Wayson Choy's *The Jade Peony* (1995), and Larissa Lai's *When Fox Is a Thousand* (1995) to Fred Wah's *Diamond Grill* (1996), Asian Canadian has emerged as a powerful cultural and socio-political sign that has put the complex history and cultural productions of the Asian Canadian community on the map. Moreover, its gradual emergence has also helped reshape the overall understanding of Canadian literature as an institution, and thus raise important questions about knowledge production and power, literature and the nation-state, as well as diaspora and postcoloniality. Consequently, the intensification of Asian Canadian literature's critical study in the last

twenty years or so has itself become the object of scholarly debates by a number of critics, from Roy Miki and Guy Beauregard, two scholars who have produced leading work in the field, to Lily Cho, Chris Lee, and Larissa Lai, notable scholars from among the younger generation of critics.

Whether as a specific course subject or through individual Asian Canadian authors included in the curricula of Canadian literature or diaspora and postcolonial studies, Asian Canadian literature has been taught for years now both at undergraduate and graduate levels. As a distinct corpus, it has also been the focus of a large number of studies in essays, books, special issues of journals, and conferences, hence the wide circulation of the eponym Asian Canadian. An aggregate moniker, Asian Canadian nevertheless belies, at least so far, the collective character its name suggests, referring as it does virtually exclusively to Chinese and Japanese Canadian authors, including also such Canadian authors coming from the Chinese diaspora in South Asia as Madeleine Thien, and their critical study.[1] Significantly, in Roy Miki's work, which spans the areas of criticism, poetry, pedagogy, and cultural activism, Asian Canadian, whether it refers to literature or critical discourse, appears, almost invariably, in scare quotes,[2] suggesting that not only is it not a long-standing term but it is not a stable concept either (see also Beauregard, "Asian" 13; Lee, "Enacting" 28–29; and Day 45). I hear Asian Canadian in a similar way, more specifically as an epithet that has a double referent: it refers to a diverse yet distinct corpus of literary works gathered together by virtue of their Chinese and Japanese cultural signatures;[3] and it refers to a critical discourse that, though equally diverse methodologically, makes this literature, along with the historical, socio-political, and cultural conditions of its production, its primary object of study. Far from suggesting that the term minus the scare quotes signifies as a singular and transparent referent within a closed circuit of meanings, I employ it as a construct marked by negative capability, and thus flexible enough to develop toward directions that we may not be able to anticipate at present.

Asian Canadian literary studies has been a field in a process of becoming rather than operating, or being conceived, as a fully institutionalized subject, with all that this entails. This is in contrast to its correspondent field of Asian American Studies, which has had a professional association since 1979 and a journal dedicated to it, is taught in a number of American universities both in major and minor programs, and includes in its purview all Asian diasporas outside the Asian continent in the U.S.[4] We could perhaps "hear" the scare quotes around Asian Canadian as a diacritical mark suggesting that the two fields may be similar but are not, or should not be, homologous.[5] Indeed, it would not be too far-fetched to argue that part of the critical power the study of Asian Canadian literature wields comes precisely from the ambivalence of its quasi-institutional status so far.[6] I say "so far" because, since the publication of Donald Goellnicht's essay, "A Long Labour: The Protracted Birth of Asian Canadian Literature" in 2000, in which he laments the (presumably) dire state of Asian Canadian literary studies and calls for its formation as a distinct area, there has been concerted action by critics in the field calling for the institutionalization of Asian Canadian studies, in effect calling for the removal of the scare quotes around its name. A recurring element in these calls is the particular ways in which the arguments, invariably spurred by an anxiety about Asian Canadian literature's belatedness vis-à-vis its American counterpart, question canonization and conventional disciplinary and pedagogical structures while employing area studies and canonization as instrumental concepts and processes.

What I am interested in exploring in this essay is not whether or not the study of Asian Canadian literature should develop as area studies; rather, I want to examine the terms or the paradigm shifts through which the call for its institutionalization occurs. What does it mean to call for the formation of an area study, in this case Asian Canadian studies? Who or what performs the calling—the critic, the field itself, the discursive and structural conditions in academic institutions and/or society at large? Who is being called upon? In the name of what or whom does this calling occur? What does this form of apostrophe entail: what does it elide or wish to make happen? how is it imbricated with the notion of belatedness? what does it tell us about the process of canon formation and the function of area studies, and how does it relate to or resist their various exigencies? and how does this call militate against this field's present conditions? I cannot possibly address in detail all these questions, but they will nevertheless shape the trajectory of my argument as I take a close look at Goellnicht's essay mentioned above, which has functioned as a recent prompt for the calls to institutionalize Asian Canadian literature, along with his more recent "Asian Kanadian, eh?" and Guy Beauregard's "Asian Canadian Studies: Unfinished Projects," both of which appeared in the 2008 "Asian Canadian Studies" special issue of *Canadian Literature* that Beauregard guest-edited.

Because my primary interest concerns the tropological and methodological moves these critics execute in making their case, my approach here privileges close reading, admittedly a way of reading that goes against the grain of most contemporary critical discourses, especially so because it involves a close reading of a critical, as opposed to a literary, text. Most critics, and I am no exception, tend to unfold their arguments by focusing on strategically selected quotations by other critics; whether they agree or disagree with them, or find good reasons to both adopt and depart from the cited comments, they employ quotations in order to situate their own views, as well as to establish the conceptual, methodological, and thematic affiliations of their comments. The length limits imposed on critical essays discourage close attention to the larger contours of the critical discourses' contexts we engage with. As a result, we have learned to practise the art of strategic quotations, finding that sentence that captures as much what its writer intends to say as what we want to say through her or him, often doing so at the expense of nuance; thus what appears to be an affirmative reading sometimes unwittingly operates as a misreading. Precisely because my interest in the call for the institutionalization of Asian Canadian literature has been stirred, in part, by the fact that a number of critics endorse Goellnicht's call without examining closely how it is formulated, and do so in contexts that do not necessarily agree with the terms of his argument,[7] my close reading of his work is also designed to suggest the imperative to read, as it were, slowly (see Miedema). The close reading I propose to offer is not meant to be exhaustive, nor does it posit itself as being immune to misreading. Indeed, close reading cannot free itself from the incommensurable problems of exemplarity, including the "translatability" issue that allows us to move from the particular to the general, and vice versa (see Harvey vii–10). Furthermore, beyond Harold Bloom's notion of "creative misprision" (xxiv), Paul de Man has shown that misreading is a fundamental element of reading literature, and a necessary aspect of the production of meaning. Thus the close look I take at selected aspects of the texts I am concerned with here is intended to shed some light on contextual specificities that are usually passed by. To situate my reading in the double perspective of area studies and canonicity that frames the call for the institutionalization of Asian Canadian studies, I begin with a brief foray into the formation of canons and area studies.

Canonization and Area Studies
Literary traditions, be they conceived as national literatures or not, are simultaneously the result of processes of differentiation based on cross-cultural encounters and of identification of common elements. But, as the 1990s canon debates in Canada and similar discussions in the US show, the principles of inclusion, which determine the identification process that shapes a tradition, and those of exclusion, which influence differentiation, display a propensity to shift their terms of reference in response to various pressures and contingencies that are not always internal to literary traditions. While earlier notions of what constitutes the canon usually reflected a belief in axiomatic principles about artistic merit, and thus "the illu-

sion of a fixed and exclusive 'canon'" (Guillory x), the recent, and in some respects ongoing, debates about the Canadian and American literary traditions, as well as the formation of area studies since the Cold War period, have been shaped as much by curricular and disciplinary concerns as by societal, cultural, political, and economic changes. We cannot afford to forget that a canon is not a body of works we happen upon but is, instead, the product of institutional practices that are inextricably, though not exclusively, related to critical discourses and academic politics. The canon has no interiority as such, no unconditional sovereignty.

An object of study constructed as much by discursive as non-discursive forces, the canon operates as a "scene of inheritance and inventory" (Derrida, *Without* 115) that reflects the processes that create it while mirroring back what we project upon it. While as critics we do not always focus on canonical texts—as Guillory reminds us, "the archive" (i.e., non-canonical works) "has always been" a chief "resource" for scholarship (15–16)—the critical enterprise is invariably marked by a disposition to identify value and systemize knowledge, as well as by the "tendency to modernize the syllabus" and critical discourses, sometimes "at the expense of older works" (Guillory 15). The latter point speaks directly to the emphasis placed in the last decades of the past century upon the literary productions by First Nations authors and authors called ethnic, diasporic, migrant, or postcolonial, an emphasis that has radically questioned the Western ideologies that have long shaped canonization. This troping toward otherness—the mark of minoritization these literatures have in common—involves a direct engagement with racialization and cultural diversity but also with the historical and systemic inequities inscribed upon minoritized cultural communities through the ways in which the hegemonic nation-state manages diversity as yet another phase of its modernity.[8] Indeed, the expansion of critical studies toward this direction has predominated academic production and curricular and pedagogical changes in this time, and there is no shortage of studies discussing the pros and cons of such developments. As David Palumbo-Liu reminds us, "canon formation and cultural crisis" (4) go hand in hand, which does not mean the emergence of a "new" or diversified canon necessarily resolves once and for all the problems it tried to address in the first place. In fact, as he writes in the mid-1990s, the "recent interest in diversity" can be seen as functioning "as a mode of managing a crisis of race, ethnicity, gender, and labor in the First World" (6). Though at first sight perhaps a cynical view, it is one reflecting the fact that mainstream literatures' canonical reformation and the emergence of different area studies and canons are entangled with global capitalism at different levels.[9]

In this regard, what constitutes aesthetic value, the difference between use value and exchange value, and how such value systems relate to the cultural capital attached to and produced by a tradition—all this influences canon formation and introduces different ways of interrogating how a tradition emerges or signifies, that is, how and where it circulates, and how, where, and why it is taught. Nevertheless, at the same time a range of discursive processes also plays a seminal role in the formation, unsettling, and re-formation of existing traditions, as well as in the development of "new" ones, such as traditions that emerge from previously non-canonical works and/or the founding of area studies—"new" in scare quotes, for in this instance newness does not necessarily signal a formerly non-existent corpus of works but, instead, speaks to a different response to and engagement with ways of knowledge production and the complex shifts that the notion of value has undergone. The process of reforming the canon is the result of our employing different reading methods that allow us to detect things we were previously oblivious to, a process that is also mediated by circumstances external to purely scholarly work. As Gayatri Spivak puts it, "whatever our view of what we do, we are made by the forces of people moving about the world" (3). Canonical reformation, then, is a semaphore bearing the triple meaning of "reform" as verb and noun: ameliorating a bad situation by "remov[ing]...abuses, or other hindrances to proper performance"; "alteration in form and content...the improvement or modernization of something"; and "restoration" to "an original form or state," or "to full strength or health, or to proper function" (*Oxford English Dictionary*, 2nd ed.). In this light, then, canon debates and calls for new areas have a disciplinary function—disciplinary understood in its double sense of disciplines and conduct—a function that serves as a reminder that the implicit teleology inscribed in the reformation of literary fields is tentative at best: hence the need to constantly revisit both particular canons and the notion and process of canonization itself, as well as the terms in which such critical turns occur or are debated.

In the context of minoritized literatures, both literary traditions that are disturbed by cultural and institutional shifts and those that emerge as new traditions as a result of such conditions have a contiguous relationship with the communities they come from and speak about. Nevertheless, despite the fact that communities, society at large, and literary traditions are imbricated with each other, and that literature helps forge a sense of community, it is debatable whether literary traditions have a natural relationship to the communities they are supposed to represent. For example, in his introduction to the essays by Terry Eagleton, Fredric Jameson, and Edward Said, gathered together in *Nationalism, Colonialism, and Literature*,

Seamus Deane speaks of Irish literature's response to "the many crises" that have created the imperative to develop a discourse "for a new relationship between our idea of the human subject and our idea of human communities" in terms that "raise[] the question of how the individual subject can be envisaged in relation to its community, its past history, and a possible future" (3–4). But reading a national literature in this manner does not necessarily suggest that there is an inherent bond between national or ethnic identity and national canon. Conjugating nation and literature in such a fashion fabricates a closed-circuit of exchange and representational containment that elides other complex conditions that generate national literary traditions, as well as area studies developed around particular cultural communities. In drawing attention to some of the conditions relevant to the formation of Canadian literature, Diana Brydon sums them up "into three somewhat overlapping categories: government departments, agencies, and arms-length institutions that depend for their funding on the state; the market sector; and civil-society non-profit organizations" (5–6). This constellation of agencies brings into relief the fact that literature as an institution, even when it is produced and studied in the name of particular communities, is formed by an administrative logic, a logic intended, more often than not, to mediate the implementation of strategies (Chow 41) that serve state and other interests.

Thus, though canons do have representational power, we cannot assume that they hold an unadulterated and homologous relationship with the communities they represent. Precisely because they operate as instruments of various hegemonies, such as those of imperialism and colonialism, nation-states, and patriarchal ideologies, they tend to reflect values and images that privilege some community members while minoritizing others. Even when a "new" canon comes about, it too is the result of a hegemonic process at work, hegemony here understood in the Gramscian sense, or as Ernesto Laclau and Chantal Mouffe's concept of the strategic emergence of a cohesive ideology that causes the displacement of the (as it were) *ancien régime* in order to promote a different value system.

The same applies to area studies that are formed precisely with the intention of focusing on a particular community, even though, as the Cold War history of area studies makes it abundantly clear, it is not that community's interests that are necessarily served. Despite its ostensible investment in the study of the other, "because of the relentless kinship area studies formed with strategic policy making, serving national interests and 'contract research,' it was never able to free itself from the pursuit of a knowledge bonded to the necessities that had given it shape" (Harootunian 157). Thus, while in many respects the strategic deployment and conservative disciplinary structures of area studies remain unabated since their inception as new regions of "interest" are identified, notably the demand for Arabic speakers and a grasp of Islamic cultures as part of the American "war against terror" (see Chow 15), area studies as an institutional and disciplinary formation no longer signifies exclusively scientific interest in others residing principally outside the borders of the nation-state. The advent of cultural studies in the late 1960s played a major role in the development of area studies. Significantly, at the same time that cultural studies appeared, and perhaps influenced by it, but primarily as a consequence of socio-political movements (e.g., the civil rights, feminist, ethnic minorities' movements), a different kind of area studies began to take shape.[10] In contrast to the Cold War model of area studies whose focus was, and in many respects continues to be, on others outside the nation-state, this kind of area studies follows the opposite trajectory, one based on social movements focusing on the need to raise awareness about the rights of others inside the state. It is this shift in the genealogy of area studies that has brought about, for example, the formation of women's studies and ethnic studies programs, as well as more specialized ones, such as Asian American studies, the kind of area studies that plays a role as much in canon reformation as in the canonization process.

It is important to recognize the instrumentalist role area studies has played since its inception in order to understand that canons and area studies are not interchangeable categories, nor are they knowledge practices that are readily reducible to each other. It is essential that we keep in mind their differences. Indeed, the structural ways in which canons and area studies work in the critical and curricular domains would insist on this. Still, although they have distinct genealogies and properties, canonization and the formation of area studies as new modes of knowledge production also occupy a contingent and contiguous space, a space that has the potential to be critically productive because it raises questions about how they relate to each other and function institutionally. Canons and area studies have an adversarial relationship in that area studies strives to address the gaps in the former, often encountering substantial resistance as it operates from within the margins of society and those of academic institutions. Shaped by its emphasis on a particular body of texts, along with its contexts, that was previously unexamined or that had its particularities suspended or co-opted by the mainstream canon and institutional structures, area studies acts as a threshold space that interrogates and throws into doubt the canon's constitutive value system while applying pressure on disciplinary and institutional boundaries for its legitimation. In this regard, the adversarial relationship between the canon and area studies operates in ways that are at once dialectical and dialogic, a structural conjunction that is played out in how canons and area studies define, claim, or defend their turfs in institutional domains.

If canon formation has only relatively recently begun to exercise a certain self-interrogation about how it is put together and operates, area studies today is marked on the whole by self-reflexiveness because of the subversive and emancipatory character of its formation. Exemplified by the interdisciplinary and often comparative and transnational approaches area studies employs, this self-reflexiveness is evidenced in the concern area studies displays with the politics of representation and the agenda of ethics about the conditions and circumstances that bring it forth. If Cold War area studies does not shake up the foundationalist logic of the racial and cultural relations it deals with, area studies as the product of new knowledge movements enters this terrain from the opposite side of the spectrum: it articulates not only a "new" object of study that is accompanied by the imperative to interrogate pedagogical, methodological, and institutional structures but also processes of identity formation and agency in relation to particular constituencies. At the same time, because area studies also functions in a partisan fashion, it holds the potential, as well as the desire, to form a new canon; what is more, it can influence the refashioning of an existing canon by means of a conversion process that coalesces already canonized works with those brought to the foreground by its particular focus. In this regard area studies not only plays a supplemental, and thus corrective, role but also employs the same exclusionary tactics that inform canonization in general for it configures its identity by establishing distinct parameters (Brzyski 3). Thus area studies, while it is formed with the intention of recalibrating the hierarchical logic of an established canon, can itself become a vehicle of exclusion. In this sense it may posit an alternative value system to that embedded in the traditional canonization process and consequently operate as a counter-canon, but this does not mean that it abrogates hierarchical logic entirely.

Indeed, marked as it is by the trauma or "stigma" of belatedness, area studies may lose its inaugural emancipatory character by practising a certain kind of commodity fetishism in its desire to counteract the fetishism of mainstream canons. I am employing the term "stigma" in Salah D. Hassan's sense, not as a term that makes "a moral or aesthetic judgment" (297) but one he defines as the "effect of the eventual canonization of formerly countercanonical works; it is as if the violence of inclusion inscribes the surface of a seemingly recalcitrant text at the moment when it passes from margin to centre" (298). What this suggests is that the internal and institutional operations of the canon and area studies invariably implicate a complex negotiation process with each other and within the cultural and institutional spaces they inhabit. Their antagonistic relationship is inflected by the nervousness each exhibits in trying to assert its importance and maintain or establish its institutional status; it is also marked by the complicity that ensues from the fact that the fulfillment of area studies' political agenda may very well result in relinquishing its liberatory character by capitulating to conditions that are requisite to the ways success is measured institutionally. In this context, calling for the formation of a particular area studies is a critical gesture that can boomerang easily, for the value production of this approach is often compromised by the ambivalent desire to privilege the other while reifying what the other is supposed to lack. Cultural difference in this value system can be fetishized as a worthy object in ways that instrumentalize it and translate the other's subjection into a power that serves the moral needs of the normative subject.

The Ambivalence of the Call for Asian Canadian Literary Studies
Ashok Mathur's statement that "if as literary and cultural critics we can agree that the notion of 'writers of colour' came into a national literary consciousness as a marginal notation in the 1980s then it is with considerable alarm that we should note the mainstreaming of many of these writers in that they have begun to *represent* CanLit in many quarters" (141) draws attention to the ambivalence that often accompanies the emergence of "new" literatures and their study. Mathur does not object to these writers' growing appeal or commercial success as such. Rather, he draws attention to the perils of the culture of celebrity in Canada, a culture that works in tandem with canonization. As I have argued elsewhere, the culture of celebrity may pay homage to our "persistent attempts to introduce cultural differences into our discipline, and translate them (both cultural differences and the discipline of English) into the classroom" ("The Culture" 39), but it has the uncanny ability to placate the dominant society's moral anxieties about colonialism and racism in ways that replicate the very history of co-optive gestures it seeks to remedy. Driven by, among other things, the Canadian nation-state's strategies of containment and by global capitalism, the culture of celebrity exudes, to use a Benjaminian trope, an aura that has the same "colour" as that surrounding the master narrative of the Canadian state's *Bildung*. The experience of this auratic effect at a time that is resolutely post-auratic is precisely the object of Mathur's, as well as my own, concern here. As he states, citing Richard Fung and Monika Kin Gagnon,

> "if no one writes about your work it's hard to gain the legitimacy to get the resources to produce the work." But the flip side, when that work *is* being

written about, read, and sought, is that such consumption is driven by a market desire for a particular direction or focus. Fung and Gagnon refer to this as one of the paradoxes created by demands for inclusionary practice: "that slippery ground that artists of colour walk between commodification and cultural pertinence." (141–42)

Interestingly, while what instigates Goellnicht's call for the institutionalization of the study of Asian Canadian literature is the presumed scarcity of its systematized critical attention, it is the celebratory character of the public and critical attention authors like Joy Kogawa, Rohinton Mistry, and M.G. Vassanji had already enjoyed by the time of Goellnicht's essay that is of concern to Mathur.

This incongruity may be answered, in part, by the distinction Beauregard makes in his essay that introduces the special issue "Asian Canadian Studies." Employing this distinction as a strategic device in his attempt to advance Goellnicht's initial call for the formation of Asian Canadian studies, he distinguishes between "scholarship on Asian Canadian topics" and "Asian Canadian studies projects": the former is defined as "the various kinds of academic work done, typically through established disciplinary approaches, about some aspects of Asian Canadian history or culture or social formations," a "body of scholarship" that "typically conveys a limited awareness of and engagement with the social movements and the intellectual histories that have, since the early 1970s, enabled 'Asian Canadian' topics to become visible as sites of knowledge production" (Beauregard, "Asian" 7); the latter is defined as "scholarly work that also addresses some aspects of Asian Canadian history or culture or social formations" but is marked by its "attempt to work out of an awareness of the social movements, the cultural activism, and the intellectual histories that have enabled the category of 'Asian Canadian' to come into being" (7–8). Moreover, while both are marked by a diversity of methods, scholarship as projects, according to Beauregard, is privileged by virtue of the fact that it is "not content with only producing new studies about Asian Canadians," that is, "with simply considering Asian Canadians as objects of knowledge," but is "instead" motivated by the desire "to understand and possibly transform various discipline-based sites of knowledge production" (8). Nevertheless, what he presents as a fruitful distinction, one intended to steer this field toward the formation of "'Asian Canadian Studies' with a capital S—in which we could recognize a stable curriculum, set standards for hiring and promotion, and a defined institutional space" (12), is marred by the unexamined value judgments it relies on, as well as by its blurring of different registers.

Beauregard's swift moves from scholarly and teaching methods to scholars engaged in academic politics, from producing a standardized curriculum to hiring practices (9) and different promotional standards from what is normative (12) do not allow him to linger long enough either to provide a careful examination of relevant contexts or to articulate what particular reconfigurations of institutional and disciplinary structures are necessary for the formation of Asian Canadian studies. For example, his statement that it was easier for "English departments in Canada in the 1990s" to "includ[e] *Obasan* as course material than [to] includ[e] people of colour as faculty members" (9) is a mislaid comparison, for it does not acknowledge the fact that it was not perforce departmental policy in the early stages of the period he is talking about that made the curriculum more inclusive but, instead, the initiative of individual teachers. This is an important distinction to consider since Beauregard makes disciplinary politics a key factor in differentiating between the two study categories he identifies, though he refrains from proposing a concrete plan for what would qualify as the kind of political action he has in mind. Indeed, individual political and cultural vested interests are a usual preliminary step for the reformation of the canon and curriculum development. In the absence of courses dedicated to particular bodies of literature that have been systematically ignored—be they women's, queer, or diasporic literatures—normally works from such bodies find their place in the curriculum first as isolated texts, subsequently as texts of variable-content courses, and eventually as texts of courses that are regularly included in the curriculum. Usually, the inclusion of such courses in the curriculum is either a prerequisite for hiring someone in that emerging field or the hiring of a scholar specializing in that field proves to be instrumental in reshaping course offerings. Though I certainly share Beauregard's frustration with the snail pace of institutional changes and the systemic racism that, despite legislative measures, often makes itself manifest in university life, it is important to not lose sight of the historical permutations that inform the changes he is concerned with. For example, it was not until 1995 that the amended Employment Equity Act came into effect, a fact relevant to understanding why universities did not feel compelled or pressured enough to hire persons of colour in the period to which he is referring.[11]

Thus the "dramatic proliferation of articles on texts such as *Obasan*" (Beauregard, "Asian" 9) that is symptomatic both of the growing interest in Asian Canadian literature in that period and of the disciplinary unconscious that encourages the internalization of norms without interrogation should not be dismissed as "simply" an instance of "academic business as usual" (8); while it may be that (and I tend to agree with Beauregard),[12] this body of criticism must also be seen in the context of the larger historical conditions inside and outside academe at the time, and examined in relation to the incremental function of critical discourses. Whatever its ideological complicity with the Canadian nation-state and its master narratives, this criticism, collectively seen, has served the important role of redirecting critical attention away from the typical, up to that point, focus on white authors. Moreover, it can also serve an institutional function as further evidence of the importance of Asian Canadian literature in relation to the calls to establish it as area studies. This does not mean ignoring the racialization process enacted by certain kinds of critical discourses, nor does it mean operating from within a liberal imagination that inevitably circumvents political questions; rather, it suggests that the necessary attention to the material conditions of the production of literature and critical discourses about race and gender, along with the structural affinities I discussed above about disadvantaged communities and representation, must be calibrated carefully.

Beauregard's indictment of what he has called "Kogawa criticism"—not because "this criticism is 'wrong'" but because it "discuss[es] a 'racist past' in a 'multicultural present'" ("After *Obasan*" 14)—raises the important question of the political and ethical efficacy of the critical act. An issue that has long concerned critics, especially since the last part of the previous century, it defies the possibility of a single, let alone easy, answer because of the complexities and complicities that inform the economy of discourses and of social spaces within which critics operate. Notwithstanding this, and despite his acknowledgement that "there is much work to be done...to connect Asian Canadian studies scholarship to the larger project of social transformation" ("Asian" 13), what mobilizes his argument in this instance is the premise that there is an unmediated relationship between scholarly projects and social change. More specifically, while he fittingly observes that one recurring element in the "Kogawa criticism" concerns "the function of attempting to manage the implications of a particular moment in Canadian history *by remembering it in a particular way*" ("After *Obasan*" 14), his treatment of how history is represented, remembered, or managed in ways that may allow us to move beyond a history of oppression does not engage with the larger theoretical and methodological questions we must confront if we are to avoid a mere recounting of past events. He may be careful in avoiding being prescriptive, but his argument embraces assumptions that expose as much the problems with "the politics of the image" (Guillory 7)[13] as with the mimetic fallacy at work in what constitutes the efficacy of the critical act vis-à-vis its object and its socio-political and disciplinary aspirations. His reference to the "unselfconscious uses of

Kogawa's novel" ("Asian" 9), in a paragraph where it could be applied as much to "Kogawa criticism" as to the teaching of this novel, also makes assumptions about pedagogy in general or the kinds of pedagogy practised in the classroom in the 1990s. One does not have to teach a novel like *Obasan* exclusively in an Asian Canadian literature course in order to problematize, for example, its historical context, its Christian humanism, or how it relates to the rest of Canadian literature. Beauregard's argument, then, is marked by the ambivalence characterizing new historicism: it is intent on bringing to the foreground repressed realities but does so in a way that does not take for granted "that we know what history is" or "whether history is ever distinct from the manner of its representation" (Jay 215); at the same time, it is also sullied by new historicism's shortcomings, namely, the propensity to produce, often inadvertently, a new kind of empiricism by offering a revisionary return to history and politics in ways that conflate the desire for action and the need to found a new field with the positivism of foundationalist ideologies.

Writing his introduction to "Asian Canadian Studies" from a vantage point that marks a major shift from his article about "Kogawa criticism" where he declares that "at the heart" of his argument "lie profound ethical questions about how we read, discuss, and teach racialized texts in contemporary Canadian literary studies" ("After *Obasan*" 6), Beauregard assigns himself the ambitious—and, it must be stressed, important—task of investigating "how might Asian Canadian studies projects matter to us now?" ("Asian" 9). A noteworthy aspect of this shift is that, despite his repeated emphasis on the importance of scholarly "awareness," he does not engage directly with how Canadian literature and Asian Canadian studies might interpolate each other methodologically, as well as in terms of inter/disciplinary and institutional formations. While semantically the "we" in his 2001 article refers to all scholars interested in Canadian and Asian Canadian literatures, his use of the same pronoun in his 2008 introduction, accompanied as it is by qualifiers ("limited awareness," "academic business as usual—but this time it's about Asian Canadians" [7], "not content with only," "not content with simply" [8], "unselfconscious uses" [9], etc.), leaves no doubt that the "we" in this instance is not meant to include those scholars who adopt the so-called topics or business-as-usual approach. Scholarly projects that operate meta-critically, engage with social history, and trouble established disciplinary constructs (irrespective of how they do all this) are granted the capacity to effect change at different planes inside and outside academia, a clear instance of the mimetic fallacy I referred to earlier. As I have argued elsewhere, "a turn to ethics is not an ethical act by default" ("The Limits" 938). Since Beauregard does not dwell directly on these issues underlying his argument, the terms in which he approaches Asian Canadian studies exhibit a see-saw effect that results from the unresolved philosophical and political ambivalences of his position. On the one hand, he suggests that *"Asian Canadian studies projects may matter now precisely because they have been developed and continue to operate in such unsettled terrain"* ("Asian" 12), an instance of Asian Canadian as a sign having overcome its condition of belatedness; on the other, he suspends this "moment of *arrival*" and the stabilization that would inevitably result from institutionalizing Asian Canadian studies to propose that "Asian Canadian studies scholarship" be employed as a "strategic base[] from which to rethink social and cultural formations in Canada" (13). While this shift reflects the open-endedness of his introduction's subtitle, "Unfinished Projects," it also reveals the tension between the poststructuralist bent and positivistic inclinations of his overall argument.

If, despite, or because of, its ambivalences, Beauregard's call to systematize Asian Canadian studies has broad implications that raise productive, though still unresolved, questions about the formation and politics of area studies, Goellnicht's call, in contrast, which precedes Beauregard's argument and is endorsed by it ("Asian" 8), raises a different host of questions.

To Whom It May Concern

The various calls for the institutionalization of Asian Canadian literature as an area study that have recently culminated with Beauregard's guest-edited 2008 special issue "Asian Canadian Studies" have Goellnicht's 2000 essay, "A Long Labor: The Protracted Birth of Asian Canadian Literature" at the starting point of their genealogy.[14] Although I do not have the space to examine how these calls are formulated by critics such as Lily Cho, Christopher Lee, or Iyko Day, they are consistently characterized by a number of critical gestures that repeat themselves. In this instance repetition suggests persistence with the task at hand, but it also implies that this initial call has failed to fulfill the imperative it announced, namely the need to establish Asian Canadian literature as a distinct area of study. Failure in this context is not to be attributed to a single author or essay. Rather, it is inscribed in the nature of such calls as it implies that the move to change the state of affairs in question demands collective and sustained action within different domains, hence the tactical nature of the trope of calling. So repetition also results from the need to reaffirm what is stake, to make those addressed listen to this call yet again—hopefully more purposefully. Indeed, as I have already indicated, some critics in the field have listened, as is apparent in the ways in which Goellnicht's call is being iterated, albeit without close examination of its permutations.

A call of this kind resembles, though it is not identical to, the classical trope of apostrophe whereby the speaker directs his or her speech to another person, moved by "grief or indignation" (*Rhetorica ad Herennium*, qtd. in Kneale 151), with the intention of invoking a cause and persuading the listener to act on it. A trope that has been studied mostly in terms of how it functions within literature, it is also employed as a form of address in other discourses, "highlight[ing]" the "inability" of the writer's "contemporaries to adequately see, judge, or appreciate" what is at stake (Fernandez 21). It is offered, then, as an insightful and corrective intervention that operates at once as a performative and constative utterance in that it does not simply announce something; as "a genre and a tone," apostrophe also announces a "detour[]" (Derrida, *The Postcard* 5) from a normative course, and seeks to execute it. Len Findlay's "Always Indigenize!" is an excellent example of this. A necessary condition for materializing what is called for is that the announcer is in a position to do precisely that, to lead the action required to effect change. How then does Goellnicht stage his call to establish Asian Canadian literature as area studies, and from what vantage point does he do so?

Goellnicht opens and closes his essay with a reference to "Asiancy: Making Space for Asian Canadian Writing," the essay Roy Miki delivered at the 1993 conference of the Association for Asian American Literature, a gesture consistent with the context of his focus. Yet, despite the fact that he rightly calls it a "pathbreaking paper" ("A Long" 1), he does not quote or engage with it directly until the essay's last paragraph, which concludes largely with a collage of various points Miki makes. Granting Miki the last word is a peculiar critical gesture, for Miki's essay cancels out much of what Goellnicht argues for, as well as the perspectives and methods through which he does it. While Miki's point that Goellnicht cites advocates for "'deterritorialization'... [as] a viable method for resisting assimilation, for exploring variations in form that undermine aesthetic norms, [and] for challenging homogenizing political systems," as well as for a "terminology and frames" that are "open-ended and flexible" (Miki qtd. in Goellnicht, "A Long" 29 and 30), the approach Goellnicht privileges is mimetic: his call for the formation of Asian Canadian literature area studies is not only emphatically informed by a singular paradigm, that of Asian American studies, but it also employs strategies of containment and territorialization intended to install Asian Canadian literary studies within a North American model. While Miki is interested in exploring the potentialities of such concepts as "unreadability" (Miki qtd. in Goellnicht, "A Long" 29), and thus does not seek to posit a single critical and/or disciplinary paradigm, and Beauregard, as I have argued, emphasizes the potential of Asian Canadian studies to effect social transformation, Goellnicht adopts a thetic approach, one that is defined by the extent to which Asian Canadian literature studies coincides with or departs from its American counterpart.

More specifically, his own argument takes its cue from a second-hand reference in Asian American critic Sau-ling Cynthia Wong's *Reading Asian American Literature: From Necessity to Extravagance*, a footnote reference to Shelley Wong. The footnote offers neither a date or place nor a direct citation, a detail Goellnicht does not mention. Sau-ling Cynthia Wong paraphrases "Chinese Canadian scholar Shelley Wong"[15] as commenting on the lack of a civil rights movement in Canada and referring to "the state of Asian Canadian literature...as nascent" (Wong, note 28, 217; Goellnicht, "A Long" 1).[16] At the starting point of Goellnicht's essay, then, Asian Canadian literary studies is defined from the outside and staged in peripheral terms, thus being rendered a field lacking agency, a strategy that creates space for the critical intervention Goellnicht is about to make: hence his bemoaning the fact that "we in the academy seem to operate in an almost perpetual state of *announcing* Asian Canadian literature, a literature that has taken, from our snowbound perspective, twenty to twenty-five years to be 'born'" ("A Long" 2). Ironically, his use of the Canadian cliché "snowbound" reveals that his argument, despite its expressed intention to inaugurate something new, remains entangled with the inherited Canadian national imaginary; operating as a metaphor for being Canadian, "snowbound" reproduces structurally the garrison mentality that has shaped a big part of the early stages of Canadian literature's formation. This evocation of the normative view of the Canadian nation-state and culture unwittingly "announces" the dubiousness of Goellnicht's position.

Area studies, as the concept itself makes obvious, delimits its object of study by the geographical terrain it inhabits, a terrain that also reflects and inflects the identity formations and histories it accommodates.[17] But the manner in which Goellnicht launches his argument not only takes for granted the marginality of Asian Canadian literary studies, it also situates it, to quote from Miki's "Asiancy," within a "paradigm of centrality in which the 'other' is the necessary border/margin" (105). The centre in this paradigm is not, as one would expect, the institution of Canadian literature but rather, as Goellnicht states, "the North American academic literary establishment [that] was not interested in a literary tradition called 'Asian Canadian'" ("A Long" 1). This is not surprising since "North American" here really stands for American. When Canadian authors like Margaret Atwood or Joy Kogawa do "make it" south of the Canadian border, it is usually because they have their Canadianness suspended or strategically co-opted; a lot of critical work on *Obasan* produced by Asian American scholars barely nods to its Asian *Canadian* origins. Though Goellnicht acknowledges this instance of "U.S. cultural imperialism" (21), he holds back from problematizing it because he takes it to be a "natural" condition of affairs to be reconciled with. Thus, while he concedes that "Asian American literary studies has needed Asian Canadian literature for some time," he does not address what this need to establish a (borrowed) founding moment, specifically by claiming "the Eaton sisters as the *first* Asian *American* writers" (21), entails; nor does he examine what such a fashioned genealogy means in terms of the history of literary traditions and/or the ways in which disciplinary and institutional structures are shaped by the particularities of national-states. Instead, he seeks to translate this gesture of co-optation into a productive transaction, a quid pro quo, by exhorting "Asian Canadian artists and cultural critics...to take advantage of the leverage provided by that need...both to build coalitions and to remind Asian American cultural critics to pay closer attention to national differences between the two traditions" (21).

The kind of pro-Canadianness inscribed in this statement (and elsewhere in the article), along with the ways in which it is articulated, reveals the uncertainty of the ideological underpinnings of his argument. In attempting to justify both the means and the end of the transactions he describes, Goellnicht straddles the porous borderline between the US and Canada, and Asian American and Asian Canadian literary studies, for now he speaks from within a Canadian collective "we," now from within the "maturity" ("A Long" 3) status of Asian American literary studies with which he has long been affiliated. He does not interrogate the conditions that have shaped the formation of Asian American studies, a crucial thing to do since it is the chief model he employs for the advancement of its Canadian equivalent; nor does he engage with the concepts of the nation-state and national differences, especially as they pertain to minoritized groups for, as he says, he does not want "to play directly into the hands of those Canadian cultural nationalists who use the United States as the bogeyman whom we in Canada are called on to unite against by eliding internal 'difference'" ("A Long" 21). The fact that he proceeds from within this space of national, ideological, and methodological equivocations gives away the hierarchical logic of his argument at the same time that it prepares the ground for how and why he proposes to remove Asian Canadian literary studies from its (alleged) stagnancy, as is suggested by the misfortune implied in his metaphor of "protracted birth."

That "North American" in Goellnicht's lexicon is a designation that signifies in a highly ambivalent and troubling fashion becomes apparent in the introduction he has co-authored with Eleanor Ty to their co-edited volume, *Asian North American Identities* (2004). While "North American" in this introduction is supposed to be inclusive of both American and Canadian writers of Asian origins, contrary to the editors' good intentions, Asian Canadian barely figures in. Only a feeble attempt is made to bring these two bodies of work together; with the exception of two short paragraphs and a few passing references, their entire introduction privileges Asian American studies. Moreover, that of the nine contributions to the volume only one essay is about Asian Canadian culture speaks of tokenism rather than providing evidence that there is an Asian North American critical discourse, the kind of coalition Goellnicht thinks is possible. There is no attempt to rationalize this discrepancy, though perhaps Goellnicht and Ty's reference to the former's 2000 essay that bemoans the "nascent" state of Asian Canadian things is intended to account for the glaring absences in their volume. Yet, this reference only operates in a vicious circle as it historicizes the study of Asian Canadian literature in relation to the parameters Goellnicht sets up in that essay. Despite acknowledging that including "Canadians of Asian origins" in the "particularly vexed term" Asian American "seems to negate our political and national differences and…performs a colonizing embrace of Asian Canadian cultures" (2), Goellnicht and Ty propose a corrective that inadvertently replicates this co-optive process, as does Goellnicht's own 2000 essay.

> Insisting on using a "pan-Asian designation," they posit "Asian North American" as a more useful umbrella term because Asian subjects who reside in the United States and in Canada face many of the same issues regarding identity, multiple cultural allegiances, marginalization vis-à-vis mainstream society, historical exclusion, and postcolonial and/or diasporic and/or transnational subjectivity. "Asian North American" should be employed, however, with the proviso that both the national differences between the U.S. and Canada and the significant heterogeneity within the purview of the term are acknowledged and explored. (Ty and Goellnicht 2)

Their critical discourse of pan-Asianness, which has its roots in Yen Le Espiritu's concept of pan-ethnicity that advocates solidarity across different ethnic Asian American groups by privileging their commonalities, discloses at once the vantage point from which they launch their argument and the critical lens through which they operate. Beyond a single brief reference to the fraught relations between the Chinese and Vietnamese Canadian communities (4), Espiritu's concept of pan-ethnicity clearly derives exclusively from within the histories of Asian American cultures and the political dynamics vis-à-vis ethnicity in the US, the latter being substantially different from, among other things, the official multicultural politics in Canada. This is one of the many critically differential points between the Asian Canadian and Asian American fields that Goellnicht acknowledges but refrains from pursuing in a sustained fashion. "Asian Canadians never attained the status of a mass, panethnic social movement but remained localized groups" ("A Long" 9), he writes, thus rendering the historical and socio-political particulars of the Asian Canadian community as a failing. Though he quickly qualifies his "claim" by saying that this does not mean "that they lack agency or are apathetic victims acted on by others" (10), this statement, along with his observation that "Asian Canadian literary studies have been languishing in the wilderness" (3), further situates his argument within one of the grand meta-narratives of Canadian culture. He cannot possibly be oblivious to the colonial legacy of the trope of the wilderness, not to mention the many critiques mounted against it since the critical purchase it acquired following Atwood's *Survival* and its theory of victimhood. Still, he employs this metaphor in a fashion that allows his call to institutionalize Asian Canadian literary studies to perform as an act of deliverance, an act, however, whose political unconscious remains decidedly embedded within the nationalist paradigm of Canadian literature's canonization.

Ironically, it is these historical differences between Asian American and Asian Canadian literary traditions that Goellnicht proceeds to morph in his essay as evidence for the latter's weakness, as proof for its "protracted birth." As he writes, "the cultural production of the various Asian Canadian ethnic/national groups" has failed "to unite under a single sign such as 'Asian Canadian literature'" ("A Long" 19), a "failure" (19) he attributes to Asian Canadian literary studies' inability to develop a "history of national panethnic activism" (23). Though Goellnicht asks questions pertinent to his call for the institutionalization of Asian Canadian literature—for example, "What and whose purposes are served by classifying literature according to racial and ethnic origins?" (18)—he does not interrogate his own operative terms. For example, he takes for granted that unity or unification of different Asian Canadian discourses is a desired development, not considering that such alliances often occur as a result of reductive processes and at the expense of particularities subsumed in the name of solidarity. Thus, though he casts himself in the role of a midwife that will put an end to the painful labour evoked by his metaphor of protracted birth, the strategies he employs have an abortive effect. Forming Asian Canadian literature as area studies does not then involve either a questioning of the Canadian canon and the canonization process or the tradition of Asian American studies. In fact, despite the polemical tone of this essay, it would seem that, at the fundamental level of methodology and disciplinary politics, it is an instance of what Beauregard would call academic business as usual.

Even though Goellnicht's essay is punctuated by cautionary remarks that anticipate some of the critical questions his argument raises—for example, he asks: "Doesn't this approach run the risk of simply presenting Asian Canadian literary studies as a supplement to the larger Asian American Movement...?"—the "justification" he offers for his "valid comparison," namely the opportunity to "learn...valuable lessons from that use/abuse" ("A Long" 3) paradigm, does not trouble adequately its constitutive elements. What is there to learn from a use/abuse paradigm if one does not confront head-on the abuse in question? Instead, here Asian Canadian studies remains locked in a structurally binary relation that forecloses the possibility of contestation, an element normally inscribed in the formation of area studies—contestation both of Canadian literature as an institution and of Asian American studies. Indeed, Asian American studies is the only model he considers. Constructing Asian Canadian literary studies as a field through this paradigm, a paradigm he does not attempt to question in any substantial way either internally (as a specialist in that field) or externally (as someone writing from an Asian Canadian perspective), let alone consider its internal crises at the time he is writing, discloses that, unlike Beauregard who is keen to see Asian Canadian studies "develop" into a new episteme, Goellnicht operates within an already existing, and thus deterministic, monologic epistemic frame.

As implied by the terms of his call, Asian Canadian studies is to enter the critical terrain of "North American Asian Studies" from a position of lack that is also a position of desire, a twin trope that renders Asian Canadian literary studies both marginal and assimilable. Thus, Goellnicht's 2000 call for a systematic approach to Asian Canadian literature, far from dislodging the centre/periphery structure he has identified, is a gesture that operates in a manner resembling the power structure of the Althusserian mode of interpellation. Asian Canadian literature studies can be declared "born" only insofar as it is recognized as such by Asian (North) American studies, hence the fact that the way Goellnicht proposes to remedy the situation is articulated through a reverse co-optation process. Far from gesturing toward a hemispheric model of studies, or the kind of comparative and dialogic model that informs the formation of minoritized literatures into area studies, or recent developments in the field of comparative literature,[18] he adopts a hegemonic approach, albeit one couched in liberalist terms. The contents included in his chief strategy to North-Americanize, as it were, Asian Canadian literary studies do not have an isomorphic relationship to each other but are decidedly marked by a trope that is tainted, no matter how inadvertently, by hegemonic intentions. The fact that he presents the different character and history of Asian Canadian literary studies in a manner that renders difference as "failure" ("A Long" 3) further substantiates this. Indeed, "failure" and "weakness" are conditions that remain key to his argument; what is more, such terms as "minority" and "ethnic" punctuate his essay with great frequency without being questioned, thus operating as veritable and legitimate concepts with their racializing, essentializing, and othering tactics left intact. What this methodological practice suggests, reinforced as it is by the biologism of his key trope (birth), is that his call for the formation of Asian Canadian literary studies does not set out to shake up the systemic historical conditions and cultural and national ideologies of normativity that have produced racialized subjects and minoritized cultures.

The Coming Out of the Asian Canadian "Canon"
The Asian Canadian canon Goellnicht announces, then, in his 2008 essay, "Asian Kanadian, eh?", a canon he identifies with the work of Roy Kiyooka and Fred Wah, authors he did not engage with in his 2000 essay, is the result of deferred action, an instance of belated reading that draws attention to what he could have read at the time of producing his earlier essays but, for some reason, did not. Thus, it is not Asian Canadian literature (read Kiyooka and Wah) that is belated, but Goellnicht's own reading. If belatedness is marked by latency and forgetting, then a compelling question here is why Goellnicht "forgot" to consider this material in his earlier work. Elevating to canonical status what he previously ignored or treated in a desultory fashion creates expectations of radical rereading and contextualization. Nevertheless, without questioning his operative terms (e.g., canon and canonization, ethnic, minority, etc.) or methodology, he offers instead a revisionist reading of an already familiar cultural terrain. The lengthy sections on both Kiyooka and Wah, which, as he states, ask "questions... [that] have been posed previously" ("Asian" 73), offer a survey of these authors' literary production and cultural activities the aim of which is to assert how "the themes that they tackle... resonate in a profound fashion with the minority community so that they are deemed to speak with the voice of the collective" (72). Marked by a critical fallacy that assumes the force and value of a canon are symptomatic of its ability to speak for a community—be it universally conceived or defined in terms of particular locations—Goellnicht's "Asian Canadian canon" raises questions, at least for this reader, if for no other reason than because neither Kiyooka nor Wah "speak[s] with the voice of the collective"—if indeed there is such a voice. What is more, assuming that this messianism is possible, or

inscribed in Wah and Kiyooka's texts, Goellnicht makes no attempt to show how it is constructed. Pertinent in a discussion of a canon devised with the express purpose of representing a presumably cohesive community would be to explain what constitutes the "collective" and its "voice." Nevertheless, these constructs are left unexamined, and are thus granted unmediated and transparent status.

Goellnicht's canonizing intentions regarding Kiyooka and Wah follow his "adapt[ation]" of Deleuze and Guattari's notion of "minor literature" ("Asian" 72), but Goellnicht's approach, blurring as it does the textual and the biographical, the literary and the canonical, and subject formation/positioning and community, along with its privileging of thematics at the expense of linguistic and formal elements, is akin to Deleuze and Guattari's theory of minor literature only insofar as he employs the term "minor." Deleuze and Guattari emphasize minor literature's "immediacy to politics" (17), but they stress that the "message" of this politics "doesn't refer back to an enunciating subject who would be its cause...[any] more than to a subject of the statement (*sujet d'énoncé*) who would be its effect" (18). Their approach to what they call minor literature, though published before the second volume of their capitalism and schizophrenia project, is already inscribed by their concept of the rhizome they developed in *A Thousand Plateaus: Capitalism and Schizophrenia* (1987). The rhizome points to a radical break from traditional epistemological formations and, more specifically, speaks against linear genealogies. As they write, "the rhizome is antigenealogy. It is a short-term memory, or antimemory" (*A Thousand* 21). Reflecting, then, the rhizome's "continuous, self-vibrating region of intensities whose development avoids any orientation toward a culmination point or external end" (22), their notion of minor literature cannot possibly be seen as supporting canon formation, let alone Goellnicht's canon that derives from an overdetermined act that reduces the complex texts of these two authors to transparent representations of personal and community histories. Thus, far from being an adaptation, Goellnicht's approach is anti-Deleuzian/Guattarian, for it renders their notion of "collective assemblages of enunciation" (Goellnicht, "Asian" 72; Deleuze and Guattari, *Kafka* 18) as a positivistic construct that reifies the cultural and textual semiosis of Kiyooka's and Wah's work.

The same critical gesture marks the title of this essay, "Asian Kanadian, eh?", obviously an attempt to inscribe Kiyooka into the Asian Canadian tradition. But if the "K" reflects Kiyooka's "athwarted" (Miki, "Inter-Face" 51) relationship with the Canadian nation-state, the Canadian idiomatic "eh" Goellnicht inserts in his formulation suggests that the nation as construct here remains intact, that the intention is to seek a place of visibility and comfort for minority and ethnic communities within it. His reading, for example, of the *Tish* group that Wah was affiliated with may offer a valid critique of it vis-à-vis its lack of concern with the "profoundly racist past (and present)" of what Frank Davey calls "'the political and social life' of Vancouver" ("Asian" 81) at the time, but it misses the point that a lot of the *Tish* work about language, form, genre, and localism developed ways of reading the nation-state against the grain, hence the resistance they encountered at the time within conventional nationalist discourses. The same contradiction emerges from his reading of Kiyooka's and Wah's writing. Though he acknowledges its radicality, rather than engaging with its "difficulty" and "experimentation," he elides discussions of form, language, or genre and adopts, instead, an instrumentalist thematics that allows him to turn these writers into spokespersons for his own cause. Thus, the truncated survey he offers of Kiyooka's life and work makes it possible to call him "a lonely prophet" and a "Romantic artist" marked by "insistent individualism" (88), characterizations that, at least in my view, completely belie Kiyooka's politics and poetics.[19] If Goellnicht's recurring concern in this essay is how to reconcile his canon of two experimental writers with the notion that "experimental poetic practice often alienates the ethnic communities that it is intended to appeal to and to serve as they consider such art to be elitist, academic, divorced from 'reality' rather than speaking with the voice of the collective" (88–89), then he neutralizes this issue by consistently employing an interpretive practice that fetishizes as much this writing as ethnic communities.

The canon he announces, then, a canon, he claims, he "has had a hand in shaping" ("Asian" 73), is not a new canon. It is, instead, a (re)reading of two authors as central figures in a belated attempt to (re)organize and (re)orient a study area for strategic reasons. While Kiyooka and Wah have gained critical prominence relatively recently, they have always been important figures among those critics and writers, Asian or non-Asian Canadian alike, interested in the kinds of poetics and politics their work articulated in particular and the postmodern and post-structuralist contexts they have been associated with in general. It is not a coincidence that both these writers attracted wider critical attention after the publication of texts that are more accessible, Kiyooka's mother's narrative, *Mothertalk*, and Wah's *Diamond Grill*, texts that tease the reader with the promise of transparency as they offer easier points of entry into their textuality. Goellnicht has a point when he argues that poetry does not "hold[] the foundational place held by novels and autobiographies" in the formation of "Asian North American literary tradition," and he is right to argue, too, that "poetry is [not] an apolitical form" (87). Nevertheless, it is equally important to acknowledge that engaging with the politics of poetry or of texts that defy easy generic definitions should not be limited to a merely thematic approach, an approach that privileges "perceptual semiotics" (Deleuze and Guattari, *A Thousand* 23). Such an approach runs the risk of imposing a cultural authenticity on texts and elides the ways they produce meaning.

In this regard, that Goellnicht calls Wah's statement about "coming to the discourses of multicultural, racialized, and ethnic writing" in the early 1990s "a stunning revelation" because "discourses of racialized and ethnic writing had been circulating on the West Coast since the early 1970s" ("Asian" 84) is "stunning" itself. Not only does Goellnicht's response reveal an attachment to the notion of homogeneous time, a linear understanding of history and temporality that works against the semiosis operating in both Wah's and Kiyooka's texts, but it also assumes an unmediated process of subject formation. Goellnicht's canon, then, a canon that conflates its authors' discursive realities and textualities by ignoring their incommensurabilities, is not a canon as such. Rather, the result of blurring the textuality of the referential with the referentiality of the textual, it is a gesture that must be read in the context of the institutional values Goellnicht attaches to canonization. If his canon of Kiyooka and Wah is offered as a response to his earlier call to institutionalize Asian Canadian literature, if it means that Asian Canadian studies has come out of its "wilderness," then it has "arrived" in an overdetermined and skewed fashion that belies as much its own potentialities as the potential of area studies to make a critical difference institutionally and otherwise.

The Mark of Belatedness

Belatedness, and its variant "lateness" employed by Chris Lee, is certainly a term that punctuates frequently as much the essays I have discussed here as others that deal with similar issues. Belatedness is always accompanied by ambivalence and by nervousness—nervousness as employed by Homi Bhabha but also as it is thematized by Ato Quayson (see Bhabha and Quayson). It speaks at once of the condition of being peripheral and of the desire to rectify this state of marginalization by "*catching up*" (Beauregard, "Asian" 13). Thus a belated culture, even after it arrives, remains marked by its anxiety about its "cultural inauthenticity" (Szeman 187), by its ideologically produced self-image of being late, "derivative," and "imitative" (187). Often the result is "a social and cultural malaise that seems to be impossible to throw off" (187). But belatedness not only is a condition that characterizes minoritized literatures, it also epitomizes many aspects of national literatures, including those in Canada. As Szeman reminds us, "this [belatedness] is a feeling that Canadians are well aware of, and, at least in part, it is the attempt to break free of this malaise that has fuelled a great deal of Canadian writing throughout its history" (187).

What is significant in how belatedness operates is that it is configured in relation to an antecedent that, though it may be responsible for holding back the emergence of a new discourse, cannot be entirely superseded. Nevertheless, while what comes before tends to shape the terms in which something different arrives, the dialectical interplay of the past and the present, of presence and absence, in the structure of belatedness initiates a process whereby "the 'after' becomes constitutive of the 'before'" (Nägele 1). Thus, in the dialectical structure of belatedness, the before is not an object to be reproduced;[20] rather, signalling a response to "situations of a crisis that demand a reordering, reorganization, and reassessment of our lived experiences" (Nägele 5), belatedness involves "retroactive *illusion*" (Laplanche and Pontalis 112) in that it "return[s] to something which was not exactly *there* in the first place" (Levine 169). In this way, the "memory-traces" (Laplanche and Pontalis 111) of a traumatic event that has remained "latent," as Jacques Lacan would say (48), are "revised at a later date to fit in with fresh experiences or with the attainment of a new stage of development" (Laplanche and Pontalis 111).

Given this dialectical temporal structure of belatedness, the announcement of a "new" canon does not necessarily alter the relationship of Asian Canadian literature to the nation-state and CanLit as a national formation. Positing it in canonical terms, while doing so without problematizing what this canonization process entails, relocates Asian Canadian writing in a familiar ground, namely, "within the boundaries of the nation that initially justified its appearance as a nation-based formation" (Miki, *In Flux* 9). In this context, Goellnicht's desire to release Asian Canadian writing from the discursive contexts that have acknowledged it only as a minoritized corpus performs a paradoxical movement: Asian Canadian writing as a canonized construct may appear to enact an emancipatory gesture but, because its canonization process does not deal with how the before and after of its belatedness are constitutive of each other, it falls short of "expos[ing] the limits through which the politics of difference" has previously "scripted" it as peripheral to the nation-state (Miki, *In Flux* 11). It is this complex temporal structure of belatedness that is eschewed in Goellnicht's call for the formation of Asian Canadian studies. The before—be it Asian American studies, the history of individual authors, or such terms as those of race/racism, ethnicity, minority, and the nation—is granted a foundational force that undermines the terms of the call. It is because his initial call to bring together the Asian American and Canadian traditions has not materialized as envisaged that he answers his own call by turning his critical gaze toward the Canadian literary tradition to retrieve Kiyooka and Wah as the central figures in the canon he announces. But if such a call, as I mentioned earlier, must cause a detour from normative patterns in order to effect change, this act of retrieval does not constitute the formation of something new.

Such a turn toward a "new" canon raises a host of questions that remain unanswered. For example, how would an Asian Canadian canon as defined via Kiyooka's and Wah's writing change the centrality of *Obasan* in that tradition?[21] How would this "new" tradition, retrieved from, yet still contained within, the before of belatedness, trouble CanLit? How would it relate—politically, culturally, and institutionally—to, say, South Asian Canadian, Caribbean Canadian, and Asian American literatures? Why opt for a canon and not for area studies? What would the institutional, disciplinary, and pedagogical implications of such a canon be? Or, to put it bluntly, what is lost or gained by Goellnicht's approach? To pursue fully the permutations of these questions here I would need to address how critics—for example, Lily Cho, Larissa Lai, and Chris Lee—reference Goellnicht's work in the affirmative while, at the same time, positing arguments that do not necessarily endorse his approach and conclusions; and I would need to do so by broadening up the overdetermined landscape of anxiety regarding minoritized literatures, institutional formations, canons, and areas studies in order to engage with the political and cultural economies that it is inflected by. This pursuit, however, falls beyond the parameters of this essay.

Calling (yet again)

As I explained in the opening of my argument, my intention here has not been to provide an alternative answer to the limits of the epistemic shift announced by Goellnicht's call. Nor should my assiduous focus on his work be perceived, as the anonymous readers of my work feared it would be the case, as a personal attack. Rather, my argument has been primarily motivated by my goal to examine the tensions that might emerge in the process of attempting to institute minoritized discourses beyond the condition of otherness allotted to them by dominant narratives, as well as by my intention to tease out some of the implications of how critical work that exerts influence—influence measured as much by frequent citation as by other critical gestures that register different kinds of acknowledgement—operates within the field. That I have done so by means of the kind of close reading normally not granted to critical texts reflects both my frustration with professional strictures about codes of conduct and my desire to demonstrate that, to better appreciate the production of new knowledge and how it circulates, we ought to slow down. In effect, my close reading of the tropes of Goellnicht's call for the institutionalization of Asian Canadian literature also functions here as a trope for my own call to slow down, to read closely by way of taking into account both the textual and contextual aspects of the critical work at hand. If a call is marked by its own conditions for reception, I hope that my reading of Goellnicht's influential essays will elicit responses that will continue the critical dialogue about the compelling questions with which Asian Canadian writing as a discursive formation confronts us.

Notes

I wish to acknowledge the Canada Research Chair Tier 1 in Critical Studies in Canadian Literature for the support it provided to research and write this essay. A much earlier and much shorter version of this essay was presented at the "Virtually American? Denationalizing North American Studies" Conference, organized by Mita Banerjee, University of Seigen, Seigen, Germany, 2005. I am grateful to my colleagues at that event, especially Mita Banerjee, Roy Miki, Ashok Mathur, Glen Lowry, and Kirsten McAllister, for the feedback they provided. I also owe thanks to my graduate research assistant Hannah McGregor for her help with my research.

1 This focus is, in part, the result of circumstance, as the first Asian Canadian writers to publish as well as to get organized—I am referring here to the Asian Canadian Writers' Workshop in Vancouver—were Chinese and Japanese Canadian authors, a fact that is also explained demographically. For further discussion on this point, see, for example, the Introduction of Eleanor Ty and Christl Verduyn.
2 The scare quotes in "Asian Canadian" are removed in the revised version of the essays that have been collected in *In Flux: Transnational Shifts in Asian Canadian Writing* (2011).
3 Even though I obviously rely here on the field's own self-definition, I see no good reason why other Canadian authors of Asian origins could not be included in this group. Their inclusion, however, would inevitably necessitate a recasting of some of the terms of discussion in relation to diaspora and the nation-state since their history, and as a result their literary production, though still marred by racialization, involves different temporal moments and particular conditions.
4 See the Association for Asian American Studies (AAAS) web site: http://www.aaastudies.org/statement/index.php. Beyond its express focus on its academic mandate, the AAAS also states that it "advocates and represents the interests and welfare of Asian American Studies *and* [my emphasis] Asian Americans. AAAS is also founded for the purpose of educating American society about the history and aspirations of Asian American ethnic minorities."
5 This is a point that other critics make as well. See Beauregard ("Asian"), Day, and Ty and Verduyn.

6 By "critical power" in this context I am referring to my perception that critical developments in the area of this literary field have not only been important for an understanding of Asian Canadian literature but have also played a significant role in the studies and debates about other diasporic literatures in Canada, as well as Canadian literature itself.
7 I have in mind here, for example, Lily Cho's statement in the special issue "Asian Canadian Studies" that "following Goellnicht's meditations on institutional formations... [her] paper explores the institutional futures of a field whose arrival needs less and less to be announced" (181). Contrary to her point that "Goellnicht makes clear that he is referring to the institutional space of Asian Canadian literature rather than the literary works themselves" (181), Goellnicht, as Roy Miki and myself argue, conflates the two in substantial ways. See Miki, "The Poetics of the Hyphen: Fred Wah, Or the Ethics of Reading 'Asian Canadian' Writing," paper presented at the conference "Virtually American? Denationalizing North American Studies," University of Seigen, Seigen, Germany, 2005. My earlier version of this essay, which I presented at the same conference, also addressed this issue, but this section is here deleted due to lack of space.
8 Canada's official policy of multiculturalism is one obvious example of this, but the continuous preoccupation of critics with it as the socio-cultural and political frame par excellence that has shaped these developments, despite any misgivings they might have about it, inadvertently privileges and legitimizes it in ways that distort, if not belie, the complex picture of things in the period since the 1970s.
9 I use global capitalism here as a shorthand reference as much for the material conditions of the cultural market place and institutional developments as for the new modes (including neo-colonial) of mobility and the ways all these affect the agency and production of previously or newly minoritized subjects.
10 I am referencing here Anna Brzyski's *Partisan Canons* (2007), specifically her Introduction, but also Terry Smith's contribution to her volume, "Coda: Canons and Contemporaneity" (309–26).
11 It was not until 1984 that Judge R.S. Abella released her *Report of the Commission on Equity in Employment*, commissioned by the Liberal government of John Turner, which led to the 1986 first Equity Employment Act under the Conservative government of Brian Mulroney. But this first Act did not include all the recommendations made by Abella, most importantly that concerning monitoring the implementation of the Act. Under the Liberal government of Jean Chretien and following public hearings, the Act was amended, and a revised Employment Act was passed in 1996. Two important changes, relevant to the argument made here, include that, beginning in 1997, employers are subject to audits in order to monitor compliance and are expected to "consult and collaborate with employee representatives" (Human Resources Development Canada, "Labour standards and employment equity, 1996," Employment Equity Data Report, release no. 2, June 1999, p. 3). See Carol Agocs's "Canada's Employment Equity Legislation and Policy, 1987–2000: The Gap between Policy and Practice," *International Journal of Manpower*, 23, 3 (2002): 256–76,

which also illustrates that this legislation encountered resistance in various sectors and did not begin to be implemented immediately.
12 See my chapter on *Obasan* in *Scandalous Bodies* (175–221).
13 For John Guillory "the politics of the image" does not refer to a field "opposed to the real" but to one "of 'imaginary' politics" manifested by "the sense of representation as *reflection* or image" (7).
14 I identify Goellnicht's essay as the first such call because this is how, as I understand it, he situates his essay.
15 Though identified as Chinese Canadian, Shelley Wong specializes in Asian American literature and teaches in the US.
16 In the same note, Sau-ling Cynthia Wong goes on to observe that "it is noteworthy that both *Obasan*, the first Japanese Canadian novel, and Sky [sic] Lee's *Disappearing Moon Cafe* (1990), the first Chinese Canadian novel, were marketed and critically received as part of Canadian literature rather than specifically Asian Canadian literature" (note 28, 217). This is a moot point, given that she sees these texts as being the first ones of their kind.
17 Area studies, of course, can also be delimited by its particular focus on a singular subject, for example, gender, that is not defined by geographical parameters, though it can certainly inflect the subject in particular ways.
18 See, for example, Pearl T. Robinson, "Area Studies in Search of Africa" (2002), John Bowen, "The Development of Southeast Asian Studies in the United States" (2003), and Nicholas B. Dirks, "South Asian Studies: Futures Past" (2003), all part of the University of California International and Area Studies Digital Collection (see http://escholarship.org/uc/gaia_gaia_books); J.K. Gibson-Graham, "Area Studies after Poststructuralism," *Environment and Planning*, 36 (2004): 405–19; and John Canning, "Disciplinarity: a barrier to quality assurance? The UK experience of area studies," *Quality in Higher Education*, 11, 1 (April 2005): 37–46.
19 That two of the most important works of Kiyooka, *Transcanada Letters* (2005) and *Pacific Rim Letters*, ed. by Smaro Kamboureli (2005), are letters show that, far from being a "lonely prophet" without an audience, he was in constant dialogue with a diverse community of artists, scholars, and friends.
20 I employ here Freud's concept of *Nachträglichkeity (normally translated as "deferred action")*. Though the concept never received full treatment by Freud, it appears in different parts of his work, including his correspondence with Fliess.
21 See in this context Goellnicht's "Joy Kogawa's" (2009).

Works Cited

Beauregard, Guy. "After *Obasan*: Kogawa Criticism and Its Futures." *Studies in Canadian Literature* 26. 2 (2001): 5–22.

Beauregard, Guy. "Asian Canadian Studies: Unfinished Projects." "Asian Canadian Studies" Special Issue of *Canadian Literature* 199 (2008): 6–27.

Bhabha, Homi. "Anxious Nations, Nervous States." *Supposing the Subject*. Ed. Joan Copjec. London: Verso, 1994. 201–17.

Bloom, Harold. *The Anxiety of Influence: A Theory of Poetry*. 2nd ed. New York: Oxford UP, 1997 [1973].

Brydon, Diana. "Metamorphosis of a Discipline: Rethinking Canadian Literature within Institutional Contexts." *Trans.Can.Lit: Resituating the Study of Canadian Literature*. Ed. Smaro Kamboureli and Roy Miki. Waterloo, ON: Wilfrid Laurier UP, 2007. 1–16.

Brzyski, Anna. "Introduction: Canons and Art History." *Partisan Canons*. Ed. Anna Brzyski. Durham, NC: Duke UP, 2007. 1–25.

Cho, Lily. "Asian Canadian Futures: Diasporic Passages and the Routes of Indenture." "Asian Canadian Studies" Special Issue of *Canadian Literature* 199 (2008): 181–201.

Chow, Rey. *The Age of the World Target: Self-Refentiality in War, Theory, and Comparative Work*. Durham, NC: Duke UP, 2006.

Day, Iyko. "Must All Asianness Be American? The Census, Racial Classification, and Asian Canadian Emergence." "Asian Canadian Studies" Special Issue of *Canadian Literature* 199 (2008): 45–70.

Deane, Seamus. Introduction. *Nationalism, Colonialism, and Literature*. By Terry Eagleton, Fredric Jameson, and Edward Said. Minnesota: U of Minneapolis P, 1990. 3–19.

Deleuze, Gilles, and Félix Guattari. *Kafka: Toward a Minor Literature*. Trans. Dana Polan. Minneapolis: U of Minnesota P, 1986.

Deleuze, Gilles, and Félix Guattari. *A Thousand Plateaus: Capitalism and Schizophrenia*. Trans. and Foreword by Brian Massumi. Minneapolis: U of Minnesota P, 1987.

de Man, Paul. *Blindness and Insight: Essays in the Rhetoric of Contemporary Literary Criticism*. 2nd ed. Minneapolis: U of Minnesota P, 1983 [1971].

Derrida, Jacques. *The Postcard: From Socrates to Freud and Beyond*. Trans. Alan Bass. Chicago: U of Chicago P, 1987.

Derrida, Jacques. *Without Alibi*. Ed., trans., and with an Introduction by Peggy Kamuf. Stanford: Stanford UP, 2002.

Espiritu, Yen Le. *Asian American Panethnicity: Bridging Institutions and Identities*. Philadelphia: Temple UP, 1992.

Fernandez, James D. *Apology to Apostrophe: Autobiography and the Rhetoric of Self-Representation in Spain*. Durham, NC: Duke UP, 1992.

Findlay, Len. "Always Indigenize! The Radical Humanities in the Postcolonial Canadian University." *Ariel: A Review of International English Literature* 31, 1–2 (2000): 306–26.

Goellnicht, Donald. "Asian Kanadian, eh?" "Asian Canadian Studies" Special Issue of *Canadian Literature* 199 (2008): 71–99.

Goellnicht, Donald. "Joy Kogawa's *Obasan*: An Essential Asian American Text?" *American Book Review* (November–December 2009): 5–6.

Goellnicht, Donald. "A Long Labour: The Protracted Birth of Asian Canadian Literature." *Essays on Canadian Writing* 72 (2000): 1–41.

Guillory, John. *Cultural Capital: The Problem of Literary Canon Formation*. Chicago: U of Chicago P, 1993.

Harootunian, H.D. "Postcoloniality's Unconscious / Area Studies' Desire." *Learning Places: The Afterlife of Area Studies*. Ed. Masao Miyoshi and H.D. Harootunian. Durham, NC: Duke UP, 2002. 150–74.

Harvey, Irene E. *Labyrinths of Exemplarity: At the Limits of Deconstruction.* Albany, NY: State U of New York P, 2002.

Hassan, Salah D. "Canons after 'Postcolonial Studies.'" *Pedagogy: Critical Approaches to Teaching Literature, Language, Composition, and Culture* 1.2 (2001): 297–304.

Jay, Gregory S. "American Literature and the New Historicism: The Example of Frederick Douglass." "New Americanists: Revisionist Interventions into the Canon" Special Issue of *boundary 2* 17.1 (1990): 211–42.

Kamboureli, Smaro. "The Culture of Celebrity and National Pedagogy." *Home-Work: Postcolonialism, Pedagogy, and Canadian Literature.* Ed. Cynthia Sugars. Ottawa: U of Ottawa P, 2004. 35–55.

Kamboureli, Smaro. "The Limits of the Ethical Turn: Troping toward the Other, Yann Martel, and *Self.*" "The Ethical Turn in Canadian Literature and Criticism" Special Issue of *University of Toronto Quarterly* 76. 3 (2007): 937–61.

Kamboureli, Smaro. *Scandalous Bodies: Diasporic Literature in English Canada.* Foreword by Imre Szeman. Waterloo: Wilfrid Laurier UP, 2009 [2000].

Kneale, J. Douglas. "Romantic Aversions: Apostrophe Reconsidered." *Rhetorical Traditions and British Romantic Literature.* Ed. Don H. Bialostosky and Lawrence D. Needham. Bloomington, IN: Indiana UP, 1995. 149–66.

Lacan, Jacques. "The Function and Field of Speech and Language in Psychoanalysis." *Écrits: A Selection.* Trans. Alan Sheridan. New York: Norton, 1977. 30–113.

Laclau, Ernesto, and Chantal Mouffe. *Hegemony and Socialist Strategist.* New York: Verso, 1985.

Laplanche, J., and J.-B. Pontalis. *The Language of Psycho-analysis.* Trans. Donald Nicholson-Smith. New York: Norton, 1973.

Lee, Christopher. "Enacting the Asian Canadian." "Asian Canadian Studies" Special Issue of *Canadian Literature* 199 (2008): 28–44.

Lee, Christopher. "The Lateness of Asian Canadian Studies." *Amerasia Journal* 33.2 (2007): 1–17.

Levine, Michael G. *The Belated Witness: Literature, Testimony, and the Question of Holocaust Survival.* Stanford, CA: Stanford UP, 2006.

Mathur, Ashok. "Transubracination: How Writers of Colour Became CanLit." *Trans.Can.Lit: Resituating the Study of Canadian Literature.* Ed. Smaro Kamboureli and Roy Miki. Waterloo, ON: Wilfrid Laurier UP, 2007. 141–51.

Miedema, John. *Slow Reading.* Duluth, MN: Litwin Books, 2009.

Miki, Roy. "Asiancy: Making Space for Asian Canadian Writing." *Broken Entries: Race Subjectivity Writing.* Toronto: Mercury, 1998. 101–24.

Miki, Roy. *In Flux: Transnational Shifts in Asian Canadian Writing.* Edmonton, AB: NeWest, 2011.

Miki, Roy. "Inter-Face: Roy Kiyooka's Writing, A Commentary/Interview." *Roy Kiyooka.* By Roy Kiyooka. Vancouver: Artspeak Gallery; Or Gallery, 1991. 41–54.

Nägele, Rainer. *Reading after Freud: Essays on Goethe, Hölderlin, Habermas, Nietzsche, Brecht, Celan, and Freud.* New York: Columbia UP, 1987.

Palumbo-Liu, David. *The Ethnic Canon: Histories, Institutions, and Interventions.* Minneapolis: U of Minnesota P, 1995.

Quayson, Ato. *Aesthetic Nervousness: Disability and the Crisis of Representation.* New York: Columbia UP, 2007.

Spivak, Gayatri Chakravorty. *Death of a Discipline.* New York: Columbia UP, 2003.

Szeman, Imre. "Belated or Isochronic? Canadian Writing, Time, and Globalization." *Essays on Canadian Writing* 71 (2000): 186–94.

Ty, Eleanor, and Donald C. Goellnicht. Introduction. *Asian North American Identities: Beyond the Hyphen.* Ed. Eleanor Ty and Donald C. Goellnicht. Bloomington, IN: Indiana UP, 2004. 1–14.

Ty, Eleanor, and Christl Verduyn. Introduction. *Asian Canadian Writing Beyond Autoethnography.* Ed. Eleanor Ty and Christl Verduyn. Waterloo, ON: Wilfrid Laurier UP, 2008. 1–27.

Wong, Sau-ling Cynthia. *Reading Asian American Literature: From Necessity to Extravagance.* Princeton: Princeton UP, 1993.

THREE

When Race Does Not Matter, "except to everyone else": Mixed Race Subjectivity and the Fantasy of a Post-Racial Canada in Lawrence Hill and Kim Barry Brunhuber

Ana María Fraile

This essay offers a close reading of two contemporary novels that illustrate how African Canadian mixed race writers unsettle and problematize any fixed notion about Canadian identity and Canadian culture and literature by exposing the crevices of institutional Canadian multiculturalism through the experience of the shifting, ambiguous, liminal, and transnational positionality of mixed race subjectivity. The main focus will be on the *zebra poetics*[1] used to unveil the processes of racialization and racism covertly at work both in Canada and globally, as well as the fallacy of the discourses sustaining the beginning of a post-racial, colour-blind, and just era. The in-betweenness of African Canadian mixed race subjectivity unsettles the discourse not only on Canadian cultural nationalism but also on black nationalism. Besides, since mixed race subjectivities have historically violated "the sanctity of racial polarities" (Clarke, *Odysseys* 211), they occupy a privileged space from which to interrogate the historical intersection of race, class, gender, sexuality, and ethnicity, drawing attention to historiography and to received ontologies.

Both *Any Known Blood* (1997) by Lawrence Hill and *Kameleon Man* (2003) by Kim Barry Brunhuber stem from a tradition of African Canadian subjectivity and discourse that have only recently been made visible, having been largely disregarded by mainstream Canadian criticism until the 1980s.[2] Consequently, both novels resonate with the debates about the positionality of black Canadian subjectivity in the nation's meta-narratives and in the field of Canadian literature and criticism. In particular, with their mixed race male protagonists, Hill and Brunhuber complicate the seemingly polar positions within African Canadian criticism represented by critics George Elliott Clarke and Rinaldo Walcott. Whereas Clarke advocates the adherence of African Canadians to regional and national affiliations, thus rooting African Canadian culture deeply in Canadian soil, Rinaldo Walcott proposes a "deterritorialized strategy" that draws attention to "diaspora networks and connectedness as opposed to an explicitly national address" (Walcott 15) and reads black Canada as a transnational, diasporic space, a "black Canadian geography that requires us to think contrapuntally within and against the nation" (22). Yet, these are not clear-cut perspectives for either critic, as Clarke maintains that "African-Canadian literature [and culture] has always been international" (*Eyeing the North Star* xv), and Walcott's diasporic approach also encompasses "a discourse and grammar for blackness in Canada [that] can be located at the interstices of various histories of migration" (Walcott 139), beginning with the history of ex-slaves and moving into the twentieth and twenty-first centuries (an archival effort represented by Clarke).

The racial hybridity of Hill's and Brunhuber's protagonists is in dialogical interaction with the discourses of both Clarke and Walcott while also bringing to the forefront the illusion of a raceless society through the instability and shifting of racial identity in the highly racialized space of Canadian multiculturalism. Thus, Canada's official policy is portrayed as paradoxically hovering between essentializing race and ethnicity by trying to support and promote the different ethnic cultures in Canada, and colour-blindness and a denial of racialization in the confidence that the Constitution, through the 1988 Multiculturalism Act, guarantees and extends the same rights and obligations to all Canadians. This essay's title alludes to the pitfalls of this post-racial atmosphere, which is by no means uniquely Canadian, and which the mixed race subjectivities, due to their fluid transracial, transcultural, and transnational quality, can best disturb and reveal as a deception. I also suggest that the two novels chosen offer a critique of the current post-civil-rights, conservative multiracial discourse, as they expose the politics of colour-blindness as anti-black and as a setback to the achievements of the civil rights movement.

A Post-Racial Era?

In the international Anglo cultural and literary realms, the move toward the construct of a post-racial era is epitomized by the publication of Paul Gilroy's book *Against Race: Imagining Political Culture Beyond the Color Line* (2000), where the author challenges scholars to move beyond theories of race. Gilroy has not been alone in this demand, as sociologists, psychologists, political scientists, cultural and literary critics from different parts of the Western hemisphere—Orlando Patterson, Pierre Wacquant and Loïc Bourdieu, Antonia Darder and Rodolfo Torres, Adolf Reed Jr., and Neil Bissoondath[3]—have all insisted on the retreat from race. Furthermore, the momentous election of mixed race Barack Obama as President of the United States in 2008 may deceptively convey the idea that the Western world has definitely entered the post-racial era that Paul Gilroy longed for.[4] However, neither the current discredit of essentialist theories of race in favour of theories about its social constructedness nor the ideal of social justice for all, which characterizes the different but similarly colour-blind phenomena of institutional multiculturalism and the multiracialism movement,[5] has led to the dissolution of racism or of its accompanying scourges—social injustice and economic imbalance. In fact, as historian David Roediger laments, "as the twenty-first century starts, the idea of a colorless struggle for human progress is unfortunately back with a vengeance" (Roediger).

Contradicting any formulations about Canadian belatedness, Canada anticipated the move against race in the 1950s and '60s, only to return to reinvigorated discussions on race in the 1980s and '90s. In their illuminating introduction to the volume *Race*, "'Race' into the Twenty-first Century," Daniel Coleman and Donald Goellnicht explain how by the mid-twentieth century the country consciously shifted away from the previous race-based thinking that promoted eugenics as a nationalist principle to build a superior "'Canadian race' based on 'Nordic man,'" and supported Pierre Trudeau's vision of a colour-blind, just society. The process culminated with the State's adoption of multiculturalism as a defining principle of Canadian society and national identity, which emphasized ethnicity over race. However, critics soon started pointing out the pitfalls of such a policy. Indo-Caribbean Canadian writer Neil Bissoondath opposed the proponents of multiculturalism—as well as many of its critics—by arguing that neither race nor ethnicity should play a relevant part in Canada, and that nationhood should be based on the principle of assimilation to the foundational French- and Anglo-Canadian ethnicities. Others, mainly writers and activists of colour, complained that Canadian multiculturalism "represented the dismal failure of liberal multiculturalism precisely because it exposed the professed colour blindness of this policy as a covert strategy for maintaining the status quo, for propping up white privilege" (Coleman and Goellnicht 9). The coalescence of what Charles Taylor calls the "politics of difference" and the "politics of equal dignity" or of "boutique multiculturalism" (Fish 378) and "strong multiculturalism" (382) in Stanley Fish's terminology, results, as Smaro Kamboureli puts it, in an "impossible act of balancing differences"—"a politics that attempts to recognize ethnic differences, but only in a contained fashion, in order to manage them. It pays tribute to diversity and suggests ways of celebrating it, thus responding to the clarion call of ethnic communities for recognition. Yet, it does so without disturbing the conventional articulation of the Canadian dominant society" (*Scandalous Bodies* 82).

Contrary to Gilroy's call to do away with "the old, modern idea of 'race' [which] can have no ethically defensible place" in "multicultural social and political life" (6), the Canadian return to discussions of race during the 1980s and '90s was a consequence of a new racial awareness that materialized in "the increasing racialization of the Canadian social and literary discourse" (Padolsky 19). Therefore, the *creation* of diverse racialized Canadian literary traditions, which function as *strategic essentialisms* "in a scrupulously visible political interest" (Spivak 205), has sought to provide a space for the reconstruction of complexly racialized identities in a cultural context that, by disavowing race, perpetuates injustice. Canadian literature can be viewed not just as the mirror of society's tensions with respect to the assumed erasure of race, but as an agent of social and individual change, in that it provides a space for the contestation of an allegedly a-racial multicultural society and for the affirmation of difference. As Kamboureli explains: "While CanLit as an institution reflects this process whereby the other becomes the same, normative and therefore transparent, it also insists on positing itself as a discursive site where the other can deflect its assigned familiarity, its status as a vanishing object" (*Trans.Can.Lit* ix).

Caught in the crosscurrents of different identity-constitutive tensions, the racialized bodies of the mixed race protagonists in *Any Known Blood* and *Kameleon Man* become the catalysts for what Daniel Coleman calls *cross-cultural refraction,* meaning the distortions caused by "the transition from one culture to another," similar to the distortion produced by "the transition between elements [which] makes the straight drinking-straw appear to bend in the glass of water" (*Masculine Migrations* 3). Drifting between races and ethnicities as, simultaneously, insiders and outsiders, the protagonists Langston Cane the Fifth and Stacey Schmidt both engage and unsettle the official discourses about race, ethnicity, class, and gender, which are thereby rendered unfamiliar, while a space is created for the contestation and reinvention of Canadian identity. In contrast with Canada's ideal "multicultural project of colour-blind inclusiveness" (Coleman and Goellnicht 7), the emphasis on race in both novels offers a comment on the actual difficulties of carrying out such a project. The racialization of Canadian society is apparent from the very beginning in both novels, determining the protagonists' respective struggles to assert themselves as free male subjects in Canada.

Race occupies central stage in Lawrence Hill's novel from the very title, *Any Known Blood*, with its allusion to the US *one drop rule* as articulated in the epigraph that opens the novel: "Everybody having a known trace of Negro blood in his veins—no matter how far back it was acquired—is classified as a Negro. No amount of white ancestry, except one hundred percent, will permit entrance to the white race." The social exclusion dictated by the hypodescent rule formulated by Gunnar Myrdal in this quote is further amplified by the second epigraph citing Langston Hughes's poem "Cross," which presents the mixed race subject as excluded not just from the white but also from the black world, "Being neither white nor black." Setting up the link between Canada and the US, the novel's Prologue shatters the notion of Canadian colour-blindness and underlines the social construction of race. Thus, a "grapefruit-sized rock" (xiv) and the racist, threatening voices of young men calling, "*You will die, nigger. You will die soon*" (xiv) definitely racialize the colour-neutral shadows of a man and a woman—Langston's parents—making love in Toronto, shadows which prior to the attack revealed "nothing of her whiteness, or his blackness" (xiv). Interestingly, a very similar scene occurs in *Kameleon Man*, when the protagonist realizes that only on the reflection in the window of a half-lit room are he and his white girlfriend Melody "the same colour" (169).

From the outset, Kim Barry Brunhuber's debut novel exhibits a similar focus on race and racialization. As in *Any Known Blood*, the allusion to race is implicit in the novel's title, which underlines the social construction of race by referring to the possibility of willingly changing or choosing one's race, the same as chameleons change colours to blend with their environment. Moreover, the title *Kameleon Man* focuses on the intersection between race and masculinity, establishing that, like race, masculinity is not an essence but rather a plurality determined by its multiple intersections with other categories influencing men's identities. The title also refers to the fashion firm Kameleon Jeans, which twenty-one-year-old Stacey sees as his chance for fame and money. Kameleon Jeans will not hesitate to capitalize on Stacey's racial ambiguity, matching his undefined multiracial image with the universal staple of fashion that jeans symbolize. As Dat

Win will let Stacey know, "Jeans can make you into anything you want. Class and culture disappear. Like communism, only it works. Labourers and the proletariat wearing the same clothes. It's kind of ironic that America's uniform is Marxism's only living legacy" (201). In the novel, however, jeans do not help to erase difference, but are used as "camouflage" rather than a bridge for cross-cultural communication. Thus, Stacey's mixed race condition will be co-opted and put to the service of capitalist greed, intent on transcending all sorts of boundaries—race, class, ethnicity, gender, nationality, generation—in order to appeal to universal consumerism.

Despite the obvious focus on race and racialization in the novel, Brunhuber complains that reviewers have disregarded the importance of race in it, in a display of typical colour-blindness:

> My only disappointment has been that very few interviewers have given enough attention to the subject of race, which is one of the main themes of the novel.... This supports my view that Canadians don't want to talk about race. It's exactly that head-in-the-sand approach that I wanted to challenge with my book, and it's unfortunate that most interviewers still want to duck the issue. We can't change one of the most fundamental problems in our society if nobody's willing to acknowledge it. (Brunhuber, Interview)

It is against this background of colour-blindness that the protagonists in both novels have to negotiate their ambiguous, shifty position as mixed race African Canadians.

Colour-Blind Multiculturalism and the Rejection of Blackness

Chapter 1 of *Any Known Blood* opens with Langston Cane the Fifth's account of his evasive and burdensome racial condition as a mixed race individual: "I have the rare distinction—a distinction that weighs like a wet life jacket, but that I sometimes float to great advantage—of not appearing to belong to any particular race, but of seeming like a contender for many" (1). Claiming multiple racial identities—but never his own *zebra*, black-and-white ancestry—Langston exposes two of the fissures in the praxis of Canadian multiculturalism: namely, Canadians' latent racism, which is exposed every time he claims to be "part anything people were running down" (2), and the impracticality of an official multiculturalism policy, which since 1996 has relied on a census that encourages racial self-identification.[6] Langston's forged adoption of an Algerian identity to apply for his current job as a government speech writer for which "only racial minorities need apply" (2) serves as an ironic comment on this freedom of racial self-identification, as he tests his theory that "nobody would challenge my claim to any racial identity" (2). His misidentification, paired with his unveiling of the Ontario Government's plans "to eliminate human rights legislation and to dismantle the human rights commission" (17), refracts the distance between the multicultural ideal embodied by the affirmative action policy under which he got the job and the politicians' allegiances with the hegemonic economic powers.

By faking several racial identities and shunning his roots as white or African American/Canadian, Langston does not simply follow Langston Hughes's understanding of the mulatto as "neither black nor white," as established in his poem "Cross," which serves as an epigraph on the first page of the novel. On the one hand, by willingly refusing to partake of either whiteness or blackness, he avoids being co-opted by or profiting from the hegemonic ideology of Canadian whites. On the other hand, he also avoids identifying with blackness and the collective history of oppression and struggle for civil rights and equality. In the process, he eschews his father's code of domineering, patronizing black manhood, represented by the latter's engagement as a civil rights leader, by his professional and economic success within the capitalist system, and by his patriarchal outlook in the context of heterosexual family codes. Langston's rejection of his own African Canadian ethnicity is therefore also an attempt to distance himself from his father's disapproval of his broken, childless marriage and of his mediocre job as a government speech writer. Langston particularly eschews his father's belief that he is a kept man, that his love for his wife was just a fake front "for free rent" (46), something that definitely shatters the social codes that link masculinity to independent and male-provider figures.

Nevertheless, Langston's rejection of his African Canadian ethnicity by means of his misidentifications with various racial groups is, as Winfried Siemerling has pointed out, a disidentification (36), a term used by Judith Butler to refer to "an identification that one fears to make only because one has already made it" (*Bodies That Matter* 112). As a result, Langston simultaneously rejects and subscribes to his father's social codes, his family's legendary tradition, and Canadian multiculturalism. This ambivalent, paradoxical position resulting from his *zebra* condition leaves him powerless and abject, to the extent that he considers himself a loser who unconsciously wishes to succeed on his own terms, as his brother will tell him (Hill, *Any Known* 53). As he simultaneously identifies and disidentifies with his prestigious ancestors, Langston ironically reasserts his own courage: "But it also takes something to fall from the treadmill of great accomplishments, to fail, even at the tasks of being a husband and a potential father and a writer, to march to the gates of middle-age and look ahead and accept that you will not change the world" (3–4). Langston will be proven wrong, though, when at the end he makes his own contribution to social understanding by means of writing a novel based on his family history, thus linking his individual achievement to the collective wellbeing. In the process he will have embraced both blackness and whiteness, acknowledging by the end of the novel that he is "zebra incorporated" (400).

As in Langston's case, Stacey's mixed race in *Kameleon Man* raises the issue of authenticity, which unsettles the protagonist even at the unconscious level, as his recurrent nightmare reveals. In the opening pages, Stacey recounts the dream in which his face becomes a mask while he walks down an endless runway and the smile he thinks is the key to his success becomes "frozen, an impossible rictus stretching from ear to ear" (7–8). At this point, Stacey is not mortified by the idea of being untruthful to himself, but by the possibility that his disguise may be discovered, and his real, resilient and subversive essence or identity disclosed, putting his life at risk: "The audience sees through my face, howls at the deception, rushes the stage, tears me to bloody ribbons" (8). This nightmare also illustrates his fear of rejection by his white girlfriend, Melody, who is portrayed as a consumer of *boutique multiculturalism*, lured by the exoticism of the racially different, but rejecting *essential* or *pure* blackness, as when in the presence of two black Jamaicans she whispers to Stacey, "I'm glad you're not like them" (165). Although Stacey first believed that she was attracted to him because she considered him black, and therefore he was cheating her—"I'm not the genuine article. I come with no pedigree of negritude" (49)—he would soon realize that she is a racist at heart, only attached to him because of his tamed blackness: "She told me on our first date that she liked me because I wasn't too dark. I took that as a compliment then. Now I know better. I'm not like 'them' [pure blacks]" (169). In a Fanonian vein, Stacey's mulatto condition turns him into a ghost.

> We're shades. Insubstantial images of something real. Reduced almost to nothing. The only thing worse than living in that black-and-white world is living in a grey one, in which *race doesn't matter except to everyone else*. In which nothing's black or white and everything's both. The problem with living in grey is that one does not grow natural defences. Growing up grey is like growing up weightless on the moon. To return to earth is to be crushed by the weight of one's own skin. (49; emphasis added)

Stacey thus exposes the dangers and contradictions of Canadian liberalism's professed colour-blindness, significantly coinciding with Wayde Compton's observation that to support the view that "race doesn't matter" neutralizes any attempt on the part of the racialized subject to contest racism. To Compton, Canadians tend to allow whites to define what is and isn't black, and white Canadians do so according to the colour metaphor, which they can't seem to see *is* a metaphor—to them, unless you are literally black-skinned (and who is?), you are not black, and what's worse is they have no word for what you *are*, and are likely to tell you "race doesn't matter," which, if you allow it, will leave you absolutely powerless and abject. That's white Canadian liberalism... (135)

The result is tragic, as Stacey's comparative analyses between the animal world and his own experience as mixed race reveal. His uneasiness is illustrated through the example of the mule deer: "It's a cross between a species of deer that hides from its enemies and another species that runs away from them. When it smells a wolf or a mountain lion, the mule deer doesn't know whether to run or hide, and it's always eaten first" (Brunhuber, *Kameleon* 169). Likewise, Stacey relates the fate of a zebra in a TV documentary to his own: "Another zebra's been caught by a lion. The zebra always struggles briefly, gives a pitiful honk and a wheeze, then lies still, resigned to its fate. How can it surrender so easily? I'd scratch, bite, kick, fight to the death, like those busy beavers that would rather gnaw off their own legs than be caught in a trap. But my trap is more subtle than a lion, colder than metal" (108).

Stacey's reference to the strong drive for freedom of the beaver, this symbol of Canadian identity that he appropriates for himself, and the inevitability of the trap, again situate him in the hazardous position of abjuring his mixed race identity and espousing Canadianness. Similarly, and in spite of his awareness of racialization, Stacey's identification with white Canadian liberalism prevents him from considering his objectification as a model in racial terms, preferring to think, like the novel's first reviewers, that the moulding of models is what this business is about: "It's modeling, for Christ's sake. By the very nature of our profession, our characters are untrue, subject to question, flimsy as a nightgown" (135). Consequently, Stacey dangerously overlooks the fact that consumer culture has not only been implicated in the creation of hierarchical categories of race, but "has contributed to shifts in how racism operates, specifically to the shift *from* a racism tied to a biological understanding of race in which identity is fixed or naturalized *to* a racism in which race is a cultural category in which racial identity is represented as a matter of style, and is the subject of choice" (Lury 169).[7] As a result of the representation of race in terms of an aesthetic choice, "the political reality of racism is eradicated" (168), though racism itself is not. Brunhuber contests this attempt at camouflaging racism by bringing to the forefront the multiple racist, psychological, economic, and sociological implications of this redefinition of race both for the subject marked as non-white (and non-black) and for society at large.

Stacey's eventual rise in the modelling industry is intrinsically linked to the evolution of racialization in the West towards the enhancement of mixed race and multiracialism. At the beginning of the 1990s, Susan Willis traced two contradictory and coexisting tendencies with regards to the representation of race. On the one hand, "a move towards the representation of racial sameness and [on the other,] an emphasis on the celebration of racial difference" (Lury 162). She pointed to a *new ethnicity* in which "individuals who, in some way or other, represent all races in one are held up as ideals...an attempt to erase the political significance of race" (163). Stacey is clearly complicit by lending himself to become that ideal Lury mentions, an icon of racial sameness that supports the idea of a colour-blind, post-racial society: "What do they [the audience] see, anyway? They are not looking at Stacey—he does not exist anymore. Fashionable metallurgists have broken me down, smelted me, moulded me, sculpted me, into a model. A representation of an object. Perfectly to scale, proportioned in all dimensions. Worthy of imitation. Exemplary. Designed to be followed" (Brunhuber, *Kameleon* 7).

In the same vein, US novelist Danzy Senna ironically explained in "The Mulatto Millennium": "According to the racial zodiac, 2000 is the official Year of the Mulatto. Pure breeds (at least the black ones) are out and hybridity is in. America loves us in all our half-caste glory" (205). Hence, Stacey's racial indeterminacy turns him into the emblem of the times, as Kameleon agent Dat Win lets him know: "See, when I look at you, it's kind of hard to tell what you are exactly.... You could pretty much pass for whatever, right?" (Brunhuber, *Kameleon* 203). Thus, at the beginning of the new millennium, favouring racial sameness under the guise of multiracial attitudes seems to have won over the celebration of racial difference, as Win explains in a few words: "A couple of years ago everyone was caught up celebrating difference, the exotic. The blacker the better" (204). Now, however,

> things are different. We're done with the idea of legitimacy, pureness. The essential African, the essential Asian. All of that's done. Our ideas about race are changing. Gradually the world is swallowing the idea. That we're all the same. And I don't mean that we're all the same inside. One day, we'll all be the same outside. If we stir the pot long enough, you're what's left at the bottom. Kameleon isn't just about jeans anymore, it's about us. It's about humanity. It's about the net result, and you're it. (204)

By reverting difference to sameness, Dat Win reverses Charles Darwin's theory about the evolution of species from a single ancestor to the present diversity of life—human and otherwise. In Dat Win's questionable vision of a "multiracial democracy beneath the long shadow of 'global white supremacy'" (Sexton 5), Stacey is made into the representative hybrid man, not just in the New World, as Stuart Hall would have it, but in the globalized society of the future.[8] Because multiracialism "operates by way of a historic double standard—endorsed when it does not involve blackness in significant ways, abjured whenever it does" (Sexton 17), Stacey is asked to eschew his self-ascribed black identity: "You want me to say I'm not black?" (Brunhuber, *Kameleon* 204). By accepting Dat Win's terms, he becomes complicit with multiracialism's anti-blackness.

Fittingly, like Langston Cane, who considers himself a failure, Stacey has a deprecating self-image. As a result, both protagonists set out in search for wholeness, self-respect, and social approval, which leads them to shed their role as subversive tricksters of forged identities. In order to achieve their goals, they need first to embrace the black component of their mixed ethnicity, and they do so by retrieving and situating themselves in the historical discourse of race and racialization.

Retrieving Blackness and the Historical Dimensions of Racialization

Both Langston and Stacey belong in the current context where multiracialism is attuned to the "conservative restoration" which eschews common political actions, such as the black liberation struggle, in favour of a citizenship that is based on "one's moral integrity in putatively private affairs" (Sexton 5). Stacey's objective to become a famous top model or Langston's decision to write a book on his family history are clearly perceived as individualistic projects for their personal benefit. However, as their respective quests proceed, it becomes evident that they inevitably draw on the history of black diaspora and collective struggle for equality and liberation that precedes them.

In *Any Known Blood*, Langston's individualistic enterprise in search of himself is measured against the collective liberation struggle in which the previous generations of Langston Canes were actively engaged. Thus, the runaway ex-slave Langston Cane the First emerges as a colossal legendary figure who, in his escape from slavery, arrived in Oakville, Ontario, on the Underground Railroad, only to join John Brown in his attack on the Harpers Ferry arsenal in Virginia years later, thereby entering the annals of history; Langston Cane the Second and Langston Cane the Third became community leaders in their respective struggles against racism, both in the US and in Canada; whereas Langston's father, Langston Cane the Fourth, turned into a civil rights champion after his particular experience of racial discrimination upon his arrival in Canada in 1954, when he was denied rental accommodation. As a result of his ancestors' success and respectable position as community leaders, Langston Cane the Fifth suffers from an anxiety of influence—similar to the anxiety theorized by Harold Bloom in 1973. He feels hampered by the ambiguous relationship he maintains with his male predecessors and his belief that he will never measure up to them. Their achievements threaten his own budding individuality, and the way to overcome the impasse he has reached is to follow the advice of his old friend Aberdeen: "Your family has had some born achievers, son, but you don't have to do what they did. I know you're interested in who your people were. Why don't you write about them? You told me years ago that you wanted to do it. Write, Langston. Go write. Go do the one thing that all the achievers in your family were too busy and too important to do" (12).

Obligingly, Langston sets out to write a book which revises his ancestors' exceptional lives. As a result, their experience is not just acknowledged but also preserved, ultimately encroaching on and expanding Canadian historiography. But his book also inscribes in the big book of Canadian History the average black experience as embodied by Aberdeen's humble assessment of his own life, which according to him "never amounted to much" because he "never made history" (11–12). On the contrary, Langston's book reveals that Aberdeen's life is instrumental in illustrating race relations in Canada along time. Simultaneously, by digging into the archives and recording the history of African Canadians, Langston attains the stature of the *griot*, a venerable position as the recorder of history, its guardian and receptacle. Aberdeen's mandate to "go write" pushes Langston to do something memorable, like Mahatma Grafton when he felt driven to follow his father's dictum to "go do some great thing" in Hill's previous novel, *Some Great Thing* (1992). However, Langston not only gains in self-esteem by succeeding in writing the book, but he also ceases viewing his own identity as derivative, gains in self-respect, and finds his own place as a worthy Cane.

As his research for the book yields more and more details, his revered ancestors are also revealed as flawed human beings. Langston learns to demystify them and to assume his own public role as a mixed race individual who stands astride the US and Canada in the age of multiculturalism. His quest for self requires that he plunge into his family history and that of blacks in both Canada and the US, thereby corroborating Diana Fuss's argument that "identification names the entry of history and culture into the subject, a subject that must bear the traces of each and every encounter with the external world" (3).

Langston starts his quest for self-definition in the collective framework of his family history and the struggle for civil liberties when his career as "a deceptive insider and deceptive outsider" (Trinh T. Minh-ha qtd. in Wah 87) takes an unexpected turn after he slips an incendiary podium speech to the Ontario Minister of Wellness. Outraged by the hypocrisy of the provincial government, Langston decides to expose their double standards with respect to multiculturalism policies by letting the minister unwittingly abjure his cabinet's plans "to kill anti-discrimination legislation and junk the provincial human rights commission" (Hill, *Any Known* 13) in front of the Canadian Association of Black Journalists. Through this subversive act, Langston proves to be "a revolutionary under that placid exterior" (18) and a worthy descendant of all the Langston Canes that preceded him. As Siemerling notes, "the moment reveals a decisive identification from within that suddenly destabilizes and then derails his habitual disidentification and previous playful passing" (34).

After losing his own job for exposing the government's manoeuvre, Langston realizes that his previous disidentifications have taken him nowhere, and that to combat his mid-life identity crisis and his "lack of success at everything" (Hill, *Any Known* 58) he needs to excavate his family roots and position himself within his family history: "It's to know my past. I have to know. My life can't go on until I know these things" (360), Langston explains to his father. Therefore, Langston undoes his father's journey from the US to Canada and travels to Baltimore in the US, in a move that takes him "from politeness and ambiguity" to disambiguation (Siemerling 34). As a result of his trip, his family's generational criss-crossing of the US-Canadian border is revealed as an exercise in cross-cultural refraction. As he does research into the different Langston Canes and gathers material to write a saga based on his family's transnational experiences and interracial marriages, Hill's novel also becomes a Künstlerroman with the potential of effectively *changing the world*. It is through taking up a role as artist/writer that Langston rejects contemporary multiracialism as founded upon "an evacuation of the historical richness, intellectual intensity, cultural expansiveness, and political complexity of black experience, including, perhaps especially, its indelible terrors" (Sexton 15).

Similarly, in spite of Brunhuber's effort to write "a book that takes place in the present and moves relentlessly forward—no pauses, no flashbacks. Forget about the historical, the epistolary" (Brunhuber, "Book Club"), the history of racialization shapes Stacey's perception of himself from the very beginning, conditioning his behaviour and his position in the world. Being able to transform oneself to fit the observer's eyes is an exercise with historical resonance in the experience of the African diaspora, as W.E.B. Du Bois famously synthesized at the beginning of the twentieth century in *The Souls of Black Folk*—"It is a peculiar sensation, this double-consciousness, this sense of always looking at one's self through the eyes of others, of measuring one's soul by the tape of a world that looks on in amused contempt and pity" (2)—and as Frantz Fanon convincingly explained in his book *Black Skin, White Mask*, whose title successfully conveys the idea of the inner colonization and subversive resistance of the black subject.

As an emerging fashion product, Stacey perceives his camouflaging in the historical context of black people's resistance to racist oppression and colonial imperialism through the development of their own resources, among which is the West Indian practice of Obeah magic: "Or maybe I'm still there. Essentially Stacey, but made up, dressed, camouflaged, disguised by the art of powerful illusionists, obeah men" (Brunhuber, *Kameleon* 7). Nevertheless, Stacey tries to eschew any essentializing based on race and racial history, aspiring, like Langston, to self-definition and control over his own life: "Maybe the disguise is really my own. I'm a chameleon. A mimic, like a stick insect, like those yellow-and-black-striped flies that pretend to be bees" (7). Mimicking and masquerading bring to the forefront a history of oppression and of expropriation of identity as well as the subversive strategies to resist both.[9]

Camouflage is always an act of exclusion rather than of integration for Langston and Stacey, as they always pass as "others" but never as members of the group with which they are interacting at a specific moment, as Langston's words reveal: "In Spain, people have wondered if I was French. In France, hotel managers asked if I was Moroccan. In Canada, I've been asked—always tentatively—if I was perhaps Peruvian, American, or Jamaican" (Hill, *Any Known* 1).

In his quest for identity, Stacey is constantly criss-crossing the boundary between how he wishes to see himself and how he thinks he is perceived. Stacey's friend Siemen, a successful mulatto model, contextualizes the commodification of blackness in the history of the African diaspora, warning him of the dangers of letting his identity be defined by others and of wearing a mask hiding one's true self: "Never let them create your image for you. I don't have to tell you what happens when they do. Why do you think black people are so messed up? Our image has been repackaged and sold off to the highest bidder. Soul is for sale. Our own souls are disposable, like gloves… You can't carry two faces under one hat" (Brunhuber, *Kameleon* 135).

Hence, history, and the history of racialization, is as central to Stacey's quest as to Langston Cane the Fifth's. The main difference between the characters is that Langston has been both burdened *and* empowered by his family storytelling and by his family's insistence on the relevance of passing down the memory of the family history that positions them in the world. By contrast, Stacey is anchorless. Raised by his white mother in the mostly white town of Nepean, and severed from his black heritage by the disappearance of his African American father when he was but an infant, Stacey can neither be hampered by an Oedipal complex, like Langston, nor empowered by a model blackness as performed by his black father. His allegiance is nevertheless to blackness, as he feels *disidentified* as white. Ethnically speaking, he is an average, middle-class, mainstream Canadian, interested in "tennis, skiing, rugby, volleyball, football, horseback riding" (14), psychology, and zoology. He also plays cello, which presupposes a formal education in classical music, and views himself as "a pretty good photographer" (14). However, his experience is that of estrangement from a normative Canadian environment that tends to silence race. His cultural capital—knowledge and expertise—as well as his preferences and the use he makes of his resources—*habitus* in Bourdieu's terminology—depend heavily on his social setting, and they prove of little use to him in the modelling world. Rianne, the woman in charge of bookings at Feyenoord's, makes this very clear when, after inquiring about his special talents, he provides the list above, and she decides he has none—"we'll just put no" (14)—because his abilities do not correspond with her preconceived idea of what a black man's talents should be. Thus, devoid of the symbolic capital that characterized him as an individual, Stacey is perceived as black, and blackness in the multiracial imagined community is "an antiquated state of confinement" (Sexton 6), which society is best rid of. Consequently, Rianne lets him know that "the market for black guys, it's not really big here [Toronto]" (Brunhuber, *Kameleon* 12), and recommends that he try in New York or Miami.

Contrasting Stacey's lived experience with the professed ideal of Canadian multiculturalism, the latter is exposed as tokenism in the shape of the Toronto Caribana festival, ethnic food, or the "diversity ticket" (173–75). Furthermore, the existing racism repeatedly materializes in the symbolic figure of the monkey, which historically emerged as a colonial white sign denoting blackness as infra-human and imitative of whiteness. Stacey's girlfriend's attachment to the monkey toy he won for her at the Ottawa Exhibition, and which stands for him, conveys her suspiciously racist attraction to the exotic but tamed blackness of Stacey's mixed race looks (96). More explicitly racist are the insults thrown at Stacey by the little kid living in his same building when he calls him monkey on different occasions (102), and the "mysterious phrases like SPICY CHIMP BOY" (103) that cover the elevator's walls. However, Stacey colonizes the white sign of the monkey, in the tradition of African American rhetorical signification, by becoming the interpreter of his own condition as mixed race and by performing his mixed race identity as "repetition, with a signal difference," thus turning into Henry Louis Gates's *signifying monkey* (Gates 51). By endlessly displacing and deferring meaning in a constant play of signification and cross-cultural refraction, Stacey embodies the process and indeterminacy of interpretation (Gates 35) aimed to refute the dehumanization of blacks and other peoples of colour.

In the novel, racist dehumanization emerges on the surface when capitalist consumerism and race coalesce in Stacey's body, treated as just "fresh meat" and "cattle" (21) and establishing a historical continuum that links present-day modelling to chattel slavery and the auction block:

> "I have to hand it to them. You are the only thing they were missing. Now they've covered the spectrum." He puts his hand to his mouth, holding an invisible microphone. "Black and bald? Big and Black? You want 'em, we got 'em. Too dark? Don't worry, we got mocha. Fifty-one flavours of Negro." He laughs. "You know, they won't hire any other black models now that their collection's complete. Now that they've got their light-skinned brother, their mulatto, tragic or otherwise, they don't care, as long as you reflect those brown light waves, brother." (42–43)

Stacey's ultimate denigration before his unexpected rise as an international model for Kameleon Jeans occurs when he refuses to remove his abundant body hair, as the *Modelling Made Easy* pamphlet advises, and is transformed into "The Beast" by the art of makeup (152–54) for a photography session.

Despite his absorption of white Canadian ethnicity, Stacey's disidentification as white does not lead to an easy identification with blackness either. Echoing Langston Hughes's poem at the beginning of Hill's novel, Stacey states his astride racial position in negative terms of exclusion when he laments that his white girlfriend is "under the impression that I have the best of both worlds—dark enough to be exotic, light enough to be immune from it all [racism]. She doesn't realize you can't have the best of both worlds when you belong to neither" (169).

Moreover, the protagonist's ignorance about black culture and experience becomes evident as measured against his black apartment mates' behaviour and tastes when he moves to Toronto, a move that helps create the observer's necessary distance for cross-cultural refraction. His simultaneous position as an ethnic outsider and a self-identified racial insider also throws light on the crevices of black masculinities, which are shown as cultural constructions and performances, both impaired by the internalization of demeaning stereotypes imposed upon the black male and empowered by the simultaneous subscription and resistance to those constructions. With Crispen and Augustus, Stacey learns about the codes and performance of black urban masculinity, which is played out on what they call CPT, or "Coloured People's Time," a statement about black people's pace and priorities. He is then able to resist his white girlfriend's control over him: "Why are you always so obsessed with time? Everything has to be on time, on your time, or there's hell to pay. I don't work that way. Haven't you ever heard of CPT?" (94). An example of resistance to the white cultural economy of time and space (Gilroy) is the boys' choice of the night—a time that is "set aside as the period allocated for recovery and rest from work" (Lury 170) in the normative society—as the time for the performance of their black masculinity. Thus, they take the dance floors of night clubs as the space to vent their diurnal frustrations, which they seek to compensate by seducing white girls. Additionally, the novel's examination of the construct and performance of black masculinity is aptly met by an interest in the intersection of race, gender, and sexuality, to which I now turn.

Historicizing Sexuality and Gender through Race
In *The Amalgamation Waltz: Race, Performance, and the Ruses of Memory*, Tavia Nyong'o demonstrates how the rise of a pervasive image of the mixed race subject as racially anomalous responded to the appearance of an independent black public sphere and an organized politics of black uplift. Sex and sexuality were then linked to the newfound mobility of blacks, which was apprehended in the political imaginary as a bodily and sexual scandal. In the US South in particular, "the myth of the black rapist in lusty pursuit of white women" (Rushdy 67) originated as a reaction of "the white minority's wider struggle for social control" (66, note 28) between Reconstruction and the turn of the century in order to justify the surge of violence against the emancipated blacks. A key difference between the US and Canada is, as George Elliott Clarke notes, that "black males were not demonized in this fashion in colonial Canada—nor were interracial relationships as demonized as they were in the U.S." (email to the author).

In Hill's *Any Known Blood* the history of miscegenation is embedded in the Canes' genealogy: from Langston Cane the First and his second white wife, who caused his escape from Canada after being accused of bigamy, to Langston Cane the Fourth, who married a white Canadian, and Langston Cane the Fifth who also married and later divorced another white Canadian woman. The history of interracial sexuality in Canada is also illustrated by the story of Aberdeen Williams and Evelyn Morris (Hill, *Any Known* 327). At age eighty-eight, Aberdeen is an old friend of the Cane family, and the link between generations. His life experience brings to the forefront Canada's historical attitude against miscegenation, when his affection for white Evelyn Morris results, not just in the opposition of the girl's mother to their union, but in their persecution by a Canadian branch of the Ku Klux Klan. However, the incident is happily solved thanks to the help they get from Langston Cane the Third, from the neighbours, and, most importantly, from the police and the judicial system. Thus, the KKK members that had harassed Aberdeen and burned a cross on Langston Cane the Third's front lawn were fined and jailed (326), establishing a clear contrast with the racial atmosphere in the US during those Depression years. As Hazel—Langston Cane the Third's mother-in-law—notes, "In the States they'd swing you from a branch and there'd be no talking before or after. As for Aberdeen and that white woman, someone would have put a stop to that nonsense the moment it started" (326). Nevertheless, Aberdeen also exposes Canada's double standard concerning miscegenation, as well as the intricacies of the intersection of race and gender, when he complains: "I never understood how the mayor could carry on with a Negro gal and have nobody up in arms about it, even though the whole town was in the know. Yet, there I was, planning to marry Evelyn, and the whole world started shaking" (345). What Aberdeen's complaint reveals is that the Canadian community sanctions the extramarital coupling of a white man and a black woman, reminiscent of the sexual exploitation of black womanhood in slavery times by white owners who sought both sexual pleasure and enlargement of their capital by engendering new slaves. On the contrary, Canadians decry the union of a black man and a white woman, something that has historically been viewed in North America as an attack on white society. Hill completes the spectrum of reactions to miscegenation by having Langston's aunt, Mill, severing relations with her brother, Langston Cane the Fourth, because he had "married white" (378), which she considered a betrayal of black women (5).

Hill's novel also coincides with Sexton's assessment of the current racial situation as one where "black resistance is thought by state and civil society to be effectively contained or neutralized, both practically and symbolically" (12). In such a context, Sexton explains, the colour line becomes "considerably more fluid" (12), as the white majority feels less threatened. Sexton concludes, therefore, that there is an "inverse historical relation between white supremacy's tolerance for multiracial formations and the relative strength of black liberation struggle" (12). Following Sexton's reasoning, the current Canadian racial tolerance shows its crevices in the novel when the State's implementation of multiculturalism policies is viewed as an increase of black power by the Salvation Front, "a Toronto-based neo-Nazi hate group that denies the Holocaust and advocates the deportation of blacks and Asians" (Hill, *Any Known* 354). As a result, three young members belonging to this extremist group try to pass as black bigots who claim that "capitalists and governments must be forced by law to hire blacks and racial minorities first" (355), and who kidnap the white physician Norville Watson—Langston Cane the Fourth's erstwhile public enemy who refused to rent Langston and his white wife Dorothy an apartment. Their objective is "to discredit black militants and to foment public hostility toward racial minorities" (355), thus neutralizing black resistance and trying to reverse "controversial measures such as employment equity" (356), which can be perceived as black achievements.

The neutralization of black resistance in *Kameleon Man* is nowhere more apparent than in the co-option and commodification of the black male image as either an excelling sportsman or an urban thug. Thus, the market demands of black model Crispen that he dress "as if he should be either hitting a home run or robbing a liquor store" (18). Similarly, the fashion business could have profited from Stacey's scarred face if he had agreed to sell his image as a drug smuggler. As B tells him, "Scarifications are hot right now. Supermodels are cutting themselves up left and right. And once they find out about your disappearance and the drugs and everything, you'll be unstoppable" (279–80). The novel emphasizes how urban black thug aesthetics lose their oppositional character when co-opted, marketed, and sold to white middle-class kids all over the world.

Like Hill's novel, Brunhuber's confirms Sexton's argument that there is a parallel between racial tolerance and the neutralization of black resistance. Thus, in Stacey's world, where racial difference has been conveniently packaged and contained, interracial sex seems to be socially acceptable, and its product, the mixed race person, clearly promoted. Far from a threat to society, racial difference emerges as a profitable commodity to be consumed. However, conforming to the tune of the times exacts its toll on the black characters in *Kameleon Man*. Stacey's confession at the beginning of chapter 2, "I have always lusted after white girls, ever since I was old enough to wash my own sheets" (10), situates him on the same colonized psychological stage as his mates, Augustus and Crispen, who are always busy "chasing after white girls like mongrels" (123), as the more race-conscious Siemen laments. Whereas Stacey and his friends are aware of their own commodification as fashion products, they turn white women into luxury objects through which they can make a statement about their virility and social status. Accordingly, Crispen humorously refers to their conquests as "BMWs" or "Black Men's Women" (101). Although for them the commodification and consumption of white women becomes the measure of their success as black men, their behaviour only confirms Franz Fanon's theory about the black man's colonization and expropriation of identity.

Hence, the black man's longing to have sexual intercourse with the white woman symbolizes his embrace of whiteness: "When my restless hands caress those white breasts," Fanon wrote in *Black Skin, White Masks*, "they grasp white civilization and dignity and make them mine" (63).

Furthermore, their obsession with white women indicates their acquiescence to the stereotype of the oversexed black male, which is closely connected to the US myth of the black rapist. Stacey becomes complicit with such a myth when he asks Melody to pose naked for him. In front of his camera Melody becomes the sexual product of male chauvinism. However, as she is moulded by Stacey's eyes, her own acquiescence reflects her acceptance of (inter)racial and sexual stereotypes, and her doubly assailed position as a victim both of herself and of society's prejudices: "Melody's not hawking a product, she's selling an idea. An ideal. Vulnerability. Shame. Contempt. My ideas are expressed through her. She's both the medium and the message. And I, as the photographer, am an integral part of the scene. Like a behavioural scientist conducting an experiment, you have to factor in how much your presence affects its outcome" (Brunhuber, *Kameleon* 170).

The photographic session turns into a symbolic rape when Melody decides to stop but Stacey keeps shooting, "lost in the moment":

> Angry, scared, vulnerable, defenceless, pathetic. The uncontrived, unalloyed states a photographer searches for, almost never finds. I'm getting it all. Yeah, baby, yeah… The way her hair falls over her face, the way the makeup is smudged. Her eyes ringed with black, like a linebacker's. The way she holds out her hands—a disgraced movie star trying to block the camera with her palms, her pioneer palms. The way she tries to cover herself with a pillow, then throws it at me instead. I duck but keep shooting. "That's it! Don't stop."
>
> Through the pupil of my camera I can see hers—wide, black, glistening. "*Stop stop stop stop stop stop stop!*" she cries, jumping off the bed. She runs past me into the bedroom, still naked, sobbing louder now as she slams the door. Which is just as well, because I'm out of film. (170–71)

As Stacey captures and exposes in his photographs the interracial and inter-gender tensions of his society, he is performing his role as interpreter, as signifying monkey, which allows him to move on in his life. Yet, in keeping with the individualistic—as opposite to the collective—character of the times, he does nothing to make Melody aware of her own victimization and paradoxical reproduction of racist and sexist models of behaviour.

In a way, Stacey's highly racialized world relies on the "liberal goodwill" that assumes the biological erasure of race by means of crossbreeding, rather than the ethic deconstruction of racial categories in search of justice and equality, in the hope that "if we don't concretize racial identities, racism will wither away" (Clarke, *Odysseys* 223). Coinciding with Dat Win's theory about the evolution of the human species into a single, hybrid one, Stacey plays with the idea of miscegenation when he fantasizes about mating with Janesca, his blonde Canadian neighbour: "Our progeny would be mulattos—able to roam both hemispheres at will. A new hybrid species that would compete with local populations, eventually choke them out and replace them, spread like zebra mussels" (Brunhuber, *Kameleon* 106). Rather than a positive development, the global spread of this new species resulting from the blending of all races into one, which would effectively mean an a-racial society, is implicitly understood as a scourge, comparable to that of zebra mussels. Indeed, mixed race breeding does not guarantee survival for Stacey but, on the contrary, it results in his utter alienation as the purported obliteration of race serves only to impede the knowledge of history, to hide past and present discrimination, and to neutralize any attempt to combat it by creating alliances. Consequently, Dat Win's multiracialism can be said to suffer, in Jared Sexton's words, from "an assumptive logic that diminishes or conceals altogether the historicity of race and sexuality" (4), as well as disavowing the violence that has historically linked both. Stacey's fantasy about a single hybrid race cannot, therefore, assuage his need to interrogate his own racial identity.

A different dimension of the intersection of race and gender, in contraposition with that of the construction of the black male as sexual threat, is the feminization of the mixed race male body in such a way that it is reshaped into the subjected, colonized, marginalized, and commodified body of a woman. This is the case when Stacey is drawn as an "Indian woman" (Brunhuber, *Kameleon* 248), or when he both laughs at and tries to follow the *Modelling Made Easy* manual addressed to female models. His emasculation signals his transgender position as an object of desire. In *Any Known Blood*, the boundary of gender codes is also blurred by Langston's position as observer rather than agent, a situation that will be reversed by the end when he completes his own novel and considers publishing it, something that is perceived by those around him as an achievement, as having *done* something in the world. Langston resists fixed categorizations of gender when his aunt Mill, for instance, observes, "You like to look about you. You're more like a woman. Women like to look about them. Men charge straight ahead" (132). To which he replies, "I don't know about the man-woman thing. Some men charge ahead, others don't" (132).

The mixed race condition of Langston and Stacey brings to the forefront a history of miscegenation with direct implications in current notions about gender constructions and sexual behaviour.

Race / Canada

The new spaces that the mixed race subject creates for individual and national identity are translated in Langston's case in the alliance and reconciliation of different racial and ethnic groups. If, at the beginning of the novel, Langston rejects his father's imposition of a model blackness by passing for whatever nationality, his identity quest requires that he dive into his African American roots, leading him to acknowledge his dual racial and ethnic ancestry, as well as his family's history of struggle for dignity and civil rights. His journey is a return ticket that turns him, not just into the storyteller of a dynasty of great *men*, but into a mediator who facilitates communication between an extended family that comes in different shades of black and white and that is reunited after decades of separation due to racial grudges. Langston's definition of himself as "zebra incorporated" (Hill, *Any Known* 400) overshadows this role as mediator integrating both black and white strands in the family, a phenomenon, the novel implies, which can be extended to the Canadian nation at large. The fact that, at the end of the novel, the border official believes Mill's lie when she passes off her mixed race nephew Langston, African Yoyo, and African American Annette as her own Canadian children, and he lets them in wishing them "a safe trip home" (505), reinstates the belief in a plural, tolerant society, at the same time that it reunites the broken bonds of the Atlantic Middle Passage by acknowledging the connection between these different members of the African diaspora. Similarly, Mill's reclaiming of her Canadian citizenship after decades in the US, and her eventual reconciliation with her brother after their grunt for his marrying outside his race, underline the possibility of an integrated, plural society in Canada.

The plural and conciliatory view is less evident at the end of *Kameleon Man*, where Stacey reaffirms his previously suppressed or repressed identification with blackness and its history when he recognizes in the eyes of an African woman "the invisible nod, acknowledgement of the past" (249). B's black body becomes for Stacey what Toni Morrison calls "emotional memory—what the nerves and the skin remember" (119), or, to use Judith Butler's words, "the repository or the site of incorporated history" ("Performativity's" 114), the history of slavery and diaspora that unites Stacey and B across continents. Yet, Stacey's reconnection to history does not work towards social cohesion but, rather, towards his definitive estrangement from a time and place that is no more:

> If I could pick a time and place to live in, I would choose here [Andalusia] in the days of Tarik, when a black guy became the master of Spain and Africa began at the Pyrenees. Palaces of quicksilver and gold. While Europe was dark, life here was lit with outdoor lamps. In London they walked on mud.

Here they strolled over paved streets. In Paris monks were illiterate and baths were illegal. Here both libraries and baths were public. Nowadays the only evidence the country was once owned by brothers is that sometimes you'll come across a Jesus painted in black. (Brunhuber, *Kameleon* 273)

Stacey's escapist Afrocentric reverie simplistically reverses hegemonies without dissolving his present alienation. Less clearly Canadian-centred and much more individualistic, Stacey's catharsis takes place when he sees himself reflected on his own photographs, the photographs he had thrown away and which B had rescued to use in her installation. Thus, even though at that point in the novel Stacey says he does not wish to see himself "through the veil of someone else's eyes" (260), it is B's honest view of him that makes him recoil from the picture of his troubled self, of his trapped condition, of his refusal to take risks and be himself. When Stacey acknowledges at the end of the novel that he is "neither a good model nor a good chameleon" (280), he also eschews fame and money, his means to achieve respect and dignity, earnestly hoping "that the things I failed to get weren't really worth having, anyway" (280).

As a consequence of this revelation, Stacey exchanges the camouflage of chameleons and their fluid changing appearance for the figure of the metamorphosis, indicating his coming of age as a mature, self-assertive man who is able to see the true nature of things "through compound eyes" (281), like butterflies. This is a fitting image for a photographer, taking into account that "butterflies don't see the world as a continuous picture but as a series of still photographs" (277). Similarly, Stacey projects his own analytical subjectivity on his photographs, and it is through them, and not through modelling, that he eventually achieves the recognition he has been seeking: "They liked your work," B tells him. "The shots I used in my exhibit. They wrote about it in the paper" (280). In his role as interpreter of the reality around him, Stacey finds his place in the world, as part of it, rather than absorbed by it. He comes to this realization in the final lines of the novel, when he imagines taking an all-encompassing photograph that holds the prospect of a fulfilling future where he exists as himself: "B is still at the window, staring out over the mountains...I expand the picture, broaden it 360 degrees to include me. That's it. The first shot. I raise the loupe, hold the picture to the light, examine it from all angles. This single photograph almost makes up for everything that went into the taking. I close my eyes. For a beginning, it's not a bad start" (281–82).

His metamorphosis is offered as just one among a series of transformations to come, envisioning mixed race subjectivity as an evolving process that acknowledges the link with other black diasporic subjects and their history. Stacey thus accepts the command to BE, to exist on his own terms, implicit in the name of "B," the black woman artist to whom he feels particularly connected, as well as to Be Black, discarding any temptation to believe in the colour-blind multiracial society promulgated by Kameleon Jeans.

Both novels implicitly address the contemporary debate about Canadian cultural and literary identities, and they both do so through the protagonists' common awareness that *race matters* and that their world is far from post-racial. Eschewing the colour-blindness that can be associated to multiraciality and transraciality, they choose to acknowledge their mixed heritage, which encompasses the black history of oppression and the black struggle for liberation across national borders, as well as the democratic values that have come to be identified with Canadian (white) civility.

Nevertheless, Hill's novel seems to emphasize region(s) and place in a revisionary attempt to widen the parameters within which Canadian identity has been traditionally moulded. The novel's stress on plurality and inclusiveness is not meant to deconstruct previous notions of Canadian nationality but to enlarge them, including the African Canadian experience, one that has deep roots in the United States. Hill's excavation of the past through the historical account of a family saga is also in tune with George Elliott Clarke's black Canadian nationalism. Thus, *Any Known Blood* contests "the perpetual, white denial of Canada's own history of slavery, segregation, and anti-black discrimination [which] accents black invisibility" (Clarke, *Odysseys* 35) by bringing all of these elements to the forefront; on the other hand, the novel highlights the erasure of black Canada by African America, which sees "Canadian blackness as a lighter—and lesser—shade of its own" (*Odysseys* 26). As a result, Hill successfully overcomes that "sumptuous dilemma of African-Canadian literature," as he avoids these "two national(ist) pincer movements of exclusion" (*Odysseys* 36): Canadian and African American nationalisms.

In contrast, Brunhuber's *Kameleon Man* claims a more radical transnationality of Canadian cultural expression. Whereas at the end of *Any Known Blood* Langston and his aunt Mill claim their Canadianness and are welcomed back into Canada by the border officer, for Stacey the signifier *Canadian* seems to have been emptied of meaning as he situates himself in a global context. Stacey's fluid identity, which emphasizes metamorphosis at the end of the novel, separates itself from fixed notions of Canadian identity to embrace a disruptive "diaspora sensibility," more akin to Rinaldo Walcott's position with respect to the role of African Canadian literature and culture: "The terms of belonging within a context of diaspora sensibilities are fluid; they continually make and remake themselves within the contexts of specific nations. Diaspora sensibilities resurrect all that communities and nations destroy, foreclose and prohibit in their dominating narratives of collective belonging. Diaspora sensibilities are methods for overcoming the problem of locating oneself solely within national boundaries" (Walcott 22).

However, as this analysis shows, Brunhuber's attempt to do without history proves a dangerously de-historicizing move that leaves his protagonist stranded and in need of establishing (historical) links with other members of the African diaspora, such as his Toronto pals or B. Besides, his move out of the nation prevents him from effecting a change in Canada, although through his art he might end up having an international, global influence. All in all, neither Hill nor Brunhuber adheres completely to any of the allegedly contraposed *schools* of thought represented by Clarke's archival cultural nationalism, on the one hand, and by Walcott's diasporic sensibility on the other. Instead, their novels, like their mixed race protagonists, hybridize both positions, escaping narrowly drawn nationalisms and anchoring black Canadian experience in history, thereby adding up to the revisionist move that challenges what Howells calls elsewhere in this volume "any single ideology of nation" (39) in a world that is still far from post-racial.

Notes

1 Some writers have adopted the derogatory metaphor of the zebra to designate their particular poetics articulating the dual black-and-white (or multiple) racial status they reclaim for themselves. In his "Canadian Biraciality and Its 'Zebra' Poetics" in *Odysseys Home*, George Elliott Clarke points at Hill's autobiographical "Zebra: Growing Up Black and White in Canada" (1994), Suzette Mayr's chapbook *Zebra Talk* (1991), and Mercedes Baines's poem "Half Baked Zebra Cake" (1997) as explicitly using the symbol of the zebra to "repudiate the perilous notion of a univocal aesthetics of blackness" (*Odysseys* 232).
2 See Coral Ann Howells's essay "Rewriting Tradition," in this volume.
3 All but the last of these authors are amply discussed by David Roediger in his essay "The Retreat from Race and Class."
4 The fact that Obama largely avoided talking about race during the presidential campaign—except for a singular speech after his pastor was found to have made anti-American statements—and that his criticism on July 23, 2009, of a Cambridge, Massachusetts, cop for "stupidly" arresting African American Harvard Professor Henry Louis Gates Jr. when he tried to break into his own home, raised a national controversy, demonstrate, in his own words, that "race is still a troubling aspect of our society" and, consequently, "part of my portfolio." Obama turned the incident into what he called "a 'teachable moment.' Where all of us, instead of pumping up the volume, spend a little more time listening to each other and trying to focus on how we can genuinely improve

relations between police officers and minority communities. And that instead of pointing accusations we can all be a little more reflective in terms of what we can do to contribute to more unity" (Obama).

5   Whereas the multiracialism movement emphasizes colour-blindness and multiracial exceptionalism, official (liberal) multiculturalism focuses on achieving social cohesion by means of respecting, celebrating, and supporting the cultural and ethnic traditions of the distinct groups that conform a nation, thus advocating a society that extends equitable status to its diverse constituency and does not demand total adherence to a specific culture that is treated as the norm.

6   The US and Canadian censuses offer good examples of the evolution towards freedom in the choice of racial self-identification. The US census has always offered a racial categorization. With the country's history of segregation based on the *one-drop rule*—which established that a single drop of black blood made a person black—until 2000 a US citizen could only belong to one race from among the five categories offered. Since 2000, however, residents could identify themselves according to one or more racial group. Canada, in contrast, had until 1996 built its census around ethnic categories. According to Jessica Wegmann-Sánchez, Canadian censuses "favour flexibility and self-definition, permitting respondents to choose their ethnicity. Starting in 1981, they could also check more than one ethnicity, and, for the past fifty years, they could also claim that they are ethnically only 'Canadian'" (137).

However, since the controversial decision of Statistics Canada in 1996 "to include a 'race' category like the American one" (Wegmann-Sánchez 138) in order to tabulate discrimination against specific *visible* minorities, Canadian officialdom has increasingly relied on racial self-identification. As a result, if with the pre-1996 census model, "forty-four percent of Black people in Canada were not identifying themselves as Black on the ethnicity question" (Wegmann-Sánchez 138), after 1996, race and ethnicity seemed to have become even more malleable. Rinaldo Walcott could claim that "black Canadian might be anyone who resists in concerted ways, with a vision of emancipation, all forms of domination. Black Canadian is a counter-narrative or utterance that calls into question the very conditions of nation-bound identity at the same time as national discourses attempt to render blackness outside the nation" (120). Although David Chariandy reads this as Walcott's response to "the mainstream colonization of race by attempting to render Canadian Blackness disruptive, politically contestatory" ("Canada in US Now" 206), Carol Camper decries the co-option of race in these terms: "I did not want to end up publishing White women whose racial mixing was no more than a fervent, baseless desire on their part. People often come to this belief because they want to escape oppressor status and not deal with their own racism" (qtd. in Ifekwunigwe 178).

7   Lury follows Susan Willis's argument exposing the shift away from "the representations of natural or biological racial difference" at the turn of the nineteenth century and into the twentieth, to a representation of race as a matter of *style* (Lury 162).

8 In the wake of the 2008 US presidential election, Dat Win's assessment of the evolution of racialization in the West is nowhere more apparent than in current President Barack Obama's capitalization upon his own mixed heritage and family bonds, which embrace European American, African, and Asian stock, spanning continents.
9 Camouflage, however, is not the exclusive prerogative of mixed race people. In *Any Known Blood*, Cameroonian Yoyo, who has become an illegal immigrant in the US, moves to Baltimore because "nearly three-quarters of the people here are black—so I blend in easily" (101). His camouflaging is a subversive strategy to evade the law and avoid deportation. A more striking case is that of the three neo-Nazi white Canadians who, trying to pass as black revolutionaries, kidnap a conservative white doctor so as to get "folks riled up about black people" (359).

Works Cited

Bisoondath, Neil. *Selling Illusions: The Cult of Multiculturalism in Canada*. Toronto: Penguin Books, 1994.

Bloom, Harold. *The Anxiety of Influence: A Theory of Poetry*. Oxford: Oxford UP, 1997.

Bourdieu, Pierre, and Loïc Wacquant. "On the Cunning of Imperialist Reason." *Theory, Culture and Society* 16.1 (1999): 41–58.

Butler, Judith. *Bodies That Matter: On the Discursive Limits of "Sex."* New York: Routledge, 1993.

Butler, Judith. "Performativity's Social Magic." *Bourdieu: A Critical Reader*. Ed. Richard Shusterman. Oxford: Blackwell, 1999. 113–28.

Brunhuber, Kim Barry. "Book Club / Teachers Guide." N.d. http://www.kimbrunhuber.com/main.html.

Brunhuber, Kim Barry. Interview. "Kim Brunhuber: Kameleon Man." By James Hörner. Cancon: Interview. 5 Jan. 2004. http://www.canadiancontent.ca/interviews/050104brunhuber.html.

Brunhuber, Kim Barry. *Kameleon Man*. Vancouver: Beach Holme, 2003.

Camper, Carol. *Miscegenation Blues: Voices of Mixed Race Women*. Toronto: Sister Vision, 1994.

Chariandy, David. "'Canada in Us Now': Locating the Criticism of Black Canadian Writing." "Race" Special Issue of *Essays on Canadian Writing* 75 (2002): 196–216.

Clarke, George Elliott. Email to the author. 15 April 2009.

Clarke, George Elliott, ed. *Eyeing the North Star: Directions in African-Canadian Literature*. Toronto: McClelland and Stewart, 1997.

Clarke, George Elliott. *Odysseys Home: Mapping African-Canadian Literature*. Toronto: U of Toronto P, 2002.

Coleman, Daniel. *Masculine Migrations: Reading the Postcolonial Male in "New Canadian" Narratives*. Toronto: U of Toronto P, 1998.

Coleman, Daniel, and Donald Goellnicht. "Introduction: 'Race' into the Twenty-First Century." "Race" Special Issue of *Essays on Canadian Writing* 75 (2002): 1–29.

Compton, Wayde. "The Epic Moment: An Interview with Wayde Compton." By Myler Wilkinson and David Stouck. *West Coast Line* 36.2 (2002): 131–45.

Darder, Antonia, and Rodolfo D. Torres. *After Race: Racism after Multiculturalism.* New York: New York UP, 2004.

Du Bois, W.E.B. *The Souls of Black Folk.* New York: Dover Publications, 1944 [1903].

Fanon, Frantz. *Black Skin, White Masks.* New York: Grove, 1967.

Fish, Stanley. "Boutique Multiculturalism, or Why Liberals Are Incapable of Thinking about Hate Speech." *Critical Inquiry* 23.2 (1997): 378–95.

Fuss, Diana. *Identification Papers.* New York: Routledge, 1995.

Gates, Henry Louis, Jr. *The Signifying Monkey: A Theory of African-American Literary Criticism.* New York: Oxford UP, 1988.

Gilroy, Paul. *Against Race: Imagining Political Culture Behind the Color Line.* Cambridge, MA: Harvard UP, 2000.

Hill, Lawrence. *Any Known Blood.* Toronto: HarperCollins, 1997.

Hill, Lawrence. *Some Great Thing.* Winnipeg, MB: Turnstone, 1992.

Ifekwunigwe, Jayne O., ed. *Mixed Race Studies: A Reader.* London: Routledge, 2004.

Kamboureli, Smaro. *Scandalous Bodies: Diasporic Literature in English Canada.* Toronto: Oxford UP, 2000.

Kamboureli, Smaro, and Roy Miki, eds. *Trans.Can.Lit: Resituating the Study of Canadian Literature.* Waterloo, ON: Wilfrid Laurier UP, 2007.

Lury, Celia. *Consumer Culture.* New Brunswick, NJ: Rutgers UP, c.1996.

Morrison, Toni. "The Site of Memory." *Inventing the Truth: The Art and Craft of Memoir.* Ed. William Zinsser. Boston: Houghton, 1987. 103–24.

Nyong'o, Tavia. *The Amalgamation Waltz: Race, Performance, and the Ruses of Memory.* Minneapolis: U of Minnesota P, 2009.

Obama, Barack. "Obama Qualifies His Comments." ABC News Videos. 24 July 2009. http://abcnews.go.com/video/playerIndex?id=8167271.

Padolsky, Enoch. "Ethnicity and Race: Canadian Minority Writing at a Crossroads." *Literary Pluralities.* Ed. Christl Verduyn. Peterborough, ON: Broadview, 1998. 19–36.

Patterson, Orlando. "Race Over." *The New Republic* 222.2 (10 January 2000): 6.

Reed, Adolf, Jr. "Class-ifying the Hurricane." *The Nation* 3 Oct. 2005. http://www.thenation.com/doc/20051003/reed.

Reed, Adolf, Jr. "The Real Divide." *The Progressive* Nov. 2005. http://www.progressive.org/mag_reed1105.

Roediger, David. "The Retreat from Race and Class." *Monthly Review* 58.3 (July–Aug. 2006). http://monthlyreview.org/0706roediger.htm.

Rushdy, Ashraf H.A. *Neo-Slave Narratives: Studies in the Social Logic of a Literary Form.* Oxford: Oxford UP, 1999.

Senna, Danzy. "The Mulatto Millennium." *Mixed Race Studies: A Reader.* Ed. Jayne O. Ifekwunigwe. London: Routledge, 2004. 205–8.

Sexton, Jared. *Amalgamation Schemes: Antiblackness and the Critique of Multiracialism.* Minneapolis: U of Minnesota P, 2008.

Siemerling, Winfried. "'May I See Some Identification?': Race, Borders, and Identities in *Any Known Blood.*" *Canadian Literature* 182 (2004): 30–50.

Spivak, Gayatri C. *In Other Worlds: Essays in Cultural Politics.* New York: Methuen, 1987.

Taylor, Charles. "The Politics of Recognition." *Multiculturalism: Examining the Politics of Recognition.* Ed. Amy Gutmann. Princeton, NJ: Princeton UP, 1994. 25–74.

Wah, Fred. *Faking It: Poetics and Hybridity, Critical Writing 1984–1999.* Edmonton, AB: NeWest, 2000.

Walcott, Rinaldo. *Black Like Who? Writing Black Canada.* 2nd ed. Toronto: Insomniac, 2003.

Wegmann-Sánchez, Jessica. "Rewriting Race and Ethnicity across the Border: Mairuth Sarsfield's *No Crystal Stair* and Nella Larsen's *Quicksand* and *Passing*." *Essays on Canadian Writing* 74 (2001): 136–66.

FOUR

Of Aliens, Monsters, and Vampires: Speculative Fantasy's Strategies of Dissent (Transnational Feminist Fiction)

Belén Martín-Lucas

> Woman, as a sign of difference, is monstrous.
> —Rosi Braidotti,
> "Mothers, Monsters and Machines"

> A free woman in an unfree society will be a monster.
> —Angela Carter, *The Sadeian Woman*

The revisionist work of an important number of racialized cultural writers and critics in recent decades has exposed to the light many of Canada's obscured secrets. The introduction of the Multiculturalism Act in July 1988 was a public gesture of the Canadian state towards the inclusion of its diasporic Others into a new definition of the nation, a recognition that was accompanied in the month of September of the same year by the Redress Agreement that sought to compensate Japanese Canadians for the wrongs inflicted on them during and after the Internment of World War II. These advances were the result of a long history of struggle for visibility and of persistent demands for recognition by migrant communities in Canada. During the late 1980s and early 1990s, as Larissa Lai points out, there was a small measure of public space, and a new and highly productive language that we found, and made for ourselves, to talk about the racisms, sexisms, and other oppressions on which the Canadian nation (and, for that matter, many other nations) are founded. Histories like those of the Japanese Canadian Internment, the Chinese Head Tax and Chinese Exclusion Act, the Indian Act, the Komagata Maru incident and many others were drawn to the surface by indigenous cultural workers and cultural workers of color, against the polite repressions of the Canadian state. (Lai, *Brand* 24)

In the current decade, second generation diasporic subjects, "born in Canada of parents born elsewhere" (Brand, *What We All* 20), still grow up in a context that constantly treats them as foreigners or, in David Chariandy's words, as "that discomfortingly intimate stranger born here" ("The Fiction" 819). The implementation of the Multiculturalism Act has proven clearly inefficient in countering this imaginary. On the contrary, statistical data provides evidence that second generation racialized Canadians find it more difficult to identify as Canadian than their parents' generation because they "are made to feel they do not belong to Canada" (Dhruvarajan 167) through persistent racialization and exclusion from the nation (see also Ralston, Handa, Nakagawa, Reitz and Banerjee). Despite what Smaro Kamboureli has acutely described as the "fetishization of its multicultural make-up" (viii), the Canadian state and the nations within it, including the multicultural one, have failed to address the political issues of power imbalance nested at the heart of the predominant neo-liberal ideologies.

As Rinaldo Walcott has pointed out, "conceptually multiculturalism is a major concession, as the liberal democratic nation-state does not extend citizenship in equal fashion to all its members. Such a concession opens up vast opportunities to rethinking the nation and for state struggles, and thus for rethinking liberal versions of citizenship and national belonging" ("Against Institution" 19). Unfortunately, it seems that those opportunities have been hurriedly taken by neo-liberalism, as it has in fact profoundly altered citizenship practices with the infiltration of market logics into the political realm. As Aihwa Ong has convincingly argued: "The neoliberal exception articulates citizenship elements in political spaces that may be less than the national territory in some cases, or exceed national borders in others" (*Neoliberalism* 6). Individuals are categorized according to their market value, and granted elements of traditional citizenship (rights, or entitlement, for instance) according to the benefits they may provide to the economic market. Thus, Ong explains, "mobile individuals who possess human capital or expertise are highly valued and can exercise citizenship-like claims in diverse locations. Meanwhile, citizens who are judged not to have such tradable competence or potential become devalued and thus vulnerable to exclusionary practices" (6–7). For Himani Bannerji, the language of multiculturalism is just such a pronouncement of neo-liberal exclusion and discrimiNation whereby so-called "visible minorities" are categorized as such according to skin colour, Otherized by their race, and consequently *managed* by the state into a precise parcel within the mosaic. As Bannerji has exposed, "for non-whites in Canada, their own bodies are used to construct for them some sort of social zone or prison, since *they can not crawl out of their skins*, and this signals what life has to offer them in Canada" (Bannerji 112; emphasis added).

An important group of fantastical mutant creatures in the contemporary fiction of Canadian racialized women authors seems to, precisely, "crawl out of their skins." This essay examines a range of subversive metamorphoses of the female body in recent speculative fiction by Hiromi Goto, Larissa Lai, Nalo Hopkinson and Suzette Mayr. I propose to read their resort to shape-shifters (whether mythical or cyborgian) as a poetical and political strategy that allegorizes the "flexible citizen" model theorized by Ong (1999). I will pay attention first to the advantages for both critique and innovation that the genre of speculative fiction offers, and will focus then on specific examples of body metamorphosis in their narratives (short stories and novels), which I will analyze in relation to certain dominant ideological premises of neo-liberalism around the racialized and sexualized body. It is my main thesis in this essay that the trope of the mutant body is employed by these authors as an imaginative expression of cultural and political dissent.

Gothic, Post-Colonial, and (Post)Feminist

A common complaint of racialized writers is the pressure exerted on them to produce certain kinds of literature to fit into pre-established cultural types supposedly specific to a determined racial group. The so-called "burden of representation" interferes in the creative process and constricts the racialized author's creative energies in a way that any white artist would find unacceptable. Much has been written in Canada on the subject,[1] the volume *Asian Canadian Writing Beyond Autoethnography*, edited by Eleanor Ty and Christl Verduyn, being a recent collection that specifically addresses this question. As the editors point out in their Introduction to the essays:

> Many [racialized] authors consciously attempt to question or problematize the link between ethnic identity and literary production, while still recognizing the racialized context in which they write. Globalization, rapid shifts in technology and communication, cross-cultural and intra-community

networks, and racial and cultural hybridization have affected and challenged representations of the Other in contemporary novels, plays, poems, and films. Questions of sexuality and gender have further complicated the assumptions about the ethnic subject and its representation—in particular, its autoethnographic representation. (Ty and Verduyn 3)

Pilar Cuder-Domínguez reminds us, in her essay on Goto's and Lai's use of speculative fiction in that volume, that "since its inception, science fiction has been peculiarly useful as a vehicle for women writers' critique of patriarchy and for unpacking the contradictions of their own position within it" (116). From her point of view, "the deployment of fantasy (whether couched in the form of myth or of dystopian fiction) appears to serve the purpose of helping readers envision performances of racial identity alternative to those traditionally enforced. 'Race' in them means not just skin colour, but the conventional hierarchies of race and even sexual orientation ensuing from it" (117). Michelle Reid similarly interprets Lai's resorting to "fantasy, myth, realism and speculation" as a creative strategy "to highlight the generational divides between first-generation immigrants and their children, and to explore the alienation of living in a society which questions your authenticity and your claim to a cultural heritage" (353). In this sense, literary genre becomes in itself a political device that indicates the discomfort of the Canadian-born generation of racialized citizens with their nation's hegemonic conditions for belonging, multiculturalism notwithstanding (Walcott, "Caribbean" 131). Thus, as Christine Kim argues, "[Lai's] *When Fox is a Thousand* critically invokes [the discourses] of multiculturalism to position its discussion within the parameters of the Canadian nation and investigate notions of citizenship" (165). This statement can be extended, as I will try to demonstrate here, to the other speculative narratives that constitute the corpus of study of this essay, which thus follow an important tradition of the (post)feminist post-colonial gothic in which they can be meritoriously inscribed.[2] In the following section the diverse modes of the trope of the monstrous mutant body that they offer will be explored.

Skin-Strippers and Hopeful Monsters
Hiromi Goto's short story collection *Hopeful Monsters* (2004), as its title suggests, offers a wide spectrum of "abnormal" mutant/freak characters. Among them, we find a kappa in "Osmosis"—who reappears from Goto's novel *The Kappa Child*, to be considered below; a floating "Stinky Girl" with an excessive, "coloured" (38) body and her deceased ghost father; a new father in "Tales from the Breast" who grows breasts when his wife gets

tired of his patronizing encouragement to breastfeed and, in the story that gives title to the collection, a freakish newborn girl with a "tail" who might well be a new link in the evolutionary chain. This last story constitutes a good example of the conglomeration of diverse kinds of deviance that intersect in the critical discourse deployed by the narratives analyzed here. The very explicit and graphic descriptions of the pregnant and labouring body present a leaking, bleeding, overflowing female body at its highest level of Kristevan abjection. Confronting the glamorous representations of pregnancy and maternity in the mass media and the benevolent paternalistic discourse of the medical environment that manipulates the woman's body, Goto provides a most realistic description of the physicality of different bodily processes, including those censored out of the glossy images of the post-feminist maternal imaginary. Niall Scott summarizes Nicola Goc's views on this imaginary, emphasizing that "the media image of the celebrity mother treats maternity as a fashion accessory placed under a voyeur's gaze, whereas certain features of motherhood remain taboo. These include breastfeeding, or the experience of post-natal depression" (Scott, "Introduction" 4), both of which are addressed by Goto in this collection.

The physical "abnormality" of Goto's protagonist's newborn in "Hopeful Monsters" marks her as a freak (plus her being a mixed race child categorizes her as a hybrid). Contrasting the scientific discourse of teratology with the emotional affiliation of the matrilineal line, Goto exposes the violent control and manipulation of the "strange" body made to conform to the regulated "normal." The solidarity among those who are systematically excluded from normalcy—the "hopeful monsters" who adapt for survival despite adverse circumstances (in the story, racialized and lesbian women)—forges an alternative network of support that replaces the Western nuclear family with a kinship based on affinity, a proposal for a new social structure that will appear recurrently in all the following speculative narratives considered here (kinship and affinity will be addressed further when considering Lai's *Salt Fish Girl*).

In Goto's second novel, *The Kappa Child* (2001), an amphibianesque mythical creature temporarily embodied as a sexy female alien impregnates the unnamed Japanese Canadian female narrator, who will carry out a sort of miraculous pregnancy that involves sudden cravings for cucumbers (a favourite treat for kappas). The alien, a traditional figure of speculative fiction, fuses here with the mythical kappa of Japanese folklore, (re)producing a hybrid creature that participates in both imaginative traditions but also exceeds them.[3] The novel also plays continuously with a third traditional narrative, that of the classic pioneer, through the intertext of Laura Ingall's *Little House on the Prairie*. The narrator unfittingly takes Ingall's autobiography as a handbook (proving completely useless) to her own experience of displacement in the prairies. The fusion of this classic prairie narrative, the speculative mode, and myth in Goto's novel constitutes a good example of what I refer to as "speculative fantasy." The novel's plot is clearly located in a specific Canadian city, Calgary, in contemporary times, and we may read it as a realistic tale if we accept the explanation that the narrator's analyst offers: that the narrator's pregnancy is a psychological one and that she is distressed due to the violence within her dysfunctional family. All strange events, including her mother's abduction by aliens, may be rationally explained by alluding to some kind of mental disturbance. Yet, valuing fantasy and speculation as assets—the novel won the James Tiptree Jr. Award, "an annual literary prize for science fiction or fantasy that expands or explores our understanding of gender" (James Tiptree Jr. Council)—may offer more fruitful readings, in political terms, of the alieNation of this immigrant family and their First Nations neighbours, taking into account Wolmark's remark that "science fiction provides a rich source of generic metaphors for the depiction of otherness, and the 'alien' is one of the most familiar: it enables difference to be constructed in terms of binary oppositions which reinforce relations of dominance and subordination" (2). Moreover, given the secondary position of feminist science fiction in relation to other genres, Wolmark suggests that "it is well placed to invest this and other metaphors with new and different meanings which undermine ostensibly clear-cut distinctions between self and other, human and alien. It explores possibilities for alternative and non-hierarchical definitions of gender and identity within which the difference of aliens and others can be accommodated rather than repressed" (2).

Goto's novel shares many common elements with Larissa Lai's *When Fox Is a Thousand* (1995), which also features a mythical protagonist, the Fox, a notable character in Chinese folklore. Like the Kappa, the Fox is able to travel in time by occupying recently deceased women's bodies—that is, by wearing their skins. Part of the action takes place in the Vancouver of the 1990s, the moment when the Fox will finally achieve immortality, while other sections move back to ninth-century China, in the voice of the poet Yu Hsuan-Chi. As in Goto's *The Kappa Child*, intertextual references function as connecting threads, linking the mythical Fox and the historical Yu Hsuan-Chi to Chinese Canadian Artemis. The theme of reproduction is also taken up here, not only in that the Fox gives new lives to the deceased, but also because Artemis is an adopted Chinese girl in a white home. As such, parenthood does not transmit genealogically inherited traits; instead, racial and cultural identities are interrogated within the very symbolic unit of the nuclear family (the core model basis for capitalist patriarchal nation structures) as Artemis questions whether she is an Orientalist ornament collected by her mother, curator in a museum, and her father, university professor in Asian Studies.

According to Bennet Yu-Hsiang Fu, "Lai uses Fox as a metaphorical figure for constant transformations of ethnic and sexual subjectivity, affirming both difference and resistance" (158). The dead women she reanimates, on the other hand, represent "the assimilated almost-white self required [of Asian Canadian women] by the social pressures of liberalism" (Lai, "Political" 152), and both "the trickster and the inhabited female bodies are tropes of cultural survival in a world that threatens their existence" (Fu 159–60). In her analysis of the musical *Cats*, Rosi Braidotti points out how "the hybrid morphological creature—half female, half panther—stands simultaneously for ethnic mixity, moral ambiguity, sexual indeterminacy and unbridled erotic passion. The process of trans-species nomadism, or morphological hybridity, is loaded with sexuality in that it entails the erasure of and the transgressing of bodily boundaries" (*Metamorphoses* 128). Such is the case with Lai's Fox, whose shape-shifting is intimately linked both to her ambiguous racial identification and to her "monstrous" sexuality: she is a marginalized figure chastised by other foxes "for 'haunting women,' in other words, for being a lesbian and transgressing sexual normativity" (Fu 158).

In Lai's second novel, *Salt Fish Girl* (2002), another mythical creature, Nu Wa, also metamorphoses and changes females' bodies from one era to another. Although the novel opens with the very beginning of the world ("In the beginning it was just me," Nu Wa states on the first page), it then suddenly jumps to a dystopic 2044 when Miranda takes up the narrative voice. As in her first novel, Lai has alternating narrators from different temporal and physical locations: Nu Wa's narration is set in South China in the late 1800s; Miranda's in Serendipity, "a walled city on the west coast of North America" (11) owned by one of the Big Six Corporations. In this novel we also encounter another miraculous pregnancy, this time at a late age—the mother is 63 years old—and mediated by a genetically engineered durian. Miranda, the girl born from this "artificial" pregnancy, will be forever marked by a disgusting smell of fish that links her across time and space to Nu Wa's lover, the Salt Fish Girl.[4] Towards the end of the novel, Miranda, like her own mother, will become impregnated by a durian, the source of the "neither natural nor controllable" (256) fertility of the cyborg Sonias, and she will give birth to a girl in the closing paragraph. The novel thus ends on the optimistic note of the beginning of a new life, just as the last paragraphs of Goto's *The Kappa Child* end with "new green shoots of life" (275).

The female Asian-labourer clones, the Sonias, inhabit an Unregulated Zone outside Serendipity that clearly reflects the exclusionary practices of ultra-capitalist globalization described by Ong: "Low-skill citizens and migrants become exceptions to neoliberal mechanisms and are constructed as excludable populations in transit, shuttled in and out of zones of growth" (*Neoliberalism* 16). The Sonias' design is a good example of what the Critical Art Ensemble called the "civilian cyborg," the ideal consumer-producer of late capitalism "reduced to acting out rational, pragmatic, instrumental behaviours... through the use of both technological and biological enhancement" (29–30).

Lai's critique of late capitalism through the figure of the cloned cyborg (see Lee, "Mutant" 94–95) can perhaps be more clearly understood in relation to Braidotti's reflections on the cyborg as an embodiment of resistance:

> What I want to emphasize, however, is that the cyborg as an embodied and socially embedded human subject that is structurally inter-connected to technological elements or *apparati*, is not a unitary subject position. The cyborg is rather a multi-layered, complex and internally differentiated subject. Cyborgs today would include for me as much the under-paid, exploited labour of women and children on off-shore production plants, as the sleek and highly trained physiques of jet-fighter war-pilots, who interface with computer technologies at post-human levels of speed and simultaneity. (Braidotti, *Metamorphoses* 18)

This is exactly the concept of the cyborg employed by Lai in the novel, developing from Donna Haraway's view of Asian women workers as "real-life cyborgs" ("A Cyborg" 143), doubly alienated, "disassembled, reassembled, exploited as a reserve labor force" (133).[5] The cyborgs in *Salt Fish Girl* are a further step in the morphological hybridity explored in Lai's first novel: Evie, the resisting cyborg who will awaken Miranda's consciousness, is a "patented new fucking life form" (*Salt Fish Girl* 158) made out of human and carpian biomaterial, a true "fish girl" mutating at the end of the novel into a recognizable mermaid figure that resembles the Nu Wa of the opening chapter.

Miranda's alliance with the resistant community of the cyborg Sonias thus forms a sort of extended family/community, similar to those predominant in the narratives by Goto, Hopkinson, and Mayr. This alternative mode of social vinculation constitutes an important act of resistance to neo-liberalism since "allowing the extended family to continue offers individuals participating in that institution a social and economic power base which gives them the opportunity to refuse corporate culture. In addition, it creates a social process that has the potential to be more satisfying than participation in consumption processes" (Critical Art Ensemble 122–23). In *Modest_Witness@Second_Millenium*, Haraway defines "kinship" as a relation based not on blood but on affinities and affect; in the post-human age, she asks: "Who are my kin in this odd world of promising monsters, vampires, surrogates, living tools, and aliens? How are natural kinds identified in the realms of technoscience? What kinds of crossings and offspring count as legitimate and illegitimate, to whom and at what cost? Who are my familiars, my siblings, and what kind of livable world are we trying to build?" (qtd. in Winnubst 13).

Nalo Hopkinson's *Midnight Robber* (2000) and *Skin Folk* (2001) seem intent on providing (imaginative and provisional) answers to Haraway's questions. Biotechnology and trans-species mutation play a relevant part in both texts, which share these authors' common struggle to imagine more livable worlds. In the first novel, described by Hiromi Goto as "feminist in vision, lushly detailed with cultures human and alien" (Review 33), an apparently utopian society, Toussaint, benefits from advanced computing technology: cyborg citizens of the dominant classes—descendants of all Caribbean peoples—are permanently attended by an artificial intelligence called "eshu" inbred in their ears. However, this most civil society, like Serendipity, depends for its comfort and peace on the existence of a marginalized space where criminals and those who pose a threat to the law and order of Toussaint in any way, including political dissidents, are exiled. In the wild outposts that are starting to be colonized by those human exiles, all kinds of fantastic hybrid species cohabit, often showing more humane traits—solidarity, kinship, and affection outside bloodlines, for instance—than most "civilized" humans. Hopkinson thus uses the "'thinking with animals' trope" (Dillon 72) characteristic of Afro-Caribbean culture to question colonial and neo-colonial discourses of progress and modernity that despise and devastate the indigenous: in this novel, the Taino and Arawak.

Similarly, *Skin Folk* collects stories about shape-shifters.[6] Some of them are mythological folkloric figures of the Caribbean, like the soucouyant in "Greedy Choke Puppy" or the mamadjo (mermaids) in "Money Tree";[7] others are more technological ones, like the micro-thin wetsuits designed to enhance sexual pleasure that are exchanged between a man and a woman to experience the other sex's sensations (thus "shedding skins" for a few minutes) in the story "Ganger (Ball Lightning)," or the black woman in "A Habit of Waste" who buys for herself a new slender white body just to find out that the woman now inhabiting her old discarded fat black body seems to be much happier than her new white self (thereby provoking her to recover her Caribbean family's cultural background). This last story has been used by Gina Wisker as a case study in her definition of the post-colonial feminist gothic, both in her *Key Concepts in Postcolonial Literature* (147–55) and in the essay "Moving beyond Waste to Celebration," where (like Braidotti and Haraway) she uses Deleuze and Guattari's influential notion of "becoming woman" (see Deleuze and Guattari) to read shape-changing as a "postfeminist postcolonial strategy to embody celebratory, insightful change for the women concerned" (Wisker, "Moving" 116). According to Wisker, post-colonial post-feminist Gothic fantasy and horror "are critically recognized as forms of powerful expression providing space and discourse to explore a liberating movement beyond colonial, imperial and gendered silencing and oppression" ("Moving" 117). "Liberation" is indeed a key term that embraces all these narratives, where crawling out of one's skin is more often than not a freeing act, as suggested in the opening paragraph of Hopkinson's *Skin Folk*:[8]

> Throughout the Caribbean, under different names, you'll find stories about people who aren't what they seem. Skin gives these skin folk their human shape. When the skin comes off, their true selves emerge. They may be owls. They may be vampiric balls of fire. And always, whatever the burden their skins bear, once they remove them—once they get under their own skins—they can fly. It seemed an apt metaphor to use for these stories collectively. (1)

In this context, Suzette Mayr affirms in her first novel, *Moon Honey* (1995), that "metamorphosis always signals a happy alternative" (113). The novel opens with a quote from Ovid's *Metamorphoses*, an explicit connection with classical mythology that Mayr intends to subvert from a racialized feminist perspective, in the same way that Goto, Lai, and Hopkinson rewrite other classic references (see Martín-Lucas, "On the 'Dark Side'"): "*My purpose is to tell of bodies which have been transformed into shapes of a different kind*" (n.p.; italics in the original). The main mutation is that of its protagonist Carmen, a white-middle-class-good-civic Canadian who happens to find herself suddenly transformed into a young abandoned-by-her-white-boyfriend black girl. Carmen is the embodiment of the normative Canadian woman; she has interiorized racist values of the dominant national ideology, though, of course, she naïvely considers herself a modern and tolerant model Canadian. During a discussion over racism with her Indo-Canadian boss Rama, Carmen reproduces the liberal discourse of official multiculturalism in her idyllic appeal to common universal humanness, and she demands this of Rama: "Educate me, says Carmen. Show me where all this racism is, why you are so angry and bitchy all the time. Show me. If I cut you you bleed, if I cut me I bleed, we're all the same underneath. Show me the difference. Show me the difference!" (Mayr, *Moon* 21). It is at this moment that Carmen's skin turns darker, her hair "curls and frizzes, shortens" (23). From this moment on she will inhabit a new (dark) skin to experience how dramatically skin-colour change affects her social status, life standards, and emotional life.

Despite misleading appearances, all the transformations in the novel happen at times of crisis and have a clear subversive and liberatory value. For instance, a maid of honour becomes a mare and takes Mabel the bride away from her bridegroom at the altar (39–40); Fontana saves her own life when facing a she-bear by turning, as her name indicates, into a stone fountain, "*metamorphosis the happy alternative to being some bear's scratching post*" (125; italics in the original); Pascale, part-time nurse, "normal mother to her babies, a normal wife to her husband" (134), grows extra arms and eyes in her back to fulfill the innumerable duties of a superwoman and, at a certain moment of stress, becomes a basilisk, making a(n) (im)patient woman turn into stone (136). We even encounter a bride, Demeter, who is such a nightmare to the female relatives helping her to arrange her wedding that she literally becomes an asshole, her "*warm and lovely round face is now pink as [her dog] Pepe's little anus, her features squinched up until they have disappeared, the skin gathered and folded in tightly around her hole of a mouth which has drifted up to the middle of her face*" (68; italics in the original).

In Mayr's novel *Venous Hum* (2005), humour and horror mix in grotesque gothic fashion. A group of hard-working model vegetarian immigrants, whose dreams and hopes had been devotedly trusted to semi-god Pierre Trudeau and his multicultural policies, transform into vampiric cannibals who actually ingest another human's whole skin, flesh, and blood and also raise the undead from their tombs—former vampire victims—to join their already horrendous high school reunion party. The title of the novel refers, like Goto's hopeful monsters, to a medical condition, this one involving the blood flow that can be noticed by pressing the jugular vein; also known as *bruit de diable*, it is a pertinent image to evoke the vampire.

This novel is, undoubtedly, the one in this group that takes furthest the grotesque and gorish aspects of the (post)feminist gothic. If, as Braidotti maintains, "the female body shares with the monster the privilege of bringing out a unique blend of fascination and horror" ("Mothers" 65), when the monster is a vampire-cannibal mother such a blend reaches its peak; the quasi-carnivalesque scene with the final banquet description provides a delicious/delirious combination of the exquisiteness of delicatessen cuisine and the repulsion of cannibalism, in the most "normal" domestic setting of a family-and-friends reunion:

Slice with serrated steak knives through rare meat marinated in olives, capers, red wine, roasted in the oven until fragrant and perfect. Crunch through crackling, hint of rosemary, garlic, chew eagerly around the bone, suck out the fatty marrow. Smell the salt of the meat, the salt of the garlicky sauces in the little bowls over the tea lights, the slurp of skewers dipped into Thai peanut sauce, black bean sauce, black-pepper gravy, the sound of meat being chewed, the squeak and slice of incisors into the meat. Louve dips her fingers into a bowl of water and lemon slices, then wipes her hands on a napkin. Monsters are delicate eaters. Everyone knows this. (Mayr, *Venous* 227)

Perhaps it is because of its unusual combination of "dark" humour and gorish relish that this novel has not received as much critical attention as Mayr's previous works. This is unfortunate, as the narrative offers an intelligent and incisive critique of the multiple biases conflated in post-Trudeau multicultural Canada: homophobia, racism, sexism, and classism are "unpalatable" and difficult to "digest" by those who daily confront their own experience of alieNation with public discourses of Canadian "white civility" (see Coleman). Therefore, "sicker and sicker [Louve] feels, fully nauseated" (Mayr, *Venous* 222) after having sucked all the blood off the drunken heteronormative married (unfaithful) white man who happened to be the lover of her lesbian married (unfaithful) daughter Lai Fun.

Distinct from the exclusively female figure of the Caribbean soucouyant, the male and female vampire-cannibals in Mayr's narrative seem contemporary versions of popular Western representations of the myth, "the monster that threatens the white middle-class male protagonists…an exotic metaphor for an unspecified contagion which they perceive to be preying on a vulnerable, homogenous society" (Jones 152). Studying the recent cult of the vampire in popular culture, Gordon and Hollinger point out that "there are an increasing number of cases in which the vampire, if not completely sympathetic…is, at the least, portrayed with an empathy that would have been unthinkable in earlier decades" (Gordon and Hollinger 2). The renewed interest in this classic gothic character resides in its potential as a figure of subversion, since "the figure of the vampire, as metaphor, can tell us about sexuality, of course, and about power; it can also inscribe more specific contemporary concerns, such as relations of power and alienation, attitudes towards illness, and the definition of evil at the end of an unprecedentedly secular century" (Gordon and Hollinger 3). In her analysis of Jewelle Gomez's black lesbian vampire in *The Gilda Stories*, Miriam Jones remarks on the subversive turn that the metaphor of the vampire has taken, in a paragraph that I find suitable to describe Mayr's *Venous Hum*:

Gomez's *The Gilda Stories* self-consciously rewrites both the genre and the representation of the vampire figure. But most radical is her transformation of the metaphoric function of the vampire and vampirism. Her text evokes the traditional generic notions of social contagion at the same time it unmasks the metaphors. It asks: who are really made monsters in contemporary hegemonic discourse? The broad answer is: the disenfranchised." (153)

"The vampire, that crosser of boundaries extraordinaire" (Winnbust 8), is also a migrant traveller (Dracula is the Eastern rural count who moves into the Western modern city). In Mayr's novel, the vampire protagonists are immigrants to Canada, "alien" to a nation that still contradicts Trudeau's promises of multicultural conviviality and sexual freedom that preface the narrative:[9]

> In December 1967... Trudeau said, "The state has no place in the bedrooms of the nation," and the beds of many nations promptly spun out of control.
> In 1971, Pierre Elliott Trudeau, as Prime Minister of Canada, brought in an official Policy of Multiculturalism that proclaimed, Bonjour, You are invited, Hello, Vous êtes invités, to the thousands of non-European immigrants who had been flooding the country since the early 1960s. Those who never felt comfortable suddenly were *home*. At the time, Trudeau sported a long, flowing haircut.
> Canada's hair has been disheveled ever since. (Mayr, *Venous* 11)

The children of these hopeful immigrants in the novel, however, face a harsh daily reality in high school, where their peers are not that sympathetic either to homosexual or to racialized children, and teachers literally suck their blood. The high school reunion that Lai Fun organizes brings back to life all the bad spirits of her horrid experiences as a teenager, showing that, as noted above, the second generation does not always feel welcome in their own country.

AlieNation: The Monster Within

Esther Peeren and Silke Horstkotte propose that "the grotesque body's excessive materiality features a spectral fluidity and lack of borders, whereas the spectral can work on the body in a concrete manner" (13). All these metamorphosing and hybrid characters posit a challenge to stable and fixed categorizations of identity by resorting—in diverse and specific ways that rely on different cultural backgrounds—to the over-exploitation of dominant constructions of the monstrous Other. These narratives present figures of excess that transgress and overflow borders—racial, sexual, national, even galactic—making normalcy limits and expectations explode. The authors I am considering here envision diverse forms of shape-shifting and skin-stripping as enactments of resistance.

At this point, it is not difficult to establish the more than obvious connections between the trope of the monstrous Other and theories of the abject, abnormality, and alienness in relation to both femininity and to the symbolic constructions of the nation, the topic for discussion in this volume. In the "active forgetting," which according to Ernest Renan is the prerequisite for the construction of the nation (11)—firmly rooted in the notions of "home" and "belonging"—the monstrous, that is, the "alien," is marginalized and repressed into the "not belonging." In Canada, the First Nations, Inuit, Métis, and racialized collectives have been constantly conceived of as the necessary Other of the Canadian nation, be this nation English Canada, Quebec, or contemporary multicultural Canada (see, for instance, Bannerji, and Walcott, "Caribbean"). Drawing on Bhabha's version of the "unhomely" as "a paradigmatic postcolonial experience" that produces a blurring of the borders between home and the world (445), Roy Miki uses similar language of uncanny alterity in his analysis of Canadian nationalism in the age of globalization:

> the "unhomely" is the event of a disjuncture, a crisis in spatialized time, between here and there, near and far, one's own and one's alien, internal and external; the "I" as doubled, subject and object, in the alterior spaces between shifting formations. When the influx of globalization makes the nation strange to itself, the present takes on the face of the uncanny and what was (now previously) in place is set adrift—to encounter the spectres of loss, nostalgia and liminality. (47)

Canadian nationalist discourses have historically excluded racialized subjects through their insistence on the colonial past of its two founding nations and through "the legalization of policies that supported the eugenic agenda of the dominant Anglocentric group at the turn of the nineteenth century" (Miki 49). In the contemporary context of economic globalization,

> the social and cultural mechanisms that stabilized "national identity" around a centre have been compromised by global forces undermining the ability of nation-states to control their own affairs.... In this unravelling process, the nation, as if "suddenly," becomes strange to itself and appears, in effect, as a spectral nation that is no longer what it was, no longer in control of the borders of its identity—which is to say no longer normalized through its historically constituted codes of racialization and differential relations of subject positioning. (Miki 46–47)

Even in the context of globalization, the discourse of multiculturalism (though rhetorically based on diversity) continues to imagine a white Canadian normative citizen against whom all Others are termed "visible minorities," on the physical and political ground of the body, as the important corpus of writing on racialization in Canada has amply demonstrated (to which the four writers here studied have contributed with theoretical and critical works as well). The body thus becomes an important metaphor and site for intervention in the discourses on Canadian nationalisms, and it is on the body that these women writers inscribe their politics of difference, kinship, and affection. Their "abnormal" relation to the nation is not based on antagonism, as most critical studies of diasporic fiction suggest (Chariandy, "Postcolonial"), but on a demand to be considered full transnational citizens of the Canadian state, which Lily Cho has described, in her study on diasporic citizenship, as "a desire to be considered both within and without the nation" (93). Their literary production is a good example of what Chariandy described as the "inventive tactics [of historically disenfranchised peoples] for transforming even the most sinister experiences of dislocation into vibrant and revolutionary forms of political and cultural life" ("Postcolonial"). The monster, the freak, the alien, the mutant, the grotesque, have all been read as metaphors that problematize the diverse politics of exclusion/inclusion. Relying on Irigaray's and Grosz's theories of the body, Winnubst points out that the "body-in-control of the straight white male symbolic is haunted primarily by one substance—fluidity. To be a body in control, it must be rightly sealed—rigidly separated, distinctly individual, and straightly impermeable" (6). Irigaray's "The 'Mechanics' of Fluids" and Kristeva's theories of the abject come immediately to mind in relation to this conceptualization of the Western universal subject (white, male, and heterosexual) that has been made (violently) extensive to that of the nation-state. In nationalist discourses the alien other is frequently described as the disgusting abject (the outcasts in unregulated zones). In a multicultural nation like Canada, moreover, the strange body is most obviously both part of the nation and outsider at the same time, the "intimate stranger" in Chariandy's quote ("The Fiction" 819), and "abjection is contained—through the figure of the stranger—by the very notion of multiculturalism, which legislates difference as the origin of national identity" (Mansbridge 122).

Building upon Angela Carter's famous thought that "a free woman in an unfree society will be a monster," Ben Barootes explores the empowering possibilities of women's abjection as "the monstrous female is able to exist beyond the constraints of societal forms" (187). In fact, the intimate relationship of women and monstrosity has such a long history in Western thought—since "Plato claimed that woman represented nothing more than the in-between state of animal and man [and] Aristotle associated the female with amorphous matter that can only be shaped and moulded by the male logos" (Gear 322)—that the subversive vindication of women's monstrosity has become one of the key theoretical and artistic issues in the long trajectory of (post)feminisms. As Braidotti observed in her influential essay "Mother, Monsters and Machines," "woman, as a sign of difference, is monstrous" (65), and the same has been historically true of all Others to the hetero, white, male subject. As Rosemarie Garland Thomson suggests, "bodies whose forms appeared to transgress rigid social categories such as race, gender and personhood were particularly good grist for the freak mill.... Hybridity, along with excess and absence, are the threatening organizational principles that constitute freakdom" (5).

Taking advantage of that "threatening" potential, instead of reading Otherness as having a paralyzing effect, Barootes proposes that "in order that a woman may be free within an unfree society, she must first be monstrous. It is her monstrosity—that which separates and distances her from society, that which singles her out—that enables the woman to escape her social shackles" (188). This view is then extended in his essay to other marginalized individuals and communities who "can also achieve sovereignty by embracing their monstrous natures.... Whether the monster is a woman or an immigrant, natural or constructed, these texts all argue that freedom is gained through the acceptance and celebration of one's own monstrosity" (188).[10] Barootes's assertion may seem excessively optimistic in its view of freedom being the effect of monstrosity. His consideration of the literary monster as a resisting figure that escapes the bonds of hegemony as an exile inhabiting liminal spaces (196) is appealing for its empowering aspects; however, one must not forget that social, cultural, economic, and political marginalization are not *celebrated* by the authors studied here. Instead, we may consider theirs as "reowning the body in all its ambivalence and impurity," to use Tara Lee's phrase in her analysis of Goto's and Lai's fictions (*Promising* 178). Barootes's positive reading of Otherness is in line with Braidotti's view of contemporary female subjects; Braidotti's vocabulary of metamorphosis and mutation is apt to describe the kind of subjectivity that these Canadian speculative narratives propose:

> One of the aims of feminist practice is to overthrow the pejorative, oppressive connotations that are built not only into the notion of difference, but also into the dialectics of Self and Other. This transmutation of values could lead to a re-assertion of the positivity of difference by enabling a collective re-appraisal of the singularity of each subject in their complexity. In

other words, the subject of feminism is not Woman as the complementary and specular other of man but rather a complex and multi-layered embodied subject who has taken her distance from the institution of femininity. "She" no longer coincides with the disempowered reflection of a dominant subject who casts his masculinity in a universalistic posture. She, in fact, may no longer be a she, but the subject of quite another story: a subject-in-process, a mutant, the other of the Other, a post-Woman embodied subject cast in female morphology who has already undergone an essential metamorphosis. (*Metamorphoses* 11–12)

These monstrous natures are explored by an innovative fusion that exceeds generic conventions. The narratives by Lai, Goto, Hopkinson, and Mayr typically employ myths and folklore transported to technologically sophisticated (dystopic) societies, thus disrupting the already loose conventions of less prestigious (and more popular) cultural modes like folklore, fantasy, and speculative fiction. Their narrative techniques defy categorization into any particular single mode. Although cyborgs and mythical shape-shifters like the Kappa, Nu Wa, or the skin folk belong in very different and seemingly opposite cultural traditions (the first group associated with technology and science, the second with orality and "primitivism"), the mutant characters in these narratives conjugate both in the same present tense. While each of the different figures well deserves a much deeper and more extensive scrutiny that cannot be undertaken in this chapter, I have linked all of them together to examine their interconnections, rather than their specificities. Nina Lykke has pointed out that monsters, goddesses, and cyborgs are "signifiers of chaos, heterogeneity and unstable identities.... In spite of their differences, the three metaphorical figures are therefore related through their metonymical closeness to the non-orderly, non-stable, non-identical and so on" (5). Striking a similar point, Braidotti remarks on the recent "invasion" of monstrous figures in all kinds of cultural modes:

> The monstrous, the grotesque, the mutant and the downright freakish have gained widespread currency in urban post-industrial cultures also known as "postmodern Gothic."... Quite significant is also the contemporary trend for borderline or liminal figures of sexuality, especially replicants, zombies and vampires, including lesbian vampires and other queer mutants, who seem to enjoy especial favour in these post-AIDS days. This is not only the case as far as "low" popular culture genres are concerned, but it is equally true of relatively "high" literary genres. (*Metamorphoses* 177–79)

For Braidotti, feminism participates significantly in this culture of monstrosity placing "an emphasis on hybrid and mutant identities and transgender bodies" (179). The female grotesque, defined by Mary Russo as a site of transgression, emerges renewed among transnational (post)feminist writers as a political vindication of a Bakhtinian carnivalesque culture of excess and of the abject.

The symbolic identification of the nation as a woman, widely studied by feminist theorists like Floya Anthias and Nira Yuval-Davis, Wenona Giles and Jennifer Hyndman, Mary N. Layoun, Anne McClintock, or Lois West, among others, is of crucial importance to understand the subversive political statement in the fantasy tropes and speculative genres used by these racialized queer authors in their novels.[11] The control over women's (reproductive) bodies is intrinsically linked to the conceptualization of the motherland in terms of racial and ethnic purity, as Anne McClintock has vividly shown by stating that "all nationalisms are gendered; all are invented; and all are dangerous—dangerous...in the sense that they represent relations to political power and to the technologies of violence" (89). The symbolic use of women's bodies in masculinist nationalisms turns real women's bodies into the physical site of dispute between men in times of conflict, as the omnipresent resort to war rape reveals, where the violated woman stands for the invaded nation. In the nationalist rhetoric of the "mOtherland" (see Martín-Lucas "Metaphors"), the racialized female body is also strictly regulated in the name of national racial purity. Discussing legislative and medical measures on reproduction in Canada, Bannerji reveals "the white supremacist desire 'To Keep Canada White'" (69) behind the popular notion that white women should reproduce more while non-white women should reproduce less.

The queer narratives of the speculative fantasies I have discussed above further problematize such masculinist envisionings of the nation, entangling, as we have seen, issues of sexuality and gender with those of race, ethnicity, and class in their questioning of Canadian normative citizenship, while also explicitly and innovatively addressing the theme of reproduction. These authors participate with their creative and critical works in a wider attempt to construct "more ethically structured nations" (Walcott, "Caribbean" 139). By using the trope of skin as a permeable border, they propose fluid transgender, transsexual, transnational, trans-species, and/or even trans-galactic modes of what has been theorized as "deterritorialized citizenship" (Basch, Schiller, and Blanc; Walcott "Caribbean")—that is, of being a civilian (whether human, cyborg, alien, or "becoming-animal") related to others in diverse social forms of kinship and community not dependent on the "narratives of blood, land, tribe and more multifarious discourses such as generations and citizenship" (Walcott, "Caribbean" 133) that have traditionally defined national belonging.

Notes

1 See for instance Vernon's interview with Suzette Mayr and Dhaliwal's interview with Shani Mootoo.
2 See Brabon and Genz's and Gina Wisker's works on post-feminist and postcolonial gothic. Due to the controversial and conflicting uses of the term "post-feminism," I use "(post)feminism" to include both feminism and post-feminism, and I will use "post-feminism" to refer to the popular use of the word "post-feminism" in the media, which represents feminism as an outdated, old-fashioned, and overcome struggle. Wisker uses the term "postfeminism" to refer to "black and Asian women's postcolonial engagement with and assertion of women's equality and right to identity and voice. Not surprisingly," she then adds, "there is no consensus here, and actually postfeminism, like 'becoming woman', can be seen as metamorphosing, not merely stuck, rigidly, as a backlash against the 1970s and 1980s" (*Key Concepts* 119).
3 Goto's most recent novel, *Half World* (2009), also portrays a fantasy world inhabited by hybrid mutant beings. For matters of coherence and space limitations, I will not consider her juvenile fiction here.
4 Miranda's odour also links her to Hiromi Goto's "Stinky Girl"; of course the ominous relation of "smell" to racism is well known.
5 For a detailed analysis of Lai's novel in the light of Haraway's thesis of the cyborg, see Tara Lee 2004 and 2006 (chapter 6). The anthology *The Gendered Cyborg*, edited by Kirkup et al., has collected the most influential feminist essays on this figure.
6 The story "Tan-Tan and Dry Bone" included in this collection is an excerpt from the novel *Midnight Robber*.
7 Hopkinson's novel *The New Moon's Arms* (2007) again takes up the myth of the sea people in the Caribbean, whom she presents here as the descendents of the slaves in a sinking ship that are granted a new life as mermaids by the goddess Uhamiri, one of the African Mami Wata water divinities. The "mamadjo woman" and "River Mumma" in the story "Monkey Tree" are other Caribbean names of Mami Wata.
8 Giselle Liza Anatol (2004) provides a detailed analysis of the skin-shedding metaphor as a feminist liberating move in Hopkinson's collection, paying special attention to the figure of the soucouyant.
9 On the relation of sex to nationalism in Canada, see Cavell and Dickinson's "Sex and Canada: A Theoretical Introduction" in their anthology *Sexing the Maple*.
10 Barootes analyzes here British contemporary fiction, using texts by Fay Weldon, Jeannette Winterson, and Salman Rushdie.
11 I have dealt more extensively with the implications of this identification in the Canadian context in a previous essay also produced for the Penelope's Embroidery project (Martín-Lucas, "On the 'Dark Side'"). A telling literary example can be found in Shauna Singh Baldwin's story "Toronto 1984," when Piya confronts her racist boss and thinks "for now I am not only myself, but I am all of India and Pakistan and Bangladesh. I am a million and a half people sitting in one small office in Mississauga. I wear a label and will take pride in being a damn Paki" (57).

Works Cited

Anatol, Giselle Liza. "A Feminist Reading of Soucouyants in Nalo Hopkinson's *Brown Girl in the Ring* and *Skin Folk*." *Mosaic* 37.3 (2004): 33–51.

Anthias, Floya, and Nira Yuval-Davis. *Racialized Boundaries*. London: Routledge, 1992.

Baldwin, Shauna Singh. *English Lessons and Other Stories*. New Delhi: HarperCollins, 1996.

Bannerji, Himani. *The Dark Side of the Nation: Essays on Multiculturalism, Nationalism and Gender*. Toronto: Canadian Scholars' P, 2000.

Barootes, Ben. "Nobody's Meat: Freedom through Monstrosity in Contemporary British Fiction." *Monsters and the Monstrous: Myths and Metaphors of Enduring Evil*. Ed. Niall Scott. Amsterdam: Rodopi, 2007. 187–99.

Basch, Linda, Nina Glick Schiller, and Cristina Szanton Blanc. *Nations Unbound: Transnational Projects, Postcolonial Predicaments, and Deterritorialized Nation-States*. London: Routledge, 1994.

Bhabha, Homi. "The World and the Home." *Dangerous Liaisons: Gender, Nation, and Postcolonial Perspectives*. Ed. Anne McClintock, Aamir Mufti, and Ella Sohat. Minneapolis: U of Minnesota P, 1997. 445–55.

Brabon, Benjamin A., and Stéphanie Genz. "Introduction: Postfeminist Gothic." *Postfeminist Gothic: Critical Interventions in Contemporary Culture*. Ed. Benjamin A. Brabon and Stéphanie Genz. Houndmills, Basingstoke, Hampshire: Palgrave Macmillan, 2007. 1–15.

Braidotti, Rosi. *Metamorphoses: Towards a Materialist Theory of Becoming*. Cambridge: Polity, 2002.

Braidotti, Rosi. "Mothers, Monsters and Machines." *Writing on the Body, Female Embodiment and Feminist Theory*. Ed. Katie Conboy, Nadia Median, and Sara Stanbury. New York: Columbia UP, 1997. 59–79.

Brand, Dionne. *What We All Long For*. Toronto: Vintage, 2005.

Carter, Angela. *The Sadeian Woman and the Ideology of Pornography*. New York: Pantheon, 1978.

Cavell, Richard, and Peter Dickinson. "Sex and Canada: A Theoretical Introduction." *Sexing the Maple: A Canadian Sourcebook*. Ed. Richard Cavell and Peter Dickinson. Peterborough: Broadview, 2006. xiii–xliii.

Chariandy, David. "'The Fiction of Belonging': On Second-Generation Black Writing in Canada." *Callaloo* 30.3 (2007): 818–29.

Chariandy, David. "Postcolonial Diasporas." *Postcolonial Text* 2.1 (2006). http://www.postcolonial.org/index.php/pct/article/view/440/159.

Cho, Lily. "Diasporic Citizenship." *Trans.Can.Lit.: Resituating the Study of Canadian Literature*. Ed. Smaro Kamboureli and Roy Miki. Waterloo, ON: Wilfrid Laurier UP, 2007. 93–109.

Coleman, Daniel. *White Civility: The Literary Project of English Canada*. Toronto: U of Toronto P, 2006.

Critical Art Ensemble. *Flesh Machine: Cyborgs, Designer Babies, and New Eugeni Consciousness*. New York: Autonomedia, 1998.

Cuder-Domínguez, Pilar. "The Politics of Gender and Genre in Asian Canadian Women's Speculative Fiction: Hiromi Goto and Larissa Lai." *Asian Canadian

Writing Beyond Autoethnography. Ed. Eleanor Ty and Christl Verduyn. Waterloo, ON: Wilfrid Laurier UP, 2008. 115–31.

Deleuze, Gilles, and Félix Guattari. *A Thousand Plateaus: Capitalism and Schizophrenia.* Trans. Brian Massumi. Minneapolis: U of Minnesota P, 1987.

Dhruvarajan, Vanaja. "People of Colour and National Identity in Canada." *Journal of Canadian Studies* 35.2 (2000): 166–75.

Dillon, Grace L. "Totemic Representations in Recent SF." *Extrapolation* 49:1 (2008): 70–96.

Fu, Bennett Yu-Hsiang. "From Meta-Morphing T'en Hu: Sexual Transgression and Textual Transposition in *When Fox Is a Thousand.*" *West Coast Line* 38.2 (2004): 157–63.

Gear, Rachel. "All those Nasty Womanly Things: Women Artists, Technology and the Monstrous-Feminine." *Women's Studies International Forum* 24.3–4 (2001): 321–33.

Giles, Wenona, and Jennifer Hyndman, eds. *Sites of Violence: Gender and Conflict Zones.* Berkeley: U of California P, 2004.

Goc, Nicola. "'Monstrous Mothers' and the Media." *Monsters and the Monstrous: Myths and Metaphors of Enduring Evil.* Ed. Niall Scott. Amsterdam: Rodopi, 2007. 149–65.

Gordon, Joan, and Veronica Hollinger. "Introduction: The Shape of Vampires." *Blood Read: The Vampire as Metaphor in Contemporary Culture.* Ed. Joan Gordon and Veronica Hollinger. Philadelphia: U of Pennsylvania P, 1997. 1–7.

Goto, Hiromi. *Chorus of Mushrooms.* Edmonton: NeWest, 1994.

Goto, Hiromi. *Half World.* Toronto: Puffin Canada, 2009.

Goto, Hiromi. *Hopeful Monsters.* Vancouver: Arsenal Pulp Press, 2004.

Goto, Hiromi. *The Kappa Child.* Calgary: Red Deer Press, 2001.

Goto, Hiromi. Review of *Midnight Robber*, by Nalo Hopkinson. *Herizons* 16.1 (2002): 33.

Handa, Amita. *Of Silk Saris and Mini-Skirts: South Asian Girls Walk the Tightrope of Culture.* Toronto: Women's Press, 2003.

Haraway, Donna. "A Cyborg Manifesto: Science, Technology, and Socialist-Feminism in the Late 20th Century." *The International Handbook of Virtual Learning Environments.* Ed. Joel Weiss et al. Dordrecht: Springer, 2006. 117–58. http://www.springerlink.com/content/u531k271421h4940/fulltext.pdf.

Haraway, Donna. *Modest_Witness@Second_Millennium.FemaleMan©_ Meets_ OncoMouse™: Feminism and Technoscience.* New York: Routledge, 1997.

Hopkinson, Nalo. *Midnight Robber.* New York: Warner Books, 2000.

Hopkinson, Nalo. *The New Moon's Arms.* New York: Warner Books, 2007.

Hopkinson, Nalo. *Skin Folk.* New York: Warner Books, 2001.

Horstkotte, Silke, and Esther Peeren. "Introduction: The Shock of the Other." *The Shock of the Other: Situating Alterities.* Ed. Silke Horstkotte and Esther Peern. Amsterdam: Rodopi, 2007. 9–22.

Irigaray, Luce. "The 'Mechanics' of Fluids." *This Sex Which Is Not One.* Trans. Catherine Porter. Ithaca, NY: Cornell UP, 1985. 106–18.

James Tiptree Jr. Literary Award Council. "What Is the Tiptree Award?" http://www.tiptree.org/#TiptreeAward.

Jones, Miriam. "*The Gilda Stories*: Revealing the Monsters at the Margins." *Blood Read: The Vampire as Metaphor in Contemporary Culture*. Ed. Joan Gordon and Veronica Hollinger. Philadelphia: U of Pennsylvania P, 1997. 151–67.

Kamboureli, Smaro. Preface. *Trans.Can.Lit. Resituating the Study of Canadian Literature*. Ed. Smaro Kamboureli and Roy Miki. Waterloo, ON: Wilfrid Laurier UP, 2007. vii–xv.

Kim, Christine. "Troubling the Mosaic. Larissa Lai's *When Fox Is a Thousand*, Shani Mootoo's *Cereus Blooms at Night*, and Representations of Social Differences." *Asian Canadian Writing Beyond Autoethnography*. Ed. Eleanor Ty and Christl Verduyn. Waterloo, ON: Wilfrid Laurier UP, 2008. 153–77.

Kirkup, Gill, Linda Janes, Kath Woodward, and Fiona Horenden, eds. *The Gendered Cyborg: A Reader*. London: Routledge, 2000.

Lai, Larissa. "Brand Canada. Oppositional Politics, Global Flows, and a People to Come." *Reading(s) from a Distance: European Perspectives on Canadian Women's Writing*. Ed. Charlotte von Sturgess and Martin Kuester. Augsburg: Wissner-Verlag, 2008. 23–32.

Lai, Larissa. "Political Animals and the Body of History." *Canadian Literature* 163 (1999): 145–54.

Lai, Larissa. *Salt Fish Girl*. Toronto: Thomas Allen, 2002.

Lai, Larissa. *When Fox Is a Thousand*. Vancouver: Press Gang, 1995.

Layoun, Mary N. *Wedded to the Land? Gender, Boundaries and Nationalism in Crisis*. Durham, NC: Duke UP, 2001.

Lee, Tara. "Mutant Bodies in Larissa Lai's *Salt Fish Girl*: Challenging the Alliance between Science and Capital." *West Coast Line* 38.2 (2004): 94–109.

Lee, Tara. "Promising Transnational Births: The Womb and Cyborg Poetics in Asian Canadian Literature." Ph.D. diss. Simon Fraser U, Department of English, 2006. http://ir.lib.sfu.ca/dspace/retrieve/3663/etd2307.pdf.

Lykke, Nina. Introduction. *Between Monsters, Goddesses and Cyborgs: Feminist Confrontations with Science, Medicine and Cyberspace*. Ed. Nina Lykke and Rosi Braidotti. London: Zed Books, 1996. 1–10.

Mansbridge, Joanne. "Abject Origins: Uncanny Strangers and Figures of Fetishism in Larissa Lai's *Salt Fish Girl*." *West Coast Line* 38.2 (2004): 121–33.

Martín-Lucas, Belén. "Metaphors of the (M)Otherland: The Rhetoric and Grammar of Nationalism." *Her Na-rra-tion, Women's Narratives of the Canadian Nation*. Ed. Françoise Le Jeune and Charlotte Sturgess. Nantes: CEC/CRINI, Université de Nantes, 2009. 105–17.

Martín-Lucas, Belén. "On the 'Dark Side of the Nation': Racialized Women's Critique of Canadian Nationalism(s)." *Canada Exposed / Le Canada à découvert*. Ed. Pierre Anctil, André Loiselle, and Christopher Rolfe. Brussels: P.I.E. Peter Lang, 2009. 195–211.

Mayr, Suzette. Interview. "Suzette Mayr in Conversation with Karina Vernon." *Matrix* 58 (2001): 14–18.

Mayr, Suzette. *Moon Honey*. Edmonton: NeWest, 1995.

Mayr, Suzette. *Venous Hum*. Vancouver: Arsenal Pulp Press, 2005.

McClintock, Anne. "'No Longer in a Future Heaven': Gender, Race and Nationalism." *Dangerous Liaisons: Gender, Nation, and Postcolonial Perspectives*. Ed.

Anne McClintock, Aamir Mufti, and Ella Sohat. Minneapolis: U of Minnesota P, 1997. 89–112.

Miki, Roy. "Altered States: Global Currents, the Spectral Nation, and the Production of 'Asian Canadian.'" *Journal of Canadian Studies / Revue d'études canadiennes* 35.3 (2000): 43–72.

Mootoo, Shani. Interview. "Shani Mootoo: Shifting Perceptions, Changing Practices." By Sarindar Dhaliwal. *Fuse* 22.2. (1999): 18–25.

Nakagawa, Anne Marie, dir. *Between: Living in the Hyphen*. National Film Board of Canada, 2006.

Ong, Aihwa. *Flexible Citizenship: The Cultural Logics of Transnationality*. Durham, NC: Duke UP, 1999.

Ong, Aihwa. *Neoliberalism as Exception: Mutations in Citizenship and Sovereignty*. Durham, NC: Duke UP, 2006.

Ralston, Helen. "Identity and Lived Experience of Daughters of South Asian Immigrant Women in Halifax and Vancouver, Canada: An Exploratory Study." International Migration and Ethnic Relations Conference on "Youth in the Plural City: Individualized and Collective Identitites." Norwegian Institute, Rome: 25–27 May 1999. http://pcerii.metropolis.net/Virtual%20Library/ConferencePapers/ralston99.pdf.

Reid, Michelle. "Rachel Writes Back: Racialised Androids and Replicant Texts." *Extrapolation* 19.3 (2008): 353–67.

Reitz, Jeffrey G., and Rupa Banerjee. "Racial Inequality, Social Cohesion, and Policy Issues in Canada." *Belonging? Diversity, Recognition and Shared Citizenship in Canada*. Ed. Keith Banting, Thomas J. Courchene, and F. Leslie Seidle. Montreal: Institute for Research on Public Policy, 2007. 489–545. http://www.utoronto.ca/ethnicstudies/ReitzBanerjeeRev.pdf.

Renan, Ernest. "What Is a Nation?" *Nation and Narration*. Ed. Homi Bhabha. London: Routledge, 1990. 8–22.

Russo, Mary. *The Female Grotesque: Risk, Excess and Modernity*. New York: Routledge, 1994.

Scott, Niall. Introduction. *Monsters and the Monstrous: Myths and Metaphors of Enduring Evil*. Ed. Niall Scott. Amsterdam: Rodopi, 2007. 1–6.

Thomson, Rosemarie Garland. "Introduction: From Wonder to Error—A Genealogy of Freak Discourse in Modernity." *Freakery: Cultural Spectacles of the Extraordinary Body*. Ed. Rosemarie Garland Thompson. New York: New York UP, 1996. 1–19.

Ty, Eleanor, and Christl Verduyn, eds. *Asian Canadian Writing Beyond Autoethnography*. Waterloo, ON: Wilfrid Laurier UP, 2008.

Walcott, Rinaldo. "Against Institution: Established Law, Custom, or Purpose." *Trans.Can.Lit. Resituating the Study of Canadian Literature*. Ed. Smaro Kamboureli and Roy Miki. Waterloo, ON: Wilfrid Laurier UP, 2007. 17–23.

Walcott, Rinaldo. "Caribbean Pop Culture in Canada; Or, the Impossibility of Belonging to the Nation." *Small Axe* 9 (2001): 123–39.

West, Lois A., ed. *Feminist Nationalism*. London: Routledge, 1997.

Winnubst, Shannon. "Vampires, Anxieties, and Dreams: Race and Sex in the Contemporary United States." *Hypatia* 18.3 (2003): 1–20.

Wisker, Gina. *Key Concepts in Postcolonial Literature*. Houndmills, Basingstoke, Hampshire: Palgrave Macmillan, 2007.

Wisker, Gina. "Moving beyond Waste to Celebration: The Postcolonial/Postfeminist Gothic of Nalo Hopkinson's 'A Habit of Waste.'" *Postfeminist Gothic: Critical Interventions in Contemporary Culture*. Ed. Benjamin A. Brabon and Stéphanie Genz. Houndmills, Basingstoke, Hampshire: Palgrave Macmillan, 2007: 114–25.

Wolmark, Jenny. *Aliens and Others: Science Fiction, Feminism and Postmodernism*. London: Harvester Wheatsheaf, 1994.

Yuval-Davis, Nira. *Gender and Nation*. London: Sage, 1997.

FIVE

The Production of Vancouver: Termination Views in the City of Glass

Eva Darias-Beautell

Many contemporary studies have examined from a wide spectrum of angles the ways in which texts and other artworks document and enact the socialization of a particular space (Anderson, Bhabha, Colley, Grosz, Lindner). A major dimension of that process of socialization would be the production of local subjects against, or at least in contrast with, that of national citizens (Appadurai). In the case of contemporary Canada, this process is often thought of as a refiguring of the relationship between the local and the national, and it may take a variety of forms: from the (analysis of the) production of the urban in relation to the natural, thus often reconsidering or undermining dichotomous national ideologies of the past (Cavell), to the discussion of local realities in the context of global economies, often intervening between contested spaces and bringing forth conflicting narratives of place (Derksen, "National"). Such multi-scaled vision permeates recent West Coast art and writing, and specifically, those works that engage in the performance of place as a form of intervention in the powerfully idealized official and mass-media images of the city of Vancouver (Delany, Dickinson, Shier).

This essay will provide an analysis of the representation of Vancouver in a selection of contemporary texts and artworks, which I will read vis-à-vis one another with the aim of disclosing the labyrinthine structures of the social construction of place. I will focus on various modes of production of locality in the manifold sense articulated by the anthropologist Arjun Appadurai as "a structure of feeling, a property of social life, and an ideology of situated community" (189), a multifarious process which proves immensely fragile and implies constant struggle. A parallel emphasis will be placed on how these works may function as "termination views," a notion referring to Bernie Miller and Alan Tregebov's deconstructive techniques and implying a particular work's capacity to block or cancel a certain spatial perspective (see Eyland). Recent developments seem to suggest the idea that the growth of Vancouver as an emblematic "world city" of the Pacific Northwest has happened at the cost not only of erasing its national ties, but of losing its social cohesiveness. I intend to engage with the ideological implications of that spatiotemporal shift by looking at texts and artwork as sites for the manufacture of discordant images of the city and as effective tools to block idealized views of Vancouver. My selection of works aspires to be as representative as possible of the wide and rich spectrum available and includes: Jin-me Yoon's *Group of Sixty-Seven* (1996), Douglas Coupland's photographic book *City of Glass* (2000), Madeleine Thien's novella "A Map of the City" (2001), George Bowering's story "Standing on Richards" (2004), Rebecca Belmore's performance piece "Vigil" (2002), Lee Maracle's story "Goodbye, Snauq" (2004), and Bernie Miller and Alan Tregebov's public sculpture *Street Light* (1996).

The Group of Sixty-Seven
A decisive factor in the ongoing dismantling of the idea of the nation has been (and still is) the powerful globalization trends, which have swayed not only the economy and the political functioning of Western nation-states, but also their so-called national cultures (Delany, Introduction 8). The cities have had a major role in this process, since the globalization (and now antiglobalization) movements can be defined as mostly urban phenomena and, as Paul Delany argues, "the global marketplace is presented as an urban rather than a national system" ("Hardly the Center" 188).[1] It has also been in the urban arena where the postmodern privileging of the spatial dimension of knowledge has thrived, opening up infinite possibilities of juxtapositions, simultaneity, and rhizomatic models of experience. In contrast with the unattainable nature of a rather abstract nation-state, cities occupy and represent a space that is concrete, livable, lovable, participative, and increasingly interactive. They are the spaces that produce and are produced by technology, by constantly new forms of communication and relationships, since as Delany continues, "connections jump over

the hinterlands and pass along a network linking each global centre to the others. This network supports 'virtual cities' in communicative space, uncoupled from any homeland" ("Hardly the Center" 188).

In Canada, the significant challenges that have affected the concept of the nation since the 1970s have largely come in association with an important shift in the perception of urban life. In the first place, there has been a turn in critical discourses towards the recognition and appreciation of Canada's always already urban nature. Far from simple rhetorical flourish, and by no means implying a dismissal of the myriad of smaller communities and towns in Canada that do not exactly fit in that definition of the urban, this critical turn is shifting our attention towards modes of cultural production previously shunned by cultural nationalism's emphasis on small-town and wilderness narratives. Douglas Ivison and Justin D. Edwards, editors of *Downtown Canada*, a seminal collection in this regard, strongly argue not only that "Canada is an urban country," but that "by some measures Canada is one of the most urban countries on earth, with the vast majority of its population concentrated in a handful of cities" (12). The collection's main goal is "to assert the centrality of the city and the urban within the Canadian spatial and cultural imaginaries, to help us see the city as a place of Canadian society and culture, including its literature" (13). By positing the very urban nature of Canadian life and artistic production, *Downtown Canada* attests to that turn in critical discourses, providing a much-needed analysis of key texts that debunk the classic connection with the wilderness.

Second, major perceptive changes have also been induced by the influx of new immigrants into the main Canadian cities since the late 1960s, bringing their own national or ethnic histories with them and not necessarily fitting them into a continuous Canadian narrative (if there ever was one). Vancouver-based artist Jin-me Yoon's work can provide us with a good sample of this process of rearrangement, insistently putting forth the multiple ways in which new understandings of identity happen simultaneously across the local, regional, national, and international layers of culture. Her well-known installation *Group of Sixty-Seven* (1996) is composed of two grids of sixty-seven cibachrome prints displayed on two confluent wall panels, in which sixty-seven members of Vancouver's Korean Canadian community appear twice: looking out from Lawren Harris's *Maligne Lake, Jasper Park*, on one panel, and looking at Emily Carr's *Old Time Coast Village*, on the other.[2] *Group of Sixty-Seven* asks a fundamental question about how different people relate to ideas of the national/regional and the kinds of mythologies they often need to confront or subvert. In other words, where do these sixty-seven Korean Canadian subjects fit in relation to the most traditional mythologies of the nation/region, as represented by the background paintings? There is an emphasis on the insertion of the Korean Canadian subject in the white Canadian imaginary, and on the transformation that this process of self-conscious insertion may bring to an overall sense of belonging. The subject looking at Carr's painting tries to make sense and interpret the tradition thereby rendered. The subject looking from Harris's stares directly into the viewer's eyes, intensifying the work's questioning power by bringing the viewer in and making him or her complicit in the interpretative task that the work invites. In both cases, the subject's position in the forefront and inside the framework of analysis seems to endow him or her with an extraordinary ability to transform such a framework. At any rate, the sharp, somehow deliberately awkward, juxtaposition of these sixty-seven Canadian Korean subjects and the iconic landscapes explicitly modifies and questions the natural tropes typified in varying degrees by the quoted paintings.[3]

From the point of view of the cultural nationalism of the 1970s, the focus on the urban that many Vancouver artists and writers seem to willingly foster would also talk back to the wilderness metaphor supposedly representing a national ethos, since it implicitly proposes a rethinking, or a bracketing out, of the traditional approach to the nation in land-based metaphors. There is consensus among critics and commentators that it was during the late 1970s and the first part of the 1980s that Vancouver writing took off as an oppositional form of literature against unifying, homogenizing ideas coming from Ottawa and Toronto, and officially sanctioned by academia "back East" (see Bowering "Vancouver"). Moreover, as Smaro Kamboureli asserts in her contribution to this volume, the highly experimental work of *Tish* encouraged specific modes of "reading the nation-state against the grain, hence the resistance they encountered within conventional nationalist discourses" (66). At that moment, the incipient interest in the representation of an urban Vancouver experience was seen as a way of counteracting the nationalist pressures. Today, however, the emphasis has moved to the identification of conflicting constructions of the city, and recent works expose obvious frictions between the different processes of locality production, that is, between the social production of space as lived symptom and the official production of the city as a dream place.[4] My analysis of the representations of the city of Vancouver intends to address the complexity of these social and political issues at various levels of interaction with literature and the arts.

Practising Place: Simulacra and the Hypercity's Other

Vancouver has often been posited as a quintessentially postmodern city because of its deemed newness, lightness, or superficiality, attributes which could in a sense be largely true. The city's supposed incoherence in terms of ethnicity or culture, for instance, seems evident in the fact that the apparently strongest ethnic neighbourhoods (Chinatown, Commercial, Main/49th) have become shopping districts, the ethnic communities that originally settled there being now scattered all over the city's different areas (Delany, Introduction 7–8). This idea of neighbourhoods as spaces that are emptied out of cultural, historical, and ethnic signification would shift the parameters by which we produce a sense of locality, since, as Delany commented in the early 1990s, it revalidates the insubstantial, throwing new light on Jean Baudrillard's notion of simulacra:

> The distinctive economic structure of Vancouver (based on what economists call "dynamic services"), and its ability to keep growing without producing anything obviously visible or substantial, seem a striking example of Fredric Jameson's "late capitalism" in an urban setting. However, there are contradictions in Jameson's claim that postmodern culture is specific to the latter days of the capitalist system. It does look plausible that postmodernism and post-industrialism should be two names for the same thing: a historic shift from the processing of material things to the processing of mere representations of things or "simulacra" in Baudrillard's term. (Delany, Introduction 12)

That ontological shift from the material realities to their mere representations produces what semioticians have called the "hypercity," the multiple representations of the city that act as simulacra or substitutes of the "real" one (Nas, Jaffe, and Samuels). "In the hypercity," they write, "signification proceeds through the production and consumption of signifiers.... A symbolically coherent hypercity is one in which production and consumption merge" (Nas, Jaffe, and Samuels 9). The hypercity belongs to Baudrillard's realm of the hyperreal, where reference (reality) is lost to the endless process of its own simulation. In spatial terms, this would mean that "it is the map that precedes the territory—*precession of simulacra*—it is the map that engenders the territory and... it would be the territory whose shreds are slowly rotting across the map" (Baudrillard 166).

If there is one writer/artist in Vancouver who subscribes to and exploits this postmodern formula, that is Douglas Coupland, whose *City of Glass* (2000), a collaborative book made up of descriptive text, memoir, colourful photographs and drawings, succeeds in conveying a feeling of the city at the level of the hyperreal.⁵ The very idea of this book, halfway between a city guide, a tourist brochure, and a photo documentary, being picked up as the "best iconic Vancouver novel" seems indicative of such ontological trespassing ("Writing Vancouver"). *City of Glass* documents Vancouver's rapid economic growth and development of service sectors such as tourism, technological industries, and entertainment, all of which have transformed the face of the city from a rather small provincial enclave to the cosmopolitan city we know today. Well into the 1990s, Vancouver's industrial sector, though waning, was still firmly set in the interior (mainly lumber and mining). At the same time, a booming business economy was being developed with the major Asian Pacific cities, and a flowing management of Asian capital was giving rise to the huge suburban shopping centre around the city of Richmond, just outside Vancouver, debunking in economic importance, affluence, and activity Vancouver's historic Chinatown. These changes are the subject of scrutiny and interpretation as well as the source of a light irony and buoyant contradiction in *City of Glass*, where Vancouver is figured as a conflicting site, simultaneously theme park and homeless city, post-industrial enclave and ecological city, moving uneasily between colonial, post-colonial, and neo-colonial forces. However, some critics argue, instead of engaging with the source and implications of these tensions, Coupland tends to smooth these conflicts out, the frictions erased in a quintessentially postmodern tabula rasa of "comfortable cultural fusions and leisurely imbibed vistas of rain and glass" (Deer 122). This picture clashes with other murkier views of the city as a frustrating neo-colonial enclave, a condition which, according to Jeff Derksen, "puts the city in a flux of competing and contradictory impulses that could once have been described as being part of the city's character; the blandest postmodern pastiches now exist alongside a troubled (and oppressed) colonial past. Any homogeneous view of the city and its citizens runs into this uneasy collation" ("Sites" 154).

Hinted at by Derksen's words and exposed by some of Coupland's glossy photos, the city's architecture, a mixture of impossible glass skyscrapers, pastiche, and mock-Tudor styles, would provide a material instance of the anti-aesthetic, or the reign of the insubstantial, the superficial, and the shallow. It could also act as paradigm of late capitalism's strategies of production/simulation of locality, as seen almost literally at work in the rehabilitation for Expo '86 of Granville Island, from a decayed and mostly abandoned dock-industrial area to a fashionable and overpriced marketplace, as well as in the current development of False Creek for and beyond the Olympics of 2010. Furthermore, the success of the city's thriving film industry paradoxically depends on its being disguised as another city, predicated on the logics of fake, made visible by its own invisibility, *appearing* on condition of *non-being, being* at the price of a constant exercise of self-denial. But, perhaps, the most telling case of this process of simulation of locality could be found in the very emptiness of the glass condominium towers that give Coupland's book its title: the "see-throughs" that dominate the city skyline, built, Coupland explains, "as contingency crash pads for wealthier Hong Kong citizens who were bracing themselves for the worst in the 1999 changeover of rule from England to China" (126). That the transition turned out to be more advantageous for these investors than originally planned, and that the towers remained largely uninhabited until recently (when the Olympics gave a new and definite thrust to the city's real estate business), highlight the complexities and intricacies of (post-, neo-) colonial histories and how Vancouverites are touched by them—"the power of global history to affect our lives" (Coupland 126). Intriguingly, these same colonial histories also return a view of the city as simulacrum: "An occasional landlord will put those $19.99 white plastic stacking chairs out on balconies to generate the appearance of occupation," Coupland tells us (126).

Explorations of different aspects of seeing Vancouver as stage or simulacrum can be found in both fiction and art from a myriad of perspectives. Most frequently, however, works have focused on the opposite effect of urban living, revealing the incoherence of the hypercity by exposing and articulating the gap between production and consumption. In so doing, the production of locality in these works counteracts or *blocks* the official images of the city. This is seen, for instance, in Daphne Marlatt's texts, Rebecca Belmore's performances, or Chris Dikeakos's photo-based works, mostly empowered by an archival view of the city. But alternative narratives of the city are the strongest component, I would argue, of an important body of Vancouver-based Asian Canadian fiction that has insistently claimed the city's history as its own.

As Glen Deer has shown, we can identify a first generation of Asian Canadian writers whose common project of "civic historical recuperation" (120) was often based on the exposure of the layers of historical racism against the Asian Canadian communities on the West Coast. The younger generation has now expanded its interest to the complexities of diasporic trajectories, the possibilities of interracial relations, social and class mobility, and a diverse array of topics such as the effects of globalization, urban isolation, family violence, or ecological disasters.[6] This intergenerational slippage, arguably seen as a transition from stasis to motion, also becomes manifest in the choice of captive versus mobile characters, as well as in their diverse Asian Canadian ethnic origins (see Ty and Verduyn). Most importantly in the context of this essay, the slippage is evinced in their approach to the city that they live in; that is, in their modes of appropriation of urban space. A brief analysis here of Madeleine Thien's novella "A Map of the City" (2001) can throw light into these new and affective modes of production of locality and practising place.

In "A Map of the City," an immigrant Chinese Indonesian family attempts to construct the city of Vancouver as home with varying degrees of success, intersecting the spatial and the temporal through a retrospective first-person narrator daughter, Miriam, who redraws an emotional map of the city from the inside out. Physical movement parallels social mobility in the story and, accordingly, the narrator's memories of the Sunday trips in the car driving across the city correspond to a time in the family history when social and economic success seems possible: "There is my mother, the navigator, a map of the city unfurled on her lap. Me in the back seat, watching my father's eyes as they glance in the rear-view mirror, the way he searches for what might appear" (181). But, as the direction of the father's glance in the mirror beckons, the immigrant dream fails to materialize and the family is forced to move down from a house in the suburbs to a flat in the East Side, as the father also moves down in jobs: from the owner of a family restaurant to a second-hand furniture store, to a real estate agent, ironically selling "Vancouver Specials," with a myriad of odd jobs in-between and a failed trip back to Indonesia, before he ends up unemployed and living in a bachelor apartment near Commercial Drive. Thien's Vancouver is a collapsing space, the distance unbridgeable between media images of the city, which Miriam approaches in the narrative present on motorbike rides with her husband, Will ("the line of a mountain range [...] an unbroken, hazy shadow, a separate history, a different life" [212]), and its shadow, projecting no city of glass, but of grey and rectangular buildings that smell of mould inside. In the midst of these two colliding representations, the harbour's *iconic* "pure and clean and yellow" piles of yellow sulphur celebrated by Coupland (50) acquire an eerie appearance as viewed from the narrator's father's apartment balcony:

> Up in the corners, the walls were mouldy and grey and the carpets had a lingering scent, part cigarettes, part damp. He'd done the best he could with decorations. There were Christmas cards, hung up along a string, and certificates from the real estate office framed on the wall. *For Devoted Service. For Congeniality.* I walked onto his tiny balcony, looked across the road at the ramshackle apartments, the wet leaves running bright along the gutters. Out on the harbor, two yellow sulphur hills glowed neon against the grey sky. (Thien, "A Map" 205)

The father's failure to provide for the family, the mother having to work increasingly more hours to keep the three of them afloat, is perceived as a humiliation, a loss of dignity for a generation of (male) immigrants who "didn't know how to connect with their families differently than as providers" (Thien, Interview). The commercial pressures of North American life are thus magnified through the immigrant's eyes, and his faith and pride in his daughter is ironically signified in the language of the city's real estate economy and consumption culture: "'My daughter, Miriam,' he said to everyone. 'When she grows up, she is going to buy her parents a big house'" (Thien, "A Map" 165). As a child, Miriam is easily co-opted by her father's ideas and the pressures of the market economy, and she has dreams of commercials in which her father becomes the prosperous business owner that he is not (164). Soon, however, the mirror shatters and the narrator's realization in the narrative present produces a clashing text of disturbing consequences: "Now, looking back, I see that the store had an impoverished look to it, that the couches were old and worn, and that my father, once so patient a salesman, had begun to speak to his customers with an air of quiet desperation" (185).

The growing importance of this *other* story, the story of failure, embitterment, and disappointment, is masterly expressed in spatial codes, as the father's comings and goings become less frequent and he is increasingly associated with the notion of stasis: "My father began swallowing pills.... His actions became slow and meticulous. He said my mother and I made no sense to him. We rushed everywhere, we didn't have a moment to lose. He, on the other hand, stopped answering the phone" (194). The narrative of failure is also explicitly related to his diasporic displacement, "the tragedy of place," comments the narrator: "To always be in the wrong country at the wrong time, the home that needs you less than you need it" (201–2). This irresolvable sense of dislocation is strongly signified in his inability to make sense of the names and news that he retains for casual conversation with his potential customers: "'Trudeau,' he said to one customer, then shrugged his shoulders, or 'Bill Bennet,' or 'Thatcherism,' the word hanging disturbingly in the air" (170). Memory is seen in this case as a trap, the source of a paralyzing nostalgia, occluding the mother's practical stance ("'But isn't it so much cleaner here?' she would often say" [179]) and preventing any movement forward for the family. Initially, Miriam thinks that she can escape nostalgia by walking away from her father and adopting as transient a life as possible, a life of changing temporary jobs, speedy motorbike rides, and forgetfulness, and pretending to be "the kind of person who lives with only the present in mind, who knows in her heart that no failures, however great, are immovable" (198). Her first attempts at producing locality happen through the practice of naming. As Michel de Certeau has argued, "in the spaces brutally lit by an alien reason, proper names carve out pockets of hidden and familiar meanings. They 'make sense'; in other words, they are the impetus of movements, like vocations and calls that turn or divert an itinerary by giving it a meaning (or direction) (*sens*) that was previously unforeseen" (104). The family Sunday drives across the city strive to turn space into place in this fashion, to produce a map of the city as home. But the illusory simplicity of Miriam's project is undercut by the parallel production of other family maps, the *other* maps drawing an *elsewhere* of places, becoming part of and complicating the city's map:

> My parents and I would drive across the city, going nowhere in particular, all of us bundled into the Buick. Through downtown and Chinatown—those narrow streets flooded with people—then out to the suburbs. On the highway, we caught glimpses of ocean, blue and sudden.
>
> I was the only one of us born in Canada, and so I prided myself on knowing Vancouver better than my parents did—the streets, Rupert, Renfrew, Nanaimo, Victoria. Ticking them off as we passed each set of lights, *go, go, go. Stop.*
>
> But nothing in Vancouver had the ring of Irian Jaya, where my parents lived in the first years of their marriage. In 1963, the country was annexed by Indonesia. They outlawed the Papuan flag, named the territory Irian Jaya, and flooded their own people onto the island. My parents, Chinese-Indonesians, arrived during this wave and lived there through the 1960s. "There were no roads," my father said, on one of our Sunday drives. "Nothing." (Thien, "A Map" 178–79)

The practice of naming is thus haunted by conflicting notions of *here, there, home*, the characters' almost obsessive repetition of locative phrases—"I am here," "you are here," "I am home"—signalling the labyrinthine paths of diasporic citizenship (see Cho). By juxtaposing, in the narrative present, Miriam's depiction of Vancouver in media-sanctioned images and the news about the social and political turmoil in Indonesia, the story further foregrounds the inescapable complexities of colonial processes and how they continue to affect the characters' lives in Vancouver. Far from Coupland's comfortable transparency, the diasporic text acts here as a shadow city: "I ached for the country I had never seen," Miriam writes, "the loss that seemed so unresolvable" (Thien, "A Map" 214).

Yet, in a sense, the story itself embodies the change demanded: in her act of storytelling, Miriam defines a movement towards that shadow text, producing a cognitive map that is no longer defined by nostalgia for the specular simplicity of her childhood memories (see Nimura). In other words, Miriam's narrative map of the city, her story, becomes an instance of production of place only inasmuch as it incorporates that sense of "diasporic exhaustion" (Deer 122) that paralyzes the father and that she had previously wanted to discard from her life as if it "had no root" in her (Thien, "A Map" 209). In this context, Miriam's shift from driving at high speed across the city to a practice of walking the familiar neighbourhoods could be read as a gesture towards the other (de Certeau 224) and hints, in so doing, at some form of textual resolution. Such transit from self to otherness (as well as the implied juxtaposition of the spatial and temporal dimensions of being) sustains one of the final scenes in which Miriam walks out of the Vancouver General Hospital, where her father is being treated after having attempted suicide:

> A thick fog had settled over the skyline. It wiped the sky clear of mountains and water. I walked along Broadway, past Main Street, where paper cups and newspapers littered the sidewalk. Past the sign that, years ago, my father told me was the tallest free-standing sign in the world. "There it is," my father said proudly. "Bowmac. Biggest sign in the world." He also showed me the narrowest building that still stands in Chinatown. My father, the tour guide who took me everywhere. He must have loved this city. Now it was coated with snow. A white-out, everything vanished, as if this were a game, as if I could bring it back from memory. (Thien, "A Map" 224)

In this final walk, the commercial aspects of urban North American life are juxtaposed with Miriam's emotional map, which includes both her memories ("My father, the tour guide") and her desire to forget ("A whiteout, everything vanished"). Her movement across the streets discloses the hypercity's various shadows as intensely personal moments or experiences, her body slowly taking stock of one shadow at a time ("He must have loved this city"), and her mind attaching each memory to a particular location (Main Street, Chinatown). "A Map of the City" shows how any process of production of locality must be an affective practice of place.

(A)History, Location, Affect

There are, in addition, very many different forms of producing affective space. Side by side with globalizing or diasporic approaches to the city of Vancouver, we find affective engagements with local histories that range from chauvinistic vindications of the city's colonial past to transformative cartographies of the unofficial lives of invisible communities.

The chauvinistic topic is brilliantly taken up by George Bowering's short story "Standing on Richards" (2004), in which a disillusioned professor of English leaves his job at the university to become a mind-prostitute, for which he starts frequenting a particular corner of Richards Street in downtown Vancouver, a prostitutes' area, offering to sell his mind to potential clients, astonished passersby, and curious drivers. Not surprisingly, this English-professor-rents-his-mind project turns out to be "a harder sell than the typical wares offered on the street" (Evans).

The story's strength is in its eloquence, ironic humour, and absurdity, but we also find an exceptional signifying power in its attempt at being firmly set in Vancouver's soil, that is, in its odd hinting at the mechanisms of production of locality. Disappointed by the city's ignorance of its own history (who was the Richards of Richards Street?) and tired of his students' lack of interest in literature, the narrator's eccentric venture aims at bringing reality back in, as it were. In hilarious contrast with an impersonal and frustrating life in academia, his unusual plan creates high expectations as, if nothing else, it promises to revalidate the small daily gestures and conversations between people, the text allowing "a kind of confident relating of little incidences of strangers meeting or making slight human connections" (Bowering, "Introduction" xi). His plan, in other words, would succeed in "delay[ing] not death, exactly, but abandonment, perhaps, a loneliness to which the writer stand-in on Richards Street is prey" (Burns). And that loneliness is broken as the initial body/mind dichotomy, the opposition between brain and mind on which the narrator's plan seems based, is also broken. This is wittily unveiled in the funky final discussion between our inexperienced mind-prostitute and his only client:

> "Well, I figure brain is worth a lot less than mind, it being just (a) physical and (b) personal."
> "Ah," I countered, making the "ah" last as long as possible while I thought about my next move. "Ah, but mind, well, you can just tap into mind like the internet. But brain is individual. If you get someone to deliver brain, that's service. The provider has to make a living, eh?"
> He was looking at me now instead of his old shimmer.
> "Okay, I guess you're right," he said.
> I smiled.
> "What about a kiss?" he said.
> What the hell. I gave him a kiss. (Bowering, "Standing" 19)

If, as some critics have recently pointed out, postmodern theories about the production of meaning have tended to overlook the level of emotional energy that we invest in the process, Bowering's narrator seems focused on that parallel production of affect-meaning, consciously moving towards what can be called the "micro-level" of socialization: what people actually do with their culture and how they interact through and with it (see

Allan). Paradoxically, the textual production of affect-meaning succeeds only inasmuch as the narrator's mind-renting project is a sound failure. Before his radical decision of standing on the said corner makes him literally vulnerable—his body physically occupying the space of the derelict and marking the location of a historical neglect (who was the Richards of Richards Street?)—the narrating location (a commenting one sliding in and out of the narrated world) ironically exposes the first-person narrator's "stand," his fixed position, as a sexist, ethnocentric, chauvinistic, and elitist white male. This narrative/narration gap both marks and undermines the location of the Cartesian subject as well as its connection with the white colonial masculinist project (of which the Richards of Richards Street was undeniably a part). In fact, while the reader is "in" for a lecture on the colonial history of the province (Bowering, "Standing" 5–7), the origin of the "genuine Harris Tweed jacket," (3) and the Austro-French Piedmontese War (13–15), the narrator/narration is "out" on the street to find "whether men who drove slowly down certain streets in downtown Vancouver were as lonely for knowledge as they were for physical spasms" (10).

The striking gap between the narrator's two projects breaks the illusion of dissociation between knowledge and involvement, between action and feeling, which yields, in turn, an extremely vulnerable subject, since as Marshall McLuhan has argued: "It is this kind of specialization by dissociation that has created Western power and efficiency. Without this dissociation of action from feeling and emotion people are hampered and hesitant" (178). The production of locality fails without the affective dimension; the mind-versus-body narrative turns against itself; "objective" knowledge proves obsolescent, betraying the uselessness of knowledge without affect.

But the tropes of standing and naming, and their potential for the production of affect-meaning, can also be put to the opposite service, that is, to the recuperation of an embodied history of the city, to a transformative articulation of place that unveils power relations and makes room for agency. This strategy is powerfully rendered by Anishinabe artist Rebecca Belmore's performances. Her piece "Vigil," included as a video in the larger installation *The Name and the Unnamed* (2002), constitutes the artist's own response to the repeated murder and/or disappearance of women, many of them of Aboriginal background, from Vancouver's Downtown East Side. In it, Belmore occupies a street corner in that poorest part of town (a sex workers' and drug addicts' territory not far from Bowering's mind-prostitute) and enacts an honouring ritual:

> She scrubs the street on hands and knees, lights votive candles, and nails the long red dress she is wearing to a telephone pole. As she struggles to

free herself, the dress is torn from her body and hangs in tatters from the nails, reminiscent of the tattered lives of women forced onto the streets for their survival in an alien urban environment. Once freed, Belmore, vulnerable and exposed in her underwear, silently reads the names of the missing women that she has written on her arms and then yells them out one by one. After each name is called, she draws a flower between her teeth, stripping it of blossom and leaf, just as the lives of these forgotten and dispossessed women were shredded in the teeth of indifference. Belmore lets each woman know that she is not forgotten: her spirit is evoked and she is given life by the power of naming. (Belmore)

If Bowering's corner aspires to be "geometrical," Belmore's is definitely "anthropological" in that it declares the impossibility of reading space without the intervention of the individual body/subject, without emotion and feeling (de Certeau 93–94). As opposed to the illusion of control of space conceptualized in the map (geometrical space), anthropological space cannot be contained. Yet no approach to space will make sense without it (de Certeau 118). Belmore's works have repeatedly insisted on the affective dimension of colonial processes and on the importance, for an effective resistance to them, of a reciprocated emotional involvement between artist and viewer. "What Belmore helps to create," writes Gerald McMaster, "is a moment, a sacred time, a liturgical moment, where every responsible action is subject to everybody and everything" (92). She helps to establish an ethical relation between the artist and the viewer that moves beyond (self)identification towards a notion of otherness as both "the limiting condition of myself," and yet the only way to define myself "essentially by representing precisely what I cannot assimilate to myself" (Butler 111). This ethics extends to the physical site where the performance takes place, entrusting the particular corner with a sense of magic agency, as well as to the actual body through which power relations are assessed and performed. The red dress, for instance, posing as an extension of Belmore's own skin, intensifies the work's historical signification, endowing it with great performing power (Rickard). As she nails the dress to the street pole and then struggles to break free, the red fabric turns to shreds, evoking the skin that these women have left behind, their difficulty to break free, and their lack of options. "Her performance," comments Stephanie Springgay, "does not claim to speak 'for' the missing women, nor about their lives and experiences, but rather weighs heavy with the flesh of the body" (Springgay). Belmore's ethics of otherness, in other words, is materialized through sensation rather than symbol, for it is in the materiality of the body that her performance achieves its ultimate signifying moment (see Braidotti).

Moreover, that Belmore's own body is often the centre of her art, this including being the subject of violent actions, exposes the inscription and reach of colonial and patriarchal violence: "Through her own body," Springgay continues, "Belmore embodies the crimes committed against the native body, the woman's body, and the social body" (Springgay). But, in a very literal sense, her body also fills the *collapsing space* of the absent, disappeared subjects/bodies. The artist's body and the names of the unnamed, which she reads out from the written marks on her own arms, bring those women back to presence, symbolically (in the name) and physically (in the arms, in the voice, in the site). In striking contrast with the profession's anonymity—"We don't do names in this kind of situation," Bowering's client reminds his mind-prostitute ("Standing" 15)— Belmore's performance calls the names of these women into existence, embodies their violent lives, denounces their abandonment, and registers the historical site of a forgetting.

Belmore's ethics of embodiment breaks therefore the tendency to represent the city either as outside history or as the result of dichotomous structures of thought: culture/nature, symbolic/material, subject/object, mind/body. Her art focuses on the "nodal points" between those forces, drawing the viewer's attention to the connections between them, and, in so doing, to the individual subjects and bodies that are made invisible by the traditional binary frameworks (Rickard). In Belmore's works, then, the body is the city and vice versa, since it is through the body that the production of locality as an affective, social, and ideological process seems most effective and complex (Appadurai 189).

The Archival City: Ecology/Technology
Other modes of exposing the materiality of a city have involved the construction of the city as an archive of cultures, an approach that necessarily implies the insertion of diachronic anti-colonialist views by First Nations cultures or by artists who have constructed urban space as Aboriginal place. In this context, some alternatives to the shallow, highly idealized media images of Vancouver are coming from the strategic conjunction of cultural memory and an alternation between ecology and technology. First Nations Lee Maracle's short story "Goodbye, Snauq" (2004) provides a good example of the former type. Of Salish and Cree ancestry, a member of the Sto:loh Nation, Maracle is concerned with the connections between colonial history and environmental damage, and this particular story deals with the transformation of Vancouver's False Creek, previously known as "Snauq." The story is told in the first person by a Squamish/Sto:loh teaching assistant at an unnamed West Coast institution with a prestigious MA

program in Indigenous Government, and it is triggered by the $92.5 million 2000 Settlement Agreement by which the Squamish Nation surrendered any further claim to False Creek.[7]

The spatial and the temporal dimensions of locality, geography, and history go hand in hand in this story. Against the reality of cement, artificial islands, and skyscrapers that characterize the area today, the narrator juxtaposes two different texts: the Squamish Chief Khahtsahlano's words about the devastating environmental damage caused by European settlers in the early twentieth century and her own historical research about the area:

> From the shadows Khahtsahlano emerges, eyes dead blind and yet still twinkling, calling out: "Sweetheart, they were so hungry, so thirsty that they drank up almost the whole of Snauq with their dredging machines. They built mills at Yaletown and piled up garbage at the edges of our old supermarket—Snauq. False Creek was so dirty that eventually even the white mans became concerned." I have seen archival pictures of it. They dumped barrels of toxic chemical waste from sawmills, food waste from restaurants, taverns, teahouses; thousands of metric tons of human sewage joined the other waste daily. (Maracle, "Goodbye" 207)

The story's multilayered structure composes a palimpsestic history of the place that is full of meaningful gaps and (post)colonial ironies. The transformation of the area from a shared piece of natural bounty for the enjoyment of the region's First Nations into an industrial zone in the first part of the twentieth century is expressed in terms of alchemy: "The magic of the white man is that he can change everything, everywhere" Khahtsahlano says (207). But, the reader wonders, what would he say if he saw the skyscrapers, manicured gardens, and highly gentrified neighbourhood of today? The sharp juxtaposition between the chief's words and the present triumphalist official discourses about the area's development creates a conflicting narrative of place whose source is located outside the text, for its strength depends on the reader's level of acquaintance with the present heavily developed (Olympic) False Creek. The reading process defines, then, a transaction zone between the text and the off-text, where effective parallels are drawn between the (ongoing) colonial appropriation of the territory and its present process of gentrification. And, in so doing, the text succeeds in unveiling the cryptic paths of abuse and violence that underlie any process of urbanization of rural or wild lands.

On the one hand, in suggesting the continuation of colonizing practices, Maracle's text transcends the local(ized) focus of a particular area of Vancouver and builds a critique of the national as constructed on the basis of repeated episodes of violence against, and dispossession and exclusion of, Canada's First Nations. It is in this arena that she dismantles the official project of articulation of a supposedly post-colonial national ethos: "'This is an immigrant nation,' Prime Minister Chretien said after the Twin Towers of the Trade Center in New York were felled. 'We will continue to be an immigrant nation.' How do we deal with this, the non-immigrants who for more than a century were rendered foreigners, prohibited from participation?" (217). At moments like this, the target of Maracle's critique is to be found in the larger national or even global discourses which render meaningless the term *post-colonial*. But, on the other hand, her critique of the inequalities underlying contemporary national/global dimensions of citizenship is most effective, I would argue, if read against the text's specific approach to the production of locality. This is enacted by yet another level of narration: the collective memories of life in that land before the radical environmental changes, which add a further meaning to the story, connecting not only colonial history and environmental problems, but also implicitly arguing how cultural memory *is* ecological memory. Snauq, the narrator tells us in a typically idealized description of pre-colonial life, used to be

> a common garden shared by all the friendly tribes in the area. The fish swam there, taking a breather from their ocean playgrounds, ducks gathered, women cultivated camas fields and berries abounded. On the sand bar Musqueam, Tsleil Watuth and Squamish women till oyster and clam beds to encourage reproduction. Wild cabbage, mushrooms and other plants were tilled and hoed as well. Summer after summer the nations gathered to harvest, likely to plan marriages, play a few rounds of that old gambling game *Lahal*. (Maracle, "Goodbye" 208)

There is a way in which the palimpsestic narrative structure mimics the archival work conducted about the history and the ecology of the place. The different layers of culture, history, and nature are embedded in one another in an act of storytelling that produces place. However, as the practice of naming in this text seems to suggest, this process of production paradoxically invokes the disappearance of place. "Maybe, while [Khahtsahlano] spoke to his little sweetheart, enumerating each significant non-existent landmark, vegetable patch, berry field, elk warren, duck pond and fish habitat that had been destroyed by the newcomers, he felt [mundane]" (210). If naming has often been used, as we have seen in Thien's "A Map of the City," as a practice of self-location within one's own territory, Maracle's strategy of re-appropriation of the land paradoxically implies its very dispossession, since it performs its own non-existence, literalizing the symbolic function of language and turning place into non-place *by naming it*. What "Goodbye, Snauq" names, then, is the absence of place, both material (Snauq, the place, does no longer exist) and symbolic (the name, Snauq, is no longer). The story lets go of the land as it lets go of a knowledge that, according to

Maracle, has been "expropriated and distorted, bowdlerized and then sold back to us in transformed form" (Maracle, "From Discomfort" 211).

Storytelling appears then *in (its) place*, enabling the act of transformation invoked by the presence of Raven in the first paragraph: "we are built for transformation. Our stories prepare us for it" (Maracle, "Goodbye" 205). And, accordingly, it is through the narrative act that the narrator achieves the knowledge and the acknowledgement of her own complicity with the colonial powers that have dispossessed the area's First Nations. Once this recognition of complicity is accomplished, the narrator is ready to say goodbye to both Snauq and her story:

> Surrender or dig up the hatchet. The Squamish Nation has chosen surrender. Which way will my journey take me? [....]
> In one sense, I have no choice; in another, I chose the people who made the deal. In our own cultural sensibility there is no choice. There are fifteen thousand non-Indigenous people living at Snauq, and we have never granted ourselves the right to remove people from their homes. We must say goodbye." (217)

There is a way, then, in which the narrator's emotional journey through this hopelessly lost territory points towards a hopeful future at the end: "Khahtsahlano dreamed of being buried at Snauq. I dream of living there" (217). To more than one reader, this ending may sound as unlikely as unconvincing. Yet Maracle's story succeeds in showing the function of archival historical research and highlights the role of cultural memory in any process of production of place, her own text a "bewildering palimpsest of highly local and highly translocal considerations," exposing how fragile the process of production of locality always is (Appadurai 198). Most significantly, it constructs Vancouver as Aboriginal place and, in so doing, the text becomes inserted, by means of its remarkable testimonial and ceremonial powers, in an indigenous tradition which, as Michèle Lacombe shows in her contribution to this volume, rewrites normative productions of locality within and beyond the nation-state.

Also drawing on the archival, Bernie Miller and Alan Tregebov's public sculpture Street Light (1996) provides a radically different representation of locality, constructing a historical vision of Vancouver that is at once inherently proposed and cancelled. Still, their fundamental differences notwithstanding, this sculpture can be read as in dialogue with "Goodbye, Snauq"; not only does it focus on—it actually is located in—the same area of Vancouver, foregrounding those aspects of the city that undermine highly idealized media and commercial images, but it also operates at the strategic conjunction between cultural memory and, in this case, technology. The sculpture consists of a huge stone-based, bronze I-beam structure at the foot of Davie Street, by the False Creek waters, supporting photographic images taken from the Vancouver archives: "[It] is carefully aligned to cast shadow images onto the sidewalk on the anniversary of the selected historical event. At night, from the tilted traffic circle opposite the sculpture, a light illuminates the panels. The form of the sculpture quotes a mixture of objects: railway trestles, hand-cars, turntables, billboards, drive-in movie screens, movie cameras, and suggests Vancouver's transformation from an industrial centre to an information age economy" (Cole 15).

The photos illustrate moments in the life of the place before the heavy industrialization and now gentrification of the area, and show Chief Khahtsahlano with his family on the same spot that Maracle's narrator pictures him. The monumental style of the engraved concrete pillars, supporting the beams and providing the curious viewer with information about the photos as well as their reference number at the public library, has an effect of indecisiveness on the whole structure. Like Lee Maracle's paradoxical act of naming in "Goodbye, Snauq," *Street Light* seems to acknowledge and give solid ground to a tradition of community living, to an unofficial history of the place, while, at the same time, endowing those former inhabitants of the area with an epitaph. This aporic reading is intensified by the contrast between the solidity of the base pillars and the suggested fragility of the bronze beams, on which the historical images rest and which remind us of a billboard in ruins and, by extension, of the ephemeral aspects of urban commercial lifestyles. As well, the divergence between the archival images and the highly technological device that makes their view in this site possible—they are digitalized photographs projected on the sidewalk on specific dates when the sun shines through the perforated panels—contributes to obstruct the possibility of a straightforward interpretation. This has been controversial for some critics, who have seen in the sculpture's choice of material, shape, and technological play a threat to the actual site heritage it allegedly means to foreground and honour. For example:

> The superb photographs speak of the shift from subsistence aboriginal communities to the early wharf and mill camps that grew into a town called Vancouver. The archive numbers of the photographs are engraved, overly monumentally, in concrete pillars at the base of the scaffolding. Disturbingly, the resolution of the holes in the sheets is so poor as to make most of the images unreadable—particularly for reading faces and discerning many details such as the fact that many of these early Vancouverites had non-European heritages. The excessive reduction of the images in this strategic public space effectively contributes to loss of historical memory. (Ingram 41)

Fig. 5.1 Bernie Miller and Alan Tregebov's public sculpture *Street Light* (1996) from across the street. (Photograph by Brian McMorrow)

Fig. 5.2 Bernie Miller and Alan Tregebov's public sculpture *Street Light* (1996) (detail). (Photograph by Brian McMorrow)

Adding to this problematic view of local history, G.B. Ingram also critiques the work's "cramped and obstructive position," its unfit location, "violating basic canons of site planning" (41). In my opinion, however, these comments fail to appreciate Miller and Tregebov's connection to deconstructive architecture and the ensuing interpretative context within which the sculpture's relation to the site on which it is located speaks of a "deliberate disfunctionality [sic]." In other words, *Street Light* seems to insist on a negative relation to its own context, reversing, in so doing, the expected function of the public monument (Eyland, "Terminations"). I would further argue that this is achieved through the sculpture's active engagement with what Jeanne Randolph has called "the holding environment," or, as Miller himself explains, the approach to the site as a social and civic space in which to "work out ideas about ethics, say, or social responsibility, or hope, both on an individual and a social level" (Miller, Interview). From this perspective, the technological and commercial aspects of the sculpture are both proposed and "held at bay," a strategy spatially signified by the lighting device just across the street. Sitting on a metal rail structure, reminiscent of both the site's industrial past and its present condition as a favourite film venue, the illuminating movie-camera-like gadget there reinforces the role of the sculpture as a cancellation device: viewed from that roundabout across the street, the work blocks the view of the marina just behind it; and that is probably what it is designed to do.

In this way, *Street Light* would contradict Timothy Taylor's opinion that "public art via development is an intriguing business. The work is paradoxically invisible, given that it tends to land in areas of extremely high traffic: foyers and breezeways, roundabouts and seawall bull-noses" (Taylor).[8] Miller and Tregebov's visual grammar serves the function of a public monument and imposes, at the same time, a "termination view" (Eyland, "Terminations"), a deliberate interference on the corporate projects that have changed the site from a rural to an industrial to a technological space. Seen in this light, the sculpture is a "jamming" interference by which to critique "the commercial appropriation of particular and important civic spaces" (Miller, Interview).

Termination Views

"Two Vancouvers, tied in a snot" sings Rose, the main character of Alice Munro's famous story "Royal Beatings," the text marking a moment of incongruity, the failure of reason to build a coherent narrative of place (New 22). Most of the works discussed in this essay speak of a certain dysfunctionality in that they construct a city of Vancouver as a series of contested zones. Their representations of local urban spaces are far from reproducing official ideologies, be they national or regional, global or local. That the body has featured prominently in most cases seems no coincidence in this regard, since positioning the body is the necessary condition of a perception of space that includes the material as well as the symbolic dimensions of locality building. Each Vancouver is produced as a moment of intensity that is self-consciously contextual and represents an ideological interaction between particular embodied subjects (writing, reading, painting, viewing, walking, living subject/body) and the specific site. Their proposals imply a rejection of the city as an ahistorical construct or *tabula rasa*, advancing, instead, a relational affective view of urban space as operating within the specific social and historical contexts. In their diverse forms, these works act as shadows to the official neo-liberal images of the city, and, in so doing, from certain angles, they succeed in blocking the hypercity from view. They are the residual referents supporting Appadurai's belief that "the imagination is today a staging ground for action, and not only for escape" (7).

Notes

1 For a study of the development of Vancouver as an international city in the years from the 1970s to the mid-1990s, see Cohn and Smith. According to the authors, globalist strategies of economics and politics have often been the result of a lack of support or recognition from the federal government.
2 Significantly this work was purchased in 2004 by the Portrait Gallery of Canada for the Library and Archives of Canada's national portrait collection. A further analysis of Jin-me Yoon's work in the context of a changing national mythology is provided in my essay "Prototypes for New Understandings: Literature, Arts and Ecology from Canada's West Coast" (2011).
3 Very many artists have engaged in a self-conscious deconstruction of The Group of Seven aesthetics. Rebecca Belmore's *Wana-na-wang-ong* (1993), the Anishinabe name for Sioux Lookout translating roughly into "beautiful curve," could be singled out as an early attempt at reappropriating the Northern Ontario landscape (see Townsend-Gault). See also the outstanding collection of essays *Beyond the Wilderness* (O'Brian and White).
4 A number of works have been published in the last few years that deal with conflicting representations of Vancouver with a focus on social exclusion and racial/gender alienation (Menéndez Tarrazo), colonial histories and cultural citizenship (Lowry), and the (in)visibility and (in)accessibility of (sub)urban life with special attention to the Asian Canadian nature of Vancouver (Deer). My analysis contributes to and extends these discussions by focusing on the various mechanisms of locality production in both fiction and art.
5 The photographs are by Una Knox, Derek Root, Josh Olson, Judith Steedman, Robert Linsley, Arni Haraldsson, Selwyn Pullman, Linda Chinfen, and Coupland himself.

6 According to Deer, Joy Kogawa or Sky Lee, authors of *Obasan* (1981) and *Disappearing Moon Café* (1990) respectively, would belong to the first generation, whereas the "new wave" of Asian Canadian writers would be represented by Nancy Lee, Larissa Lai or Madeleine Thien.
7 For the full details of this agreement, see http://www.squamish.net/media centreandarchives/kitsilanoagreement.htm.
8 *Street Light* was selected as part of the Roundhouse Community art program involving private developers as well as the City of Vancouver Public Art Program. For information about the process of selection and the composition of the jury, see Ingram (41).

Works Cited

Allan, Kenneth. *The Meaning of Culture: Moving the Postmodern Critique Forward.* Westport, CT: Praeger, 1998.

Anderson, Benedict. *Imagined Communities: Reflections on the Origin and Spread of Nationalism.* New York: Verso, 1996.

Appadurai, Arjun. *Modernity at Large: Cultural Dimensions of Globalization.* Minneapolis: U of Minnesota P, 1996.

Baudrillard, Jean. "Simulacra and Simulations." *Jean Baudrillard: Selected Works.* Ed. Mark Poster. Stanford: Stanford UP, 1988. 166–82.

Belmore, Rebecca. *Wana-na-wang-ong.* Installation. Contemporary Art Gallery: Vancouver. 1993.

Belmore, Rebecca, perf. "Vigil." By Rebecca Belmore. Talking Stick Festival. Full Circle First Nations Performance. Firehall Theatre: Vancouver. 2002. http://www.rebeccabelmore.com/video/Vigil.html.

Bhabha, Homi. *The Location of Culture.* London: Routledge, 1994.

Bowering, George. "Introduction: Longing for the Short." *Standing on Richards.* Toronto: Viking, 2004. ix–xi.

Bowering, George. "Standing on Richards." *Standing on Richards.* Toronto: Viking, 2004. 1–19.

Bowering, George. "Vancouver as Postmodern Poetry." *Vancouver: Representing the Postmodern City.* Ed. Paul Delany. Vancouver: Arsenal Pulp, 1994. 121–43.

Braidotti, Rosi. *Transpositions.* Cambridge: Polity Press, 2006.

Burns, John. Review of "Standing on Richards," by George Bowering. *The Georgia Straight.* 13 May 2004. http://www.straight.com/article/standing-on-richards-by-george-bowering.

Butler, Judith. "Sexual Difference as a Question of Ethics: Alterities of the Flesh in Irigaray and Merleau-Ponty." *Feminist Interpretations of Maurice Merleau-Ponty.* Ed. Dorothea Olkowski and Gail Weiss. University Park, PA: Pennsylvania State UP, 2006. 107–25.

Cavell, Richard. "'An Ordered Absence': Defeatured Topologies in Canadian Literature." *Downtown Canada: Writing Canadian Cities.* Ed. Justin D. Edwards and Douglas Ivison. Toronto: U of Toronto P, 2005. 14–31.

Cho, Lily. "Diasporic Citizenship: Contradictions and Possibilities for Canadian Literature." *Trans.Can.Lit: Resituating the Study of Canadian Literature.* Ed. Smaro Kamboureli and Roy Miki. Waterloo, ON: Wilfrid Laurier UP, 2007. 93–109.

Cohn, Theodore H., and Patrick J. Smith. "Developing Global Cities in the Pacific Northwest: The Cases of Vancouver and Seattle." *North American Cities and the Global Economy: Challenges and Opportunities*. Ed. Peter Karl Kresl and Gary Gappert. Thousand Oaks, CA: Sage, 1995. 251–85.

Cole, Barbara. *Downtown Shoreline: Public Art Walk*. Vancouver: Office of Cultural Affairs, City of Vancouver, 2002. http://vancouver.ca/commsvcs/oca/PublicArt/pdf/ShorelineWalk.pdf.

Colley, Ann C. *The Search for Synthesis in Literature and Art: The Paradox of Space*. Athens, GA: U of Georgia P, 1990.

Coupland, Douglas. *City of Glass: Douglas Coupland's Vancouver*. Vancouver: Douglas and McIntyre, 2000.

Darias-Beautell, Eva. "Prototypes for New Understandings: Literature, Arts and Ecology from Canada's West Coast." *Cultural Crossings: The Case Studies of Canada and Italy*. Ed. Biancamaria Rizzardi and Viktoria Tchernichova. Pisa: U of Pisa P, 2011. 35–42.

de Certeau, Michel. *The Practice of Everyday Life*. Trans. Steven Rendall. Berkeley: U of California P, 1984.

Deer, Glenn. "Remapping Vancouver: Composing Urban Spaces in Contemporary Asian Canadian Writing." *Canadian Literature* 199 (2008): 118–27.

Delany, Paul. "'Hardly the Center of the World': Vancouver in William Gibson's 'The Winter Market.'" *Vancouver: Representing the Postmodern City*. Ed. Paul Delany. Vancouver: Arsenal Pulp, 1994. 179–92.

Delany, Paul. "Introduction: Vancouver as a Postmodern City." *Vancouver: Representing the Postmodern City*. Ed. Paul Delany. Vancouver: Arsenal Pulp, 1994. 1–24.

Derksen, Jeff. "National Literatures in the Shadow of Neoliberalism." Conference position paper. TransCanada Two: Literature, Institutions, Citizenship. University of Guelph, Guelph, ON. October 2007. http://www.transcanadas.ca/media/pdfs/derksen.pdf.

Derksen, Jeff. "Sites Taken as Signs: Place, the Open Text, and Enigma in New Vancouver Writing." *Vancouver: Representing the Postmodern City*. Ed. Paul Delany. Vancouver, BC: Arsenal Pulp, 1994. 144–61.

Dickinson, Peter. "Cities and Classrooms, Bodies and Texts: Notes towards a Resident Reading (and Teaching) of Vancouver Writing." *Downtown Canada: Writing Canadian Cities*. Ed. Justin D. Edwards and Douglas Ivison. Toronto: U of Toronto P, 2005. 78–103.

Edwards, Justin D., and Douglas Ivison. Introduction. *Downtown Canada: Writing Canadian Cities*. Toronto: U of Toronto P, 2005. 3–13.

Evans, Bryn. "Bowering's Latest Stands Still." Review of *Standing on Richards*, by George Bowering. *Calgary's News and Entertainment Weekly*. 10 June 2004. http://www.ffwdweekly.com/Issues/2004/0610/book2.htm.

Eyland, Cliff. "Terminations of View: A Series of Proposals," by Bernie Miller and Alan Tregebov. Curatorial essay. U of Manitoba, Winnipeg, MB. 2003. http://www.umanitoba.ca/schools/art/galleryoneoneone/term2.html.

Grosz, Elizabeth. *Architecture from the Outside: Essays on Virtual and Real Space*. Cambridge, MA: Massachusetts Institute of Technology, 2001.

Ingram, G.B. "Contest over Social Memory in Waterfront Vancouver." *Art for Social Facilitation: Waterfronts of Art.* Ed. A. Remesar. Barcelona: U de Barcelona, 2005. 34–47. http://www.ub.es/escult/epolis/artfsoc/artforsocial_part1.pdf.

Kogawa, Joy. *Obasan.* Toronto: Lester and Orpen Dennys, 1981.

Lee, Sky. *Disappearing Moon Café.* Vancouver: Douglas and McIntyre, 1990.

Lindner, Christoph, ed. *Urban Space and Cityscapes: Perspectives from Modern and Contemporary Culture.* London: Routledge, 2006.

Lowry, Glen. "Cultural Citizenship and Writing Post-Colonial Vancouver: Daphne Marlatt's *Ana Historic* and Wayde Compton's *Bluesprint.*" *Mosaic* 35.3 (2005): 21–39.

Maracle, Lee. "From Discomfort to Enlightenment: An Interview with Lee Maracle." By Margery Fee and Sneja Gunew. *Essays on Canadian Writing* 83 (2004). 206–21.

Maracle, Lee. "Goodbye, Snauq." *Our Story: Aboriginal Voices on Canada's Past.* Toronto: Doubleday, 2004. 205–19.

McLuhan, Marshal. *Understanding Media: The Extensions of Man.* Cambridge: Massachusetts Institute of Technology, 1994 [1964].

McMaster, Gerald R. "Towards an Aboriginal History." *Native American Art in the Twentieth Century: Makers, Meanings, Histories.* Ed. W. Jackson Rushing III. New York: Routledge, 1999. 81–96.

Menéndez Tarrazo, Alicia. "Bridge Indians and Cultural Bastards: Narratives of Urban Exclusion in the World's 'Most Liveable' City." *Atlantis: Journal of the Spanish Association of Anglo-American Studies* 31.2 (2009): 95–109.

Miller, Bernie. Interview by Cliff Eyland. "Terminations of View: A Series of Proposals" by Bernie Miller and Alan Tregebov. U of Manitoba, Winnipeg, MB. 2003. http://www.umanitoba.ca/schools/art/galleryoneoneone/term3.html.

Miller, Bernie, and Alan Tregebov. *Street Light.* 1996. Commissioned public sculpture (for Concord Pacific Development Corporation). Davie Circle, Concord Pacific Place, Vancouver.

Nas, Peter J.M., Rivke Jaffe, and Annemarie Samuels. "Urban Symbolic Ecology and the Hypercity: State of the Art and Challenges for the Future." *Hypercity: The Symbolic Side of Urbanism.* Ed. Peter J.M. Nas and Annemarie Samuels. London: Kegan Paul, 2006. 1–20.

New, William H. "Writing Here." *BC Studies* 147 (2005): 3–25.

Nimura, Janice P. "Northwest Orient." Review of *Simple Recipes*, by Madeleine Thien. *The New York Times* 29 Sep. 2002. http://www.nytimes.com/2002/09/29/books/northwest-orient.html?scp=1&sq=madeleine%20thien&st=cse.

O'Brian, John, and Peter White, eds. *Beyond the Wilderness: The Group of Seven, Canadian Identity, and Contemporary Art.* Montreal: McGill-Queen's UP, 2007.

Rickard, Jolene. "Rebecca Belmore: Performing Power." 2006. http://www.rebeccabelmore.com/performing-power.html.

Shier, Reid, ed. *Stan Douglas: Every Building on 100 West Hastings.* Vancouver: Arsenal Pulp, 2002.

Springgay, Stephanie. "An Ethics of Embodiment, Civic Engagement and A/R/Tography: Ways of Becoming Nomadic in Art, Research and Teaching." *Educational Insights* 12.2 (2008). http://www.ccfi.educ.ubc.ca/publication/insights/v12n02/articles/springgay.

Taylor, Timothy. "A Master Plan Trapped Between Past and Present." *The Globe and Mail*. 2 July 2007. http://www.theglobeandmail.com/life/article108859.ece.

Thien, Madeleine. Interview. *Mason Fiction*. 23 June 2009. http://gmufictionmfa.blogspot.com/2009/06/interview-with-madeleine-thien.html.

Thien, Madeleine. "A Map of the City." *Simple Recipes*. Toronto: McClelland and Stewart, 2001. 159–227.

Townsend-Gault, Charlotte. "Hot Dogs, a Ball Gown, Adobe, and Words: The Modes and Materials of Identity." *Native American Art in the Twentieth Century: Makers, Meanings, Histories*. Ed. W. Jackson Rushing III. New York: Routledge, 1999. 113–32.

Ty, Eleanor, and Christl Verduyn, eds. *Asian Canadian Writing beyond Autoethnography*. Waterloo, ON: Wilfrid Laurier UP, 2008.

"Writing Vancouver." *The Vancouver Sun*. 13 October 2007. http://www.canada.com/vancouversun/news/arts/story.html.

Yoon, Jin-me. *Group of Sixty-Seven*. 1996. 134 framed c-prints. Collection of the Vancouver Art Gallery and the Portrait Gallery of Canada.

SIX

Jane Rule and the Memory of Canada

Richard Cavell

> Where national memories are concerned, griefs are of more value than
> triumphs, for they impose duties, and require a common effort.
> —Ernst Renan, "What Is a Nation?"

> This is the use of memory:
> For liberation—not less of love but expanding
> Of love beyond desire, and so liberation
> From the future as well as the past.
> —T.S. Eliot, "Little Gidding"

> What it means to be a self does not consist in some delusory
> self-knowledge, but in the acknowledgement of that part of ourselves
> that we have irretrievably lost.
> —Simon Critchley, *The Book of Dead Philosophers*

Canada has reached that moment in its national history when the movement toward acquiring a sense of identity is beginning to curve back on itself.[1] One could cite a score of novels published over the last decade and a half—from Anne Marie McDonald's *Fall on Your Knees* (1996) to Dionne Brand's *In Another Place, Not Here* (1997), Tomson Highway's *Kiss of the Fur Queen* (1998), Caroline Adderson's *History of Forgetting* (1999), Eden Robinson's *Monkey Beach* (2002), Jane Urquhart's *The Stone Carvers* (2003),

M.J. Vassanji's *The Assassin's Song* (2007), Lawrence Hill's *The Book of Negroes* (2007), David Chariandy's *Soucouyant* (2007)—that are overtly concerned with the question of cultural memory in Canada. The concern emerges from the particularly vexed context of Canadian national "identity" and the two competing narratives deployed to establish that identity: the narrative of the two founding nations, and the narrative of Canada as an avowedly multicultural nation.[2] The existence of these opposed narratives confirms, before anything else, that Canada lacks a monolithic cultural memory:[3] to remember culturally in Canada means inevitably to forget. How then does Canada memorialize itself? Who and what have been forgotten in the cultural memory of Canada? (See Cavell, "Histories.") To what extent can cultural memory be embodied, objectified, authenticated?

These questions take on a special inflection when one is dealing with identity formations outside traditional nationalist models, and it is in this context that the work of Jane Rule has special significance. Rule was an immigrant to Canada, but from the United States, which places her outside both the founders' narrative and the multicultural narrative. In addition, she identified as a lesbian, thus exposing the patriarchal limits to the identity question, and to cultural memory. Yet much of Rule's writing has been concerned with questions of memory and belonging, from her pioneering text *Lesbian Images* (1975), which was a major act of cultural retrieval, to works of fiction such as *Contract with the World* (1980) and *Memory Board* (1987), and the west coast settings of these novels adds yet another set of complexities to the questions we are dealing with here, given that the "founding" narratives of Canada tend to be concerned with central and eastern Canada.[4] The questions of identity, and more specifically of cultural memory, that Rule raises in her fiction, are especially pertinent at a historical moment when the issue of gay marriage has become a concern of the federal government, suggesting that queer cultural memory is not marginal but central to our understanding of the Canadian state and to the ways in which we seek to memorialize it. Rule's work compellingly poses questions concerning those excluded from cultural memory. Her work suggests that cultural memory is not based solely on national identity but that sexuality also forms part of a citizen's identity. This is another way of saying that sexuality is crucial to our understanding of citizenship and of nationhood, while enabling us, as well, to think those categories otherwise. The nation, as *Sexing the Maple* suggests (Cavell and Dickinson), is always already sexed, and Jane Rule's writing demonstrates her awareness of this nexus while articulating the basis for the formation of post-national identifications.

Fig. 6.1 Queer sexuality meets the state. (Reproduced with permission of *The Globe and Mail* and of Christine McAvoy).

The connections between queer sexuality and the state were brought home forcefully—if bizarrely—by an incident at the British Columbia legislature in March of 2009, when members of the gay community of Vancouver were invited to the provincial seat of government in order that their community service might be acknowledged. A protocol issue arose, however, when Empress Electra Quechua and Emperor Wolfgang Bang! asked to wear their crowns into the legislative buildings, and Ms Gay Vancouver her thirty-centimetre tiara. These adornments were considered by the sergeant-at-arms to be a threat to the dignity of the House, given that Canada's titular head of state is Her Majesty Queen Elizabeth II. The visitors, however, were allowed to wear their gowns into the legislature. As the sergeant-at-arms noted, "as long as the decorum of your dress shows respect for the dignity of the chamber, you can watch what's going on in the very foundation of the government of British Columbia" (qtd. in Hunter).[5]

Remembering Canada

Since the 1980s there has been an increasingly widespread interest in the notion of memory. In part this is to be expected at a cultural moment when media devices—from digital cameras to video recorders to camera-equipped mobile phones to YouTube to Facebook—have become the new *loci memoriae*, reminding us both of how fleeting our contract with the world is and of how that fleeting contract strangely persists in an increasingly archived society, where the building of new museums remains a growth industry and public memorials proliferate (see Cavell, "Architectural"). The generations that had direct experience of the world wars are disappearing, and this further exacerbates questions of memory and mediation. Questions of memory are also raised as a result of the massive diasporic movements launched via colonialism and in the aftermath of the two world wars (and these contexts are especially relevant to cultural memory in Canada), as well as by cultural genocide (including that directed by the Canadian state at Aboriginal peoples) and their attendant truth commissions, by acts of terror, and by homogenizing elements of cultural and economic globalization. We thus find ourselves in a cultural moment of remembering and of forgetting, and because these acts are meant to be collective within a given community that can extend from the family to the nation to the globe, they inevitably raise questions of belonging and exclusion, as well as of reclamation and loss.

Memory studies have proceeded along two major axes, that of the nation—the so-called *lieux de mémoire* closely associated with the work of Pierre Nora—and that of communities, as theorized by Maurice Halbwachs in his work on *mémoire collective*. As my preamble to this chapter indicates, however, it is difficult to separate these axes; indeed, they become most productive theoretically when interfaced. Nor can the individual act of memory be transposed seamlessly onto the memory of the community, let alone that of the nation—historically, nations have often sought to forget what individuals cannot help but remember, at times breaking communities in order to rupture memory. There is a powerful political dimension in the memory of individuals and communities, thus, since their memories can contest, subvert, and supervene those memories that have statist approbation. Collective memory can supervene history in a similar way, insofar as it is bottom-up rather than top-down in its orientation, and insofar as memory tends to contest the notion of a linear and progressive history with the notion of culture, which is based "on a multi-temporal concept of history where past and present commingle and coalesce, capturing simultaneously different and opposing narratives and privileging topics of representation and memory interpreted in terms of experience, negotiation, agency, and shifting relationship" (Confino 82). This is not to suggest, however, that memory is somehow outside of history; as Anne Whitehead notes, "memory...is historically conditioned; it is not simply handed down in a timeless form from generation to generation, but bears the impress or stamp of its own time and culture" (Whitehead 4). Nor is it to suggest that memory always trumps history. In fact, the two remain in uneasy dialogue.[6]

The *lieux de mémoire* model does not map easily onto Canada. Nora had proposed this concept as a way of preserving French identity at a moment when discussions about the formation of a European Union, with its emphasis on political integration, were being broached; the integrationist model of the EU was much more at home in Canada (even taking into consideration the aspirations of Quebec) than in France, which has tended to be invested in ideas of cultural exceptionalism. As well, Nora's model devolved from the universalism that France inherited from the Revolution and its principle that all citizens are equal, and which manifests itself today—paradoxically—in President Sarkozy's plan to ban the Muslim headdress in France, a situation which, although not completely unparalleled in Canada, tends to jar with Canada's multicultural programs and with its configuration in terms of many nations in one.[7]

It was Halbwachs who demonstrated that "memory is a matter of communication and social interaction," which "enables us to live in groups and communities" (Assman 109). Memory, for Halbwachs, is thus less an individual phenomenon than a collective one. A family, in his view, is not defined exclusively through kinship relations; memory plays a role in heightening certain relationships within the family and decentralizing other relationships. To put it another way, "for a group to have an idea of what it needs in order to persist, it must begin by developing as clear as possible a representation of itself" (Marcel and Mucchielli 145). Such a representation might be a work of art, or it might be a configuration of social space, as in a neighborhood, its spatial coordinates defining—though never absolutely because it is always in process—a group. Memory, in these terms, belongs as much to the present as it does to the past, as much to space as it does to time (see Olick).

What is missing from both Halbwachs's and Nora's accounts, however, is any sense of the relationship between gender, sexuality, and identity, on the one hand, and cultural memory on the other.[8] Sexuality is excluded as much from Nora's account of the state as it is, surprisingly, from Halbwachs's account of the family. Yet, as Anne Whitehead notes, *mémoire(s)*, in Derrida's reading, is deeply gendered:

> *La mémoire*, in the feminine, designates the faculty or aptitude of memory, while its plural form refers to "memories." The masculine, *un mémoire*, signifies a document, a report, a memorandum, and the masculine plural form can refer either to a number of such documents, or to writings that tell of a life: what we would term "memoirs." Derrida thus notes that in French there is discrimination between what can be said in the masculine and feminine forms, such that the masculine always implies "a recourse to...the written mark." (Whitehead 9)[9]

Fig. 6.2 Re-membering across gender and sexuality (from Rafael Goldchain, *I Am My Family* [2008]. Reproduced with kind permission of the author/photographer)

More pointedly, Marianne Hirsch and Valerie Smith have noted that "what a culture remembers and what it chooses to forget are intricately bound up with issues of power and hegemony, and thus with gender" (6). To this observation, Whitehead adds that "public media and official archives memorialize the experiences of the powerful and it has therefore been necessary to turn to alternative archives, such as…oral testimony archives…to hear the voices of women and other disenfranchised groups" (13). The reference to orality reminds us that there is an embodied dimension to memory, and this is another way in which memory is spatial (rather than exclusively temporal) and, as such, gestures toward the sexual dimension of cultural memory. If Proust's body—to take the classic instance—becomes the site of memorialization in his encounter with the *madeleine* it is because what he is remembering, in part, is how he became sexual in a particularly queer way. Queer memory emphasizes this aspect of embodied cultural memory; through embodiment, queer memory recalls that the *mens* that stands behind remembering can refer to the act of literally or metaphorically putting together again the members of a body: *re-member-ing*.

This notion emerges powerfully in Rafael Goldchain's photographic essay *I Am My Family* (2008), which seeks to reconstruct Goldchain's family—some of whom emigrated in the 1930s from Poland to South America, others of whom died in the Holocaust—by recreating a family album in which the photographer takes on all the family roles. This process at once foregrounds the problematic of "post-memory" while producing a work of highly affective memorialization.[10] Goldchain, who emigrated to Canada in the 1970s, and is thus part of a diasporic culture rather than representative of a particular *lieu de mémoire*, found that his memory work would require him to transvest, thus emphasizing the gendered and sexualized dimension of memory. Furthermore, Goldchain had no qualms about inventing relatives for his archive, commenting, in this way, on the generations of the unborn who were also the victims of the death camps (Langford 13). But there is another dimension to this process as well; as Goldchain remarks in his "Artist Statement," the "collection and assembly of memories, starting with my own, was a process that fueled the creation of more and more self-portraits and the gradual creation of a 'family' of sorts" (18); "by looking at family photographs one seeks to know one's ancestors and, in turn, one seeks to construct oneself" (21). What this process of memorialization emphasizes, in other words, is the constructedness of "family" itself, and that families are haunted by what (and who) has been lost.

It is in this context that the Romantic inheritance of memory can be addressed, the notion that the self is constructed from a series of affective memories, as in an autobiography; Rousseau states in his *Confessions*, Whitehead remarks, that they are "the story of his feelings" (74). This suggests not only that the self is a construct but also that it is in process, and part of that process derives from what has been lost—lost to memory and also lost to the self. Concomitantly, because confessions are written to be read by others, they represent the basis on which a community can come into being; public and private are shown to be interrelated. These notions take on a psychological dimension in Freud's writings about memory, where the discovery of loss, even traumatic loss, may become the basis for experiencing the self in a different way.

The concept of the "sexual citizen" has been crucial to the development of the notion of "queer cultural memory." As Jeffrey Weeks has written,

> the sexual citizen...could be male or female, young or old, black or white, rich or poor, straight or gay.... The sexual citizen exists—or, perhaps better, wants to come into being—because of the new primacy given to sexual subjectivity in the contemporary world. The claim to a new form of belonging,

which is what citizenship is ultimately about, arises from and reflects the remaking of the self and the multiplicity and diversity of possible identities that characterize the late or post-modern world.... This new personage is a harbinger of a new politics of intimacy and everyday life. (Weeks 35)

Weeks notes in his article that "today it is commonplace for many previously marginalized people—those belonging to sexual minorities—to define themselves both in terms of personal and collective identities by their sexual attributes, and to claim recognition, rights and respect as a consequence" (36). The reference here to "recognition" recalls Charles Taylor's notion of the "politics of recognition," which holds that individual identity achieves its full value dialogically, in relation to "significant others," a term which has an interesting resonance within the queer community,[11] although he doesn't extend his politics to sexual communities. Taylor invoked the politics of recognition as a way of countering the universalism of liberal politics, a universalism that tends to be exclusive in practice, and the notion of identity as a dialogue is a productive one, albeit one that, in Taylor's articulation, still rests firmly on ideologies associated with the family, which, in a queer context, can promote a politics of *mis*recognition.

The larger context of this politics of misrecognition is explored by developmental psychologist Carol Gilligan and historian of constitutional law David A.J. Richards in *The Deepening Darkness* (2009), which argues that the violent contradictions within democracies arise from a tension with a patriarchal inheritance from the Roman Republic that placed erotic liberty in conflict with repressive power. "The focus of our Roman sources on sexuality—the severity of its suppression and also the association of sexual freedom or the claim to freedom in intimate life with movements for political liberation—riveted us" (2), the authors write. "When Augustus passed a law criminalizing adultery—the *Lex Julia*, named after his daughter whom he exiled for the crime—he transformed what had previously been a private family matter into a crime against the state" (2). The authors anchor their study of this entry of the personal into the political with a discussion of two literary polarities, the *Aeneid* of Virgil and its "heroic conception of patriarchal manhood associated with a personal history of loss" (2), and *The Golden Ass* of Apuleius, a second-century comic narrative, with its "vision of sexual love based on equality and leading to transformation" (3). They end with a discussion of why gay rights have become a "lightning-rod" issue in contemporary (North) American politics.[12]

The authors read the *Aeneid* as an ambiguous work, juxtaposing the triumphalism of Augustus with the psychological trauma of Dido, and suggest that Virgil may have come to identify with Dido: "Vergil [sic] seems to have fallen in love with Dido and perhaps saw her as himself, often in love with men whom patriarchy had rendered incapable of sustaining love. Vergil stands, in this respect, in the tradition of subsequent gay writers such as Tennessee Williams who create sexually complex, passionate, highly intelligent, and powerful women...finding perhaps in the plight of such women under patriarchy their own plight as gay men" (Gilligan and Richards 76).[13] Given that the *Aeneid* is a political foundation narrative, the authors' observations have the effect of placing sexuality, including queer sexuality, at the heart of such narratives.

The Golden Ass presents for the authors a much more liberated narrative of love and sexuality.[14] "What makes Apuleius so remarkable is that he came, presumably through his relationships with women, to see the crucial place of women's strengths in resistance to patriarchal demands" (97). This allows him, they suggest, to write a comedy in response to Virgil's tragedy, the Cupid and Psyche of his inner tale reflecting the subplot of Aeneas and Dido. "The developmental psychology implicit in Apuleius's telling of the story of Cupid and Psyche makes sense not only of the resistance of Roman women to patriarchy but also of the continuing form of such resistance today" (97).

One form such resistance takes is the preservation of cultural memory, as Apuleius's retelling of the Cupid and Psyche myth demonstrates. Memory is not, however, unmotivated (as the notion of "memory entrepreneurs" suggests), which leads to the questions of who does the remembering and what gets remembered, and which selves are thereby legitimated within statist memory (see Jelin). Timothy Findley gives these questions a Canadian context through his novel *The Wars* (1977), which is structured as a framed narrative in which the researcher in the frame seeks to discover why Robert Ross, a Canadian soldier, goes AWOL in World War I in order to rescue a barn full of horses from a fire. The researcher learns through his archival work that Robert's otherness within the nationalist context of war (as well as the peacetime context of family) is a displacement of his sexual otherness. The narrator comes to this understanding not through anything written in the national archives, however, because queers are not remembered there, but through an affective identification with Robert that is proclaimed in the novel's closing words, as the researcher takes one last look at a photograph of Robert, his sister Rowena, and their pony, Meg:

> The archivist moves among the tables—turning out lights and smiling—telling us gently "late. It's late." You begin to arrange your research in bundles—letters—photos—telegrams. This is the last thing you see before your put on your overcoat:

> ROBERT AND ROWENA WITH MEG: Rowena seated astride the pony—Robert holding her in place. On the back is written: "Look! You can see our breath!" And you can. (Findley 226)

What the researcher asserts here is an affective bond outside statist and familial institutions; although his archival research fails as an act of historical recuperation, it succeeds through a form of cultural memory that supervenes historical and nationalist memorializations.

Ann Cvetkovich has built on this notion of affective memory in her book *An Archive of Feelings* (2003). Her goal in that book, as she states it, is to move "beyond narratives of assimilation or national belonging that demand feelings of unambivalent patriotism or that restrict the language of loss to sentimental forms of nostalgia" (119), and she finds in queer sexualities the possibility of a counter-memory to these statist practices. Emphasizing migration and its attendant dislocation as a major source of contemporary trauma, Cvetkovich proposes a notion of sexuality that goes "beyond gay and lesbian identity politics to consider how (homo)sexualities function in transnational contexts" (122). As she puts it,

> queer theory has taught us to revalue gay and lesbian practices as paradigmatic instances of nonnormative sexualities; it can also help illuminate how immigration produces queer, or nonnormative, versions of national identity and the nation. Migration can traumatize national identity, producing dislocation from or loss of an original home or nation. But if one adopts a queer and depathologizing approach to trauma and refuses the normal as an ideal or real state, the trauma of immigration need not be "healed" by a return to the "natural" nation of origin or assimilation into a new one.... The desire for "natural" reproduction can be understood as a way of refusing the trauma of cultural dislocation through a fantasy of uninterrupted lineage. As a more obviously recent and invented tradition, gay and lesbian culture can provide alternative models for migrant cultures. (Cvetkovich 121–22)

Part of the trauma of queer cultural memory is that it is always partial, and to the extent that identity depends on memory, that identity will likewise be partial, in process. If there is to be a queer identification within the context of cultural memory, then it must, paradoxically, apply beyond notions of queer identity. One way of understanding this is to posit queerness as the *questioning* of full identity. To argue for a notion of citizenry that includes queer identities, then, would be to argue that national and queer identifications *alike* are partial, both as a way of critiquing nationalist notions of complete identification and as a way of asserting that *no* identity is complete but, rather, in process. This is the task that Jane Rule set for herself.

Jane Rule and the Queerly Canadian

Jane Rule often said that she had chosen Canada, rather than being born a Canadian, sidestepping, thus, the reproductive imperative that stands behind citizenship and proclaiming herself, instead, *queerly* Canadian. Similarly, she chose to be a Canadian *writer*, publishing her first work in Vancouver.[15] That story was "A Walk by Himself," issued under the imprint of William McConnell's Klanak Press in 1959. McConnell was part of a literary community that extended from Malcolm Lowry to Alice Munro, and in this way Rule became part of a literary tradition that was itself queerly Canadian, at once inside and outside the Canadian literary establishment by reason of its geographical location, far from the hegemony of Canadian national publishing in Toronto; in a private press, rather than a canonical one; on a west coast that continues to be marginal in Canadian literary culture; and in the company of that other expatriate, Malcolm Lowry.[16] The story she published in *Klanak Islands* is a devastating critique of marriage, a concern that extends across Rule's fiction and into the non-fictional work she produced beyond *After the Fire* (1989).

That concern derives from the possibility of building communities outside the statist ideology of the family. Rule's 1980 novel, *Contract with the World*, is exemplary in this regard. Set in Vancouver during the mid-1970s, the novel is Rule's most extensive experiment in point of view, comprising six chapters that are self-contained but interlocking, as in a cubist composition: Joseph Walking, Mike Hanging, Alma Writing, Roxanne Recording, Allen Mourning, and Carlotta Painting. As the use of the progressive present indicates, this is a process novel, a literary counterpart to the process art of the 1960s. Not only is the novel's visual artist, Carlotta, a painter of this sort, but Rule pushes the concept further to include the reception of the work of art as part of the process of its becoming. In the last scene of the novel, Carlotta's paintings are attacked for their apparent obscenity at the opening of her exhibition and spattered with paint. This is the nature of the contract with the world; if Rule has written an artist's novel here, it is one which brings the work of art down from the ivory tower and into the world, where she shows it playing a profoundly important social function. Sculptor Mike Trasco's comment that "*form* has to be rescued from usefulness" (24) is the inverse of the poetics that Rule brings to bear on this work. Although it is Alma, the budding writer, who is uniquely given the first person singular to narrate her section of the novel, Rule's process in the novel is more akin to that of Roxanne, who is a sound artist, making sound maps of the community, and the allusion in the novel to McLuhan's global village (316) is crucial here in understanding the fleeting nature of the oral that, paradoxically, supports intensely powerful community relations. Rather than the imagined community of the nation which Benedict

Anderson associates with the abstractions of print culture, Rule proposes a queer culture which, by virtue of its grounding in orality, is an embodied culture as well.

If *Contract with the World* is Rule's first novel to "thematically incorporate gay communities, institutions, and politics," as Marilyn Shuster remarks, it does not privilege this theme. "Rather than privilege gay identities and idealize community," Shuster writes, "Rule created characters, straight, gay, or bisexual, who are all capable of intolerance, pettiness, and overblown egos as well as sensitivity, generosity, and genuine talent" ("Introduction" 10). The six characters in the novel constitute a queer community, one which Rule resolutely sets against the statist model, as in this passage from the first section of the novel:

> Joseph would no more argue with Pierre about homosexuality than he would with Mike about art or Carlotta about suicide. All his friends seemed to wear attitudes like name tags, means of identity rather than principle. It was the same with the political parties they supported or actually belonged to. Mike belonged to the New Democratic Party because of his working-class background rather than his socialist convictions. Carlotta was really to the left of the New Democratic Party but tolerated it on the ground that a country like Canada could never manage a revolution. Alma was a Liberal to maintain social superiority and annoy Mike. Allen voted Conservative out of affected cynicism to serve his own vices. Pierre? He believed in the federal government of whatever party... because, he explained, "I have embraced my enemy and become his adoring slave." With such a view Pierre would no longer be safe on the separatist streets of Montreal, but he hadn't been in Quebec for five years. Joseph himself was the worst sort of liberal, a naïve humanist who hoped for rather than believed in anything.... To be an insignificant man in an insignificant place who could carry such ordinary responsibilities as a job and a mortgage was for Joseph a protective coloring that kept him out of the eye of the eagle, for he had no desire to be claimed for a heroic or melodramatic death in the service of his country or his own imagination. (Rule, *Contract* 25–26)

Rule is consistent here as elsewhere in attacking identity politics, both on the personal and political levels, and her position has a good deal to do with her belief in the self as process. "I am a part of all that I have met" (53) says Joseph, quoting Tennyson, which suggests that identities are not absolute but accretions—relational. When Joseph loses his memory he is unable to function in the queer community that he has brought into being around him because his relationship to the community has been sundered, and he is forced to live inside himself. Politics here—even non-normative politics—is likewise processual, defined by community relations and not by identities, be they essentialist or constructivist.

Rule brings together all the characters of *Contract with the World* at the end of the novel in a scene set in Surrey,[17] a suburb of Vancouver, where Carlotta's exhibition of paintings is having its opening night. A local bigot armed with a bucket of red paint crashes the event in order to protest the inclusion of Carlotta's portrait of Allen Dent, who had been present at a raid on a gay party in Ottawa that had been reported in the national press. All of the members of the community, except for Alma, are arrested as a result of the ensuing melee: "Surely you can...paint us all again" says Alma to Carlotta:

> Quieting, Carlotta pulled back away from that multiple embrace and discordant song, seeing them all, Joseph,...Mike, Alma, Allen, and Roxanne, escaped from their destroyed portraits, survivors who had already grown far beyond her fixed ideas of them. Because they were all here now together, their lives would change again in ways she couldn't predict. (339)

Once again Rule asserts that the self is in process and no art that wishes to be faithful to this fact can portray the self in any other way; she also suggests that queer cultural memory derives its power precisely by avoiding the notion that its value lies in an abstract future: "'I can't imagine,' Carlotta said. 'I can't imagine'" (339). As Cvetkovich suggests, the trauma is not refused here, but celebrated.

Rule's portrayal of a queer community in this novel—where "queer" is not exclusively a sexual delimitation—has productive parallels with the queer community that David Caron writes about in his study of *The Marais and the Queerness of Community*. The book is at once a memoir of Caron's father and of the Marais area of Paris where his father lived—then the Jewish ghetto of Paris and now the gay ghetto. Caron makes a distinction between the *res publica* and the community, which is at once public *and* private. Unlike the statist community, which is based on filial relationships—in the Canadian national anthem we sing of "true patriot love, in all your *sons* command"—this model is based on a relationship of *non-being*, because the community affiliation is relational, dialogical—a rapport, a companionship, as Rule suggests in her configuration of the community in *Contract With the World*. This non-being suggests, paradoxically, that community is based on loss—it is comprised by a set of relationships that will not always be, indeed, which is in a constant process of change, as Rule likewise suggests. What community gains through this is a sense of difference, as opposed to the sense of the same, of "*all* your sons" (which doesn't even admit of the difference of "daughters") and a sense of self-fashioning that emerges in part from a sense of being out of place (as an immigrant would feel, as well as those considered non-foundational within the state) and thus the necessity of bringing that place into being. It is a community neither of the past (it is non-foundational) nor of the future (it will not exist in this way, or even necessarily in this place/*lieu*, in the future—"We Are Everywhere" also means that "We Are *Nowhere*") but of the here and now—*Now Here* (Caron 116). Hence Rule's *Contract With the World* deconstructs itself at the end, Carlotta's inability to imagine another community testifying to the need not for an imagined community (in Benedict Anderson's sense of relationships mediated by the state) but for a community that has a contract with the world, with the here and now (and thus the importance given to Roxanne's soundscape project). Hence too Rule has Joseph *walking*, bringing his community into existence diasporically. As Caron remarks, the "idea that impersonality may serve as the basis for community is lost on those who conceive of community as a gathering of pre-established selves rather than as the condition for singularity" (130). Caron continues:

> even understood as plural, the gay self cannot lay claim to stability, since the process of negotiation with the identity-producing system is a never-ending one. A system is never fixed; it keeps shifting its contours, or margins, in order to ensure its own survival in the face of challenge. This is why it is perfectly conceivable, indeed probable, to have a society one day that will grant complete legal equality to gay people *and* be constitutively homophobic at the same time. This is the inevitable snag met by rights-oriented gay politics. For an analogy, think of the situation of women in today's Western democracies, where the coexistence of equal rights and sexism is the norm and not a temporary stage in the process called perfectibility.
>
> To rephrase: The proposition that "being gay" = "being oneself" presupposes a coincidence between singularity and identity that is impossible, because there exists no self outside the relational. The self *is* the relational. It never comes purely from me or from the system. It is an effect, or to be exact, a plurality of effects, of a relation that it does not precede—not even as an idea. (132)

The difference between a community and a family, thus, is that a family seeks to perpetuate itself as itself; it cannot be different from itself:

> Family as the structuring metaphor for community serves two related purposes in modern Western cultures. Applied to minority communities, the metaphor seeks to privatize the tribal, the archaic *ethnos*, the old nation within the new nation, and to remove such communities from the realm of the political—the *res publica*. Applied to the state, it transcends

and naturalizes the social, universalizes it, and equates the future with reproduction. Group friendship, on the contrary, does not have a future. Its moments may come in succession but they are not connected by causation or narrative thrust.... For homosexuals, there has never been anything but the present since a community of friends, unlike a family, is neither an outcome nor a promise of birth. (198–99)

To deny that family narrative line is to delegitimate the phallus as a generative notion and make it a *de*generate one,[18] thus sundering the system that gives men power over women. As Caron notes, this would be "the end of the social as we know it and the birth of 'the group'" (203). It would even be the end of homosexual desire in that it would undo "the foundational categories of sex and gender identities and perforce of identity *in general*. Without selves capable of laying claim to distinct identities, 'all' we are left with is the perpetual interplay of difference that I call the queerness of community" (205). That, too, is the contract with the world, as Rule depicts it in her novel: a community of disidentification that, unlike a family, does not seek to perpetuate itself, and that is oriented to the present.

Mourning Jane Rule Mourning
The ending of *Contract with the World* is comic in the formal sense, in that it brings all its characters together with the suggestion that a new society might emerge out of this social reconfiguration. Rule treats this possibility with considerable irony, however, allowing us to revisit Gilligan and Richards's discussion of sexuality, literature, and politics to remark that literary form is itself gendered and sexualized and asserts its politics through these categories. Northrop Frye has argued that "the movement of comedy is usually a movement from one kind of society to another" and that the "appearance of this new society is frequently signaled by some kind of party or festive ritual" with "weddings [being] most common" (163). Frye sets these remarks within the broader context of the structure of comedy, in which "a young man wants a young woman...and...near the end of the play some twist in the plot enables the hero to have his will" (163). The comedy that Frye cites in support of his argument—Shakespeare's *As You Like It*—is somewhat more complicated, however. As Jean E. Howard notes, the play "uses the critical capacities of pastoral to explore the causes of the lovers' unhappiness and to probe the surprisingly complex issue of what is natural in matters of love and sexual desire. In this regard, the play takes little for granted—neither the stability of gender difference nor the naturalness of heterosexuality nor the invariant nature of being in love" (1593). Rule similarly critiques the sexual politics of comic structure while

at the same time rejecting the narrative line—with its future-bound orientation and its promise of cumulative plenitude so often configured in terms of marriage—as uniquely representative of the social self. In these terms, her work bears a number of similarities to Apuleius's *Golden Ass*, especially when we consider that work as a form of satire, rather than solely within the category of comedy to which Gilligan and Rogers assign it (see Frye 235, 309). Satire inflects the utopian nature of comedy while at the same time asserting a contract with the world—a connection to the here and now from which it gains its satirical purchase.

The ironic, satirical dimension of *Contract With the World*, together with the negation in Carlotta's final comment, alerts us to the fact that Rule's work is marked throughout by a sense of loss that often shades into mourning, with loss, here as elsewhere, asserting the refusal of closure. Beginning with *Desert of the Heart* (1964), which invokes Auden's elegy for W.B. Yeats in its representation of Ann's grief for the loss of her mother, Rule enters into the elegiac mode. *Contract with the World* also cites from Auden's poem and has a chapter titled "Allan Mourning"; *This Is Not for You* (1970) is a long lament for a lost love; *The Young in One Another's Arms* (1977) takes its title from Yeats's poem "Sailing to Byzantium," which meditates on "the young in one another's arms,...those dying generations"; *Memory Board* (1987) hinges on the trauma of Constance, who was buried alive with her dead mother in a bomb shelter during the London blitz; and *After the Fire* (1989) is apocalyptic in its scenes of grief and mourning.

Mourning, in Rule's work, functions as a sign of the vexed relationship between memory and identity. Since memory can only be partial, and since identity is predicated upon memory, we can never be fully present to ourselves. Mourning is a sign of that loss, a sign that goes beyond bereavement. Freud suggested, in "Mourning and Melancholia," written in the last year of World War I, that a successful mourning was one in which all ties to the dead other were transferred to a new love object, the original love object being thus idealized. Melancholia arises, according to Freud, when this transaction remains incomplete, when the lover fails to idealize the departed lover. But we would be surprised, having read *Contract with the World*, if this process of idealization were a motivating force in Rule's work, especially insofar as it requires the negation of the other and the removal of memory precisely from the political field of agency that was of prime importance to Rule.

Derrida's reading of Freud tends to invert Freud's polarities, arguing that a successful mourning in Freud's terms would "[fail] to respect the singularity of the other," and that a failed mourning, in Freud's terms, would *succeed* insofar as it "would keep the actual other close, respecting the fact that they resist all our attempts to assign them their proper and final resting place" (Dooley and Kavanagh 77). As Derrida puts it in *Mémoires for Paul de Man*, "we can only live this experience in the form of an aporia: the aporia of mourning...where the possible remains impossible...[and] where success fails" (qtd. in Dooley and Kavanagh 77). Judith Butler has built cogently on this argument in her "Afterword" to the volume *Loss: The Politics of Mourning*, stating that the

> presumptions that the future follows the past, that mourning might follow melancholia, that mourning might be completed are all poignantly called into question in these pages as we realize a series of paradoxes: the past is irrecoverable and the past is not past; the past is the resource for the future and the future is the redemption of the past; loss must be marked and it cannot be represented; loss fractures representation itself and loss precipitates its own modes of expression. And we are considering different kinds of loss here,...perhaps most difficult, the loss of loss itself: somewhere, sometime, something was lost, but no story can be told about it; no memory can retrieve it; a fractured horizon looms in which to make one's way as a spectral agency, one for whom a full "recovery" is impossible, one for whom the irrecoverable becomes, paradoxically, the condition of a new political agency. (Butler 467)

That new agency derives from the commonality of the sense of loss. To quote Butler again, "loss becomes condition and necessity for a certain sense of community, where community does not overcome the loss, where community *cannot* overcome the loss without losing the very sense of itself as community" (468). It is this paradox that Rule represents at the end of *Contract with the World*. Loss and mourning, as she represents them there, display our tie to the other in ways that are affective rather than idealized, and in ways that remind us that we perform our beings relationally. As Peggy Phelan has put it, "Queers are queer because we recognize that we have survived our own deaths" (32). In surviving our own deaths we continue to mourn and thus to assert the political necessity of mourning.

Jane Rule takes up a number of these issues in her essay "Legally Single," written in 2001 and published posthumously in *Loving the Difficult* (2008). The essay compares two encounters with census takers, the first taking place in 1961, when the fact of two women jointly holding a mortgage can find no place in the state's construction of national identities. As Rule recollects, "the mortgage broker [had] wondered if perhaps we were the first women back [then] in the late '50s to own a house together without a husband or brother to co-sign the mortgage. He had spent the whole weekend looking through regulations for a reason to refuse us and hadn't found one" (139). And because there wasn't a place on the census form for such joint ownership, and because Helen, Rule's longtime partner, was in the garden, Jane became "head of household."

Forty years later and another census: "Now I hear," writes Rule, "that in the 2001 census taking, I will have the opportunity to declare not only joint ownership of a house but the same-sex nature of my relationship" (142). This leads Rule to ponder that the

> new militants of the gay and lesbian movement are proud of this new opportunity to declare themselves, to have their relationships given the respectability of being officially acknowledged.... How will this new misinformation be used?... Those of us who do expose ourselves in the census and tax returns will find ourselves subject to more of the regulations that have plagued heterosexuals for so long, creating false dependencies and arbitrary responsibilities, where before we learned to take real care of each other in creative, communal ways. (142)

This paragraph is typical of Rule's political generosity in asserting her solidarity, through her use of the first person plural, with those against whom she is making a declaration of political difference; once again, the theme of community emerges, this time bearing its full political significance, which Rule carries over into the essay's concluding paragraph: "We don't own each other. We are not automatically unequal in relationship.... No law should force us into relationships defined by anyone but ourselves. To declare our right to be independent of such control, every adult, regardless of sexual preference or living arrangement, should declare that she or he is legally single, even if, as in my unhappy case, it happens to be true" (143).

In this essay's Moebius loop, Rule takes the terms she is opposing and embraces them, but she does so as a way of asserting her mourning for her late partner, Helen Sonthoff, implying thus that her opposition is less to the concept of gay marriage than to the idea that it could ever represent political plenitude. Queer mourning, in this sense, is about loss as agency; as Rule's character Ruth Wheeler puts it in *The Young in One Another's Arms*, "what you lose is what you survive with" (3).

Notes

This chapter is an extended version of the keynote lecture given at the conference "Jane Rule and the Queerly Canadian," University of British Columbia, 5 June 2009, on the occasion of a major donation establishing the Jane Rule Endowment for the Study of Human Relationships. I am grateful to Dr. Janice Stewart, Chair of the Critical Studies in Sexuality Program, UBC, for the invitation, and to the generous donor who made possible this celebration of the life and work of Jane Rule. The article "Drag Queens Lose Crowns" is reprinted by permission of the Globe and Mail Inc. and photographer Christine McAvoy.

1 I refer here to "the self-conscious attitude...to be *Canadian* as distinct from British or American," as Norman Shrive put it in his classic essay "What Happened to Pauline?," first published in *Canadian Literature* 13 (1962) and reprinted in *From a Speaking Place: Writings from the First Fifty Years of Canadian Literature* (58).
2 Verbeeten states that "in the hundreds of years before Confederation, Canada knew only two distinct waves of immigrant-settlers: ten thousand French subjects who, on the initiative of independent agents, were brought out to New France between 1608 and 1760; and ninety-thousand Americans who, as Loyalist 'refugees' from the Revolution or as farmers seeking cheap land, moved to the sparsely settled Maritime colonies of Nova Scotia and New Brunswick and to Upper Canada, the future province of Ontario, between 1783 and 1812.... These were the 'founding populations' of Canada. They grew prodigiously by natural increase; fertility rates were, notwithstanding later trends, often higher in these English provinces than in Quebec.... By mid-century, moreover, Quebec began to haemorrhage its native-born to the wage-paying mills of New England" (3). These comments undermine, as Saunders puts it, "our belief that Canada is built upon the communities that came from Britain and France in the years *before and immediately after* [my emphasis] Confederation—a 'core' culture that was much later supplemented by waves of non-British immigrants" (F8). In fact, as Saunders goes on to state, drawing on Verbeeten's study, "only in the Laurier era did Canada develop the 'pull' factor that made people want to stay there. Canada began developing its core, sustainable population, the bulk of people who formed our culture, only in the 20th century. And those immigrants, from the beginning, were very different from the strictly British and French faces of the Confederation era" (F8). Likewise disputed is the notion that Canada became a multicultural nation in the 1960s. In fact, multiculturalism was promoted in Canada from the 1930s as a way of *maintaining* Anglo hegemony through a "divide and conquer" philosophy. See Henshaw, and note 3 below.
3 Sonali Thakkar, in a perceptive review of Ronald Rudin's *Remembering and Forgetting in Acadie: A Historian's Journey through Public Memory* (2009), identifies the threat posed by the Acadians' wish to be recognized as founding peoples of Canada to Quebec's status as a founding nation. The Acadians resisted the alternative, multicultural model; however, if they, too, are founders of the nation, then foundationalism becomes diluted—indeed, it becomes multicultural. Thakkar comments: "By now it is common for marginalized or discriminated-against communities to make political claims in the present by way of a narrative about the past. Potentially, they empower themselves and reclaim their identity in the process. Or, as some have suggested—allies

of minority and disadvantaged populations among them—we all become obsessed with identity politics based on injury and resentment. Those of us interested in memory need to keep thinking about this last proposition and its troubling implications, and do more work on the relationship of memory to multiculturalism and to identity politics. Case studies from Canada are particularly interesting in this respect, because of Canada's very particular articulation of multiculturalism" (15).

4 The west coast setting adds yet another dimension to my discussion of mourning in Rule. See also the chapter on "Landscapes of Loss and Mourning" in Braun (109–55).

5 This scenario powerfully illustrates Lauren Berlant's notion of the political power inherent in the performance of "an iconoclastic national counter-fantasy" that can "counter-theatricalize" dominant discourses of governance in order to produce "strategic misrecognitions" such as this brilliant example of "Diva Citizenship" (Berlant 148, 163, and 221).

6 A case in point is Timothy Snyder's July 2009 article, bearing the provocative title "Holocaust: The Ignored Reality," where it is clear that this ignorance is a result of "today's confused discussions of memory" (14). What Snyder sets out to critique is the memory of Auschwitz as the epicentre of the Holocaust; instead, he argues, it represents the tip of an iceberg whose greatest mass was in Eastern Europe, and was part of a process that began before the war, not during it: "Of the 5.7 million or so Jews killed, roughly 3 million were pre-war Polish citizens, and another 1 million or so pre-war Soviet citizens: taken together, 70 per-cent of the total"; "By 1943 and 1944, when most of the killing of West European Jews took place, the Holocaust was in considerable measure complete. Two thirds of the Jews who would be killed during the war were already dead by the end of 1942" (14; I have reversed the order of these sentences), which, I would add, was the year of the Wannsee Conference (20 January) at which the National Socialist high command convened to discuss the Final Solution. According to Snyder, "Auschwitz as symbol of the Holocaust excludes those who were at the center of the historical event"—the Jews of Eastern Europe—and he argues that "to some degree, they [the Eastern European Jews] continue to be marginalized from the memory of the Holocaust" (14). Note his deployment of the words "historical" and "memory" here. Snyder concludes: "memory has made some odd departures from history, at a time when history is needed more than ever. The recent European past may resemble the near future of the rest of the world. This is one more reason for getting the reckoning right" (16).

7 Sarkozy's attempt to measure the ethnic composition of France has become a major issue in cultural memory, since it recalls for many the Vichy government's 1940 census of France, which enabled it to identify France's 300,000 Jews, many of whom were subsequently deported to death camps. The leader of Sarkozy's project, François Heran, has stated that "it's irrational in certain ways, but these memories of history will not disappear. You still have people who are the sons and daughters of the generation that disappeared in Auschwitz. These memories are being reactivated very strongly, and we have to

take this into account" (qtd. in O'Neil). In Canada, by contrast, Statistics Canada poses questions of these sorts quite commonly. See O'Neil and also Smith.
8 Sexualized cultural memory became a major issue in Berlin with the inauguration of Peter Eisenman's *Monument to the Murdered Jews of Europe*, which is in the area of Berlin defined by the Reichstag and the Brandenburg Gate. Gay groups immediately protested the absence of reference to the 6,000 homosexuals who were murdered in the death camps. In response, a monument was placed across the street from Eisenman's memorial. This then occasioned a protest from lesbian groups, who have now agreed to share the monument. Currently, there are further protests from the Roma, who argue that they too should be memorialized, but not in the same place that homosexuals are memorialized. See "Remember, Remember" (84–85) and, more broadly, Sternweiler.
9 Whitehead is quoting from Jacques Derrida, *Mémoires for Paul de Man* (1989).
10 The term is Marianne Hirsch's from her book *Family Frames: Photography, Narrative and Postmemory*.
11 "Significant other" was a term used for same-sex friend/partner by Armistead Maupin in the fifth and eponymously titled volume of his *Tales of the City* series.
12 In the July 2, 2009, issue of *The New York Review*, David Cole reviews four books on same-sex marriage in the United States, noting that "during the last decade, forty-one states have passed statutes banning recognition of same-sex marriages, and twenty-six have amended their constitutions to that effect" (12). Three arguments are made by those who oppose such unions: that the state is responsible for maintaining traditional marriage; that the state has an obligation to promote procreation; and that the state has a responsibility to oppose immoral behaviour. Cole notes that the first argument is circular; that tradition must not be used to justify discrimination; and that marriage has been construed differently at different points in history. The procreation argument founders on the fact that "no state limits marriage to couples who intend to have children, or denies marriage to couples who are infertile. Moreover, same-sex couples can and increasingly do have and raise children" (14). The moral disapproval argument "has fared poorly in the courts" but "seems to have traction in American politics" (14); this argument does not take into consideration the possibility that marriage itself might be the object of moral disapproval, on the grounds that it "has permitted society to shirk collective responsibility for dependent care by relegating it to the private sphere, where women shoulder a disproportionate share of the burden" (16); a shift to civil unions might address these inequities and "help to undermine the stereotyped conceptions of gender that contribute to marriage's flaws" (16). In the July–August 2009 issue of the *Literary Review of Canada*, Charles Blattberg reviews *In Defense of Religious Liberty* by David Novak. "Novak is an academic philosopher and a Conservative rabbi. He is also one of the Harper government's appointees to the board of Assisted Human Reproduction Canada, a body that oversees the use of new reproductive technologies" (Blattberg, "Bad Faith?" 11). Novak argues that "'religious freedom [is] the first right in a secular society, one that trumps all other rights'" and that the legalization of same-sex marriage would be an "'assault' on his religious liberty" (11). As Blattberg goes on to note, however,

Novak appears unaware of Canada's *Civil Marriage Act*; formerly a citizen of the United States, though now teaching at the University of Toronto, Novak states that "'the great issues of public morality dealt with in this book are almost always identical in both countries'" (11) and believes that in both countries "all legislation is subject to judicial review, something he would know is not true of Canada [notes the reviewer] if he had ever read our Charter of Rights and Freedoms (or 'Charter of Rights and Responsibilities,' as he calls it)" (11).

13 While many would object to the use of "gay" here, its shock value in being used out of historical context is particularly valuable, and I would defend its use on that account.

14 The authors' reading of *The Golden Ass* is somewhat presentist; however, Apuleius specifically mentions the *Lex Julia* in the sixth book (in the context of the Cupid and Psyche story) in such a way as to confirm, in its overall direction, the authors' reading (see Darton 204).

15 Marilyn Shuster, however, states that Rule's first story was published in a San Francisco newspaper in 1960. (See Shuster *Passionate*; and also Cavell, "Jane Rule.")

16 "Bill McConnell's literary circle constituted a veritable Who's Who of Canadian letters and his own considerable literary legacy well illustrates his privileged place in that circle. His companions and collaborators included: Louis Dudek, Irving Layton, Earle Birney, Ethel Wilson, Miriam Waddington, Ralph Gustafson, Dorothy Livesay, P.K. Page, A.J.M. Smith, Alan Crawley, and Alice Munro" (see Woods).

17 Readers unfamiliar with Surrey, BC, may gain a sense of how it is represented in the local media through an excerpt from a newspaper story by David Karp that was on the front page of *The Vancouver Sun* while I was completing this chapter: "Baby boy seized amid Surrey squalor: Police find eight-month-old crawling through debris with parents nowhere near." Karp writes: "An eight-month-old baby was seized from a 'disgusting' Surrey home last week after he was found amid drug paraphernalia, cigarette butts and sharp objects, the RCMP [Royal Canadian Mounted Police] reported. Langley RCMP officers went to the house...to investigate a report of property stolen from a Langley home. Once inside, they found a baby crawling among paint balls and numerous tools.... The officers said the house had no hydro and was 'disgusting.' The B.C. Ministry of Children and Family Development [*sic*] was called and seized the baby boy. On Tuesday afternoon, a man who answered the door to the house confirmed the ministry took his nephew. He declined to comment further, saying he was stressed and 'trying to get my happiness back.' The man later left the home to yell obscenities and threats at members of the media who were photographing the property" (A1).

18 The wordplay is that of Guy Hocquenghem in *Homosexual Desire* (1978): "The homosexual can only be a degenerate, for he does not generate" (qtd. in Caron 203).

Works Cited

Anderson, Benedict. *Imagined Communities*. London: Verso, 1991.

Assmann, Jan. "Communicative and Cultural Memory." *Cultural Memory Studies: An International and Interdisciplinary Handbook*. Ed. Astrid Erll and Ansgar Nünning. Berlin: Walter de Gruyter, 2008. 109–18.

Berlant, Lauren. *The Queen of America Goes to Washington City: Essays on Sex and Citizenship*. Durham, NC: Duke UP, 1997.

Blattberg, Charles. "Bad Faith?" Review of *In Defense of Religious Liberty*, by David Novak. *Literary Review of Canada* 17.6 (2009): 11–12.

Braun, Bruce. *The Intemperate Rainforest: Nature, Culture, and Power on Canada's West Coast*. Minneapolis: U Minnesota P, 2002.

Butler, Judith. "Afterword: After Loss, What Then?" *Loss: The Politics of Mourning*. Ed. David L. Eng and David Kazanjian. Berkeley: U California P, 2003. 467–73.

Caron, David. *My Father and I: The Marais and the Queerness of Community*. Ithaca, NY: Cornell UP, 2009.

Cavell, Richard. "Architectural Memory and Acoustic Space." *Architecture in/au Canada* 29.1–2 (2004): 59–66.

Cavell, Richard. "Histories of Forgetting: Canadian Representations of War and the Politics of Cultural Memory." *Mémoire de guerre et constructions de la paix: Mentalités et choix politiques—Belgique / Europe / Canada*. Ed. Serge Jaumain and Éric Remacle. Brussels: Peter Lang, 2006. 67–80.

Cavell, Richard. "Jane Rule." *Profiles in Canadian Literature*. Ed. Jeffrey Heath. Vol. 7. Toronto: Dundurn, 1991. 159–66.

Cavell, Richard, and Peter Dickinson. *Sexing the Maple: A Canadian Sourcebook*. Peterborough, ON: Broadview, 2006.

Cole, David. "The Same-Sex Future." *The New York Review* 2 July 2009: 12, 14, 16.

Confino, Alan. "Memory and the History of Mentalities." *Cultural Memory Studies: An International and Interdisciplinary Handbook*. Ed. Astrid Erll and Ansgar Nünning. Berlin: Walter de Gruyter, 2008. 77–84.

Critchley, Simon. *The Book of Dead Philosophers*. New York: Vintage, 2009.

Cvetkovich, Ann. *An Archive of Feelings: Trauma, Sexuality, and Lesbian Public Cultures*. Durham, NC: Duke UP, 2003.

Darton, Harvey, ed. *The Golden Ass of Lucius Apuleius*. Trans. William Adlington. London: Navarre Society, n.d. [1924].

Dooley, Mark, and Liam Kavanagh. *The Philosophy of Derrida*. Montreal: McGill-Queen's UP, 2007.

Eliot, T.S. "Little Gidding." *The Complete Poems and Plays: 1909–1950*. New York: Harcourt, Brace and World, 1952. 138–45.

Findley, Timothy. *The Wars*. Toronto: Clarke Irwin, 1977.

Freud, Sigmund. "Mourning and Melancholia." *The Freud Reader*. Ed. Peter Gay. New York: Norton, 1989. 584–89.

Frye, Northrop. *Anatomy of Criticism: Four Essays*. Princeton: Princeton UP, 1957.

Gilligan, Carol, and David A.J. Richards. *The Deepening Darkness: Patriarchy, Resistance, and Democracy's Future*. Cambridge: Cambridge UP, 2009.

Goldchain, Rafael. *I Am My Family: Photographic Memories and Fictions*. New York: Princeton Architectural P, 2008.

Henshaw, Peter. "John Buchan and the British Imperial Origins of Canadian Multiculturalism." *Canadas of the Mind: The Making and Unmaking of Canadian Nationalisms in the Twentieth Century*. Ed. Norman Hillmer and Adam Chapnick. Montreal: McGill-Queen's UP, 2007. 191–213.

Hirsch, Marianne. *Family Frames: Photography, Narrative and Postmemory*. Cambridge, MA: Harvard UP, 1997.

Hirsch, Marianne, and Valerie Smith. "Feminism and Cultural Memory." *Signs* 28.1 (2002): 1–19.
Howard, Jean E. "Introduction." *As You Like It. The Norton Shakespeare.* Ed. Stephen Greenblatt et al. New York: Norton, 1997. 1591–99.
Hunter, Justine. "Drag Queens Lose Crowns in Protocol Tussle." *The Globe and Mail* (British Columbia) 3 March 2009: S1.
Jelin, Elizabeth. *State Repression and the Labors of Memory.* Trans. Judy Rein and Marcial Godoy-Anativia. Minneapolis: U Minnesota P, 2003.
Karp, David. "Baby Boy Seized amid Surrey Squalor." *The Vancouver Sun* 12 August 2009: A1.
Langford, Martha. "Imagined Memories: On Rafael Goldchain's Family Album." *I Am My Own Family.* By Raphael Goldchain. New York: Princeton Architectural P, 2008. 10–15.
Marcel, Jean-Christophe, and Laurent Mucchielli. "Halbwachs's *mémoire collective*." *Cultural Memory Studies: An International and Interdisciplinary Handbook.* Ed. Astrid Erll and Ansgar Nünning. Berlin: Walter de Gruyter, 2008. 141–50.
Olick, Jeffrey K. "From Collective Memory to the Sociology of Mnemonic Practices and Procedures." *Cultural Memory Studies: An International and Interdisciplinary Handbook.* Ed. Astrid Erll and Ansgar Nünning. Berlin: Walter de Gruyter, 2008. 151–62.
O'Neil, Peter. "Measuring Minorities to Fight Racism Means First Tackling Lingering Taboo: Memories of Star-Branded Jews in the Second World War Hampering Progressive Solutions." *The Vancouver Sun* 21 Mar. 2009: B7.
Phelan, Peggy. *Mourning Sex: Performing Public Memories.* New York: Routledge, 1997.
"Remember, Remember." *Time Out Berlin.* London: TimeOut Guides, 2009. 84–85.
Renan, Ernest. "What Is a Nation?" *Becoming National.* Ed. Ronald Suny and Geoff Ely. New York: Oxford UP, 1996. 41–55.
Rule, Jane. *Contract with the World.* New York: Harcourt Brace Jovanovich, 1980.
Rule, Jane. "Legally Single." *Loving the Difficult.* Sidney, BC: Hedgerow, 2008. 139–43.
Rule, Jane. "A Walk by Himself." *Klanak Islands: Eight Short Stories.* Ed. William McConnell. Vancouver: Klanak, 1959. 59–69.
Rule, Jane. *The Young in One Another's Arms.* New York: Doubleday, 1977.
Saunders, Doug. "Mistaken Identity." *The Globe and Mail* 27 June 2009: F1+.
Shrive, Norman. "What Happened to Pauline?" 1962. *From a Speaking Place: Writings from the First Fifty Years of Canadian Literature.* Ed. William H. New. Vancouver: Ronsdale, 2009. 56–69.
Shuster, Marilyn. "Introduction." *Contract with the World.* By Jane Rule. Toronto: Insomniac, 2005. 9–11.
Shuster, Marilyn. *Passionate Communities: Reading Lesbian Resistance in Jane Rule's Fiction.* New York: New York UP, 1999.
Smith, Timothy. *France in Crisis: Welfare, Inequality and Globalization since 1980.* Cambridge: Cambridge UP, 2004.
Snyder, Timothy. "Holocaust: The Ignored Reality." *The New York Review* 16 July 2009: 14–16.

Sternweiler, Andreas. *Self-Confidence and Persistence: Two Hundred Years of History*. Berlin: Schwules Museum, 2004.

Thakkar, Sonali. "Nous aussi nous souvenons: Where Do the Acadians Fit into the Story of Canada's Founding?" Review of *Remembering and Forgetting in Acadie: A Historian's Journey through Public Memory*, by Ronald Rudin. *Literary Review of Canada* 17.6 (2009): 14–15.

Verbeeten, David. "The Past and Future of Immigration to Canada." *Journal of International Migration and Integration* 8.1 (2007): 1–10.

Weeks, Jeffrey. "The Sexual Citizen: Who or What?" *Theory, Culture and Society* 15.3–4 (1998) 35–52.

Whitehead, Ann. *Memory*. London: Routledge, 2009.

Woods, Thomas S. "Lives Lived: William C. McConnell." *The Globe and Mail* 18 January 2002: 8.

SEVEN

Confession as Antidote to Historical Truth in *River Thieves*

María Jesús Hernáez Lerena

> The advantage of conceiving of narrative as confession rather than as expression is that it allows us to see the pathos of the simultaneous pursuit and evasion of meaning in narrative.
> —Dennis A. Foster, *Confession and Complicity in Narrative*

The novel *River Thieves* by Michael Crummey recreates the world of the nineteenth-century white settlers who met the last Beothuk in Newfoundland. Despite the sweeping historical plots the novel contains, the logic that glues the events depends more on the demands of domesticity upon the characters than on the larger pressures of historical circumstance. The settlers who were in contact with the last Beothuk, John Senior and John Peyton, wake up every day to a routine of checking traplines and organizing their labourers' work in the Bay of Exploits, in Newfoundland's Northern Peninsula. These male characters also have to organize their marital and sexual lives on the island. Their need for women and the obligation to keep their desires under the cover of social institutions are also pressing daily worries.

Reimagining historical periods, events, and figures through an attention to the demands of domesticity makes epic and purposeful plot recede; characters' lives acquire the quotidian and arbitrary rhythms of everyday life. In the domestic sphere, the idea of achieving great goals or returning life to equilibrium cannot be done within the bonds of an external plot nor can it necessarily be bound by historical dates. Targets and achievements may remain distant, loose, or unacknowledged, overridden by the endless and necessary acts of family life performed for the sake of survival, comfort, and security. Little chores have to be done anew every day; a sense of finality or closure seems impossible to attain. The significance of the epic is diminished by staging characters in their most basic bodily needs and private moments, and *River Thieves* is full of embarrassing and shameful acts performed in the intimacy of the home.

Besides this deflating aspect of adventure, we find another relevant narrative context that exceeds the constraints of domestic life and their subsequent "feminization" of history: confession. Confessional narrative, defined as a religious communicative model, emerges as a paradigm of understanding in this novel. *River Thieves* also includes court depositions; it is structured around private and public confessions, around layers and layers of listening and recounting of transgressions. In a religious context, confession is performed by two subjects, confessant and listener; in an institutional context, an individual has to certify his or her adherence to truth in public. In the omniscient narrative of *River Thieves*, what is said in the trials does not correspond to what is whispered in small chambers in the home, spaces that bear a close resemblance to the darkness of confessionals.

The novel is built upon an exchange of narratives, narratives of innocence and guilt. This exchange, implicit in the activity of confession, partakes of at least two other important discursive contexts: testimony, that is, the bearing of witness to brutality, and journal writing, understood as a private record of events and emotions with personal significance. These three models of narrative communication—journal, confession, and testimony—are discourses that forcefully spring from the basic divide between the private and the public spheres and also from a sense of guilt or maladjustment. The predominance of private utterances over public discourse effects a shift of plot in *River Thieves*: adultery and abortion emerge as the true events, evil and sinful, which taint any effort of inquiry into historical circumstance. The fact that they remain undisclosed to society throughout the novel points to the epistemological dilemma of the narrative models invoked: transmission of knowledge may be hampered by lack of articulation, by self-interest, by an unwillingness to testify, or by the unauthoritative and vulnerable position of confessant and witness.

In "Lament for a Notion: Loss and the Beothuk in Michael Crummey's *River Thieves*," Paul Chafe discussed the novel within the historical and cultural parameters of Newfoundland's collective sense of loss and guilty conscience over the extinction of the Beothuk. Cynthia Sugars has also inquired into the cultural purposes of this novel with a view to deciding whether or not it represents another case of post-colonial mourning inspired by the demise of the Aborigines, an event which Canadian fiction has recurrently transformed into a common foundational trauma, fascinating both because of "the seduction of absence" (158) and because of its cathartic possibilities.[1] My essay will not weigh Newfoundland's cultural dependence on the disappearance of a race, but will attempt to identify the kind of rhetorical environments available in culture to invoke a sense of loss and enable atonement. The focus will be on the interpretive efforts that characters undertake in pursuit of a much desired catharsis. However, catharsis here will not be considered only as an outlet for historical outrage but as a means by which narrative transmits guilt. Special attention will be given to the relationship between the idea of plot or story as linguistic arrangements, which allegedly bring about clarity, and the upsetting implications of some narrative genres, which convey the idea that reality exists irrespective of language. In short, I would like to analyze this novel taking into account certain modes of discourse or narrative genres that run against the very notion of historicity and collectivity because they question the dynamics that the discipline of history uses to represent certain realities.

Intersecting Spaces: Journal, Confession, and Testimony Writing
Testimony writing, private confession, and journal writing share a common epistemological ground as discourses marked by lack of premeditation (Freixas 12; Lejeunne 56). They are "adrift" utterances in which words often do not pursue a socializing function and are indeed at odds with the accepted forms of social organization (Tacussel 67). They constitute themselves by a willingness to produce a story at a moment of anguished emotional overflow and their function is mainly to suspend historical progress by disorganizing narrative through the irrational. They disrupt the notion of historicity by de-normalizing historical accounts through layers of occurrences that are contradictory and illogical. They are often failing patterns of enquiry that try nonetheless to approximate truth by exposing the unreliability and insignificance of history as a detached discourse, which presents human existence as "standing outside itself" (Miller 15).

Dennis Foster claimed that "confession may provide a form for exploring the motives for narrative" (2) since, in its most basic structure, we find a narrator disclosing a secret knowledge. Confession allows an exploration of the narrative response to loss and guilt in connection to the metaphysical traditions of western culture, which interpret failure, error, inadequacy, or any transgressive act, as a form of sin (14). Inherent to our tradition is also the belief that the only possibility of attaining atonement is through the medium of a narrative. Sin and disease are equated, conferring on narrative a healing power.

These three narrative frames share common definitions of history and story, language, communication, transgression, and the self. Finding their common epistemological foundations may help us to elucidate Michael Crummey's specific treatment of plot, his assumptions about the communicability of story, and the positions of subjectivity that characters are allowed to assume in his novel. My approach is to consider historical fiction (at the level of narrative strategies, and also of authorial intention) as a dialogue between the personal and the transcendental or official—confessional narrative being energized by the tensions arousing from the need to recount personal experience and the demand to abide by religious and social laws.

To pursue this interpretation of narrative as a failed disclosure of transgression or scandal, I will avail myself mainly of the theories of Shoshana Felman and Horace Engdahl about testimony writing, of Les W. Smith's revision of Bakhtin's definition of "author" in fiction, and of Denis A. Foster's interpretation of confessional narratives. Their conclusions about the finality and lack of finality of narratives reveal the nature of the conflict between those discourses that seek completion and closure (history, law, biography, some forms of omniscient fiction) and those that avoid coherence and consummation (testimony, the lyric, confession, ranting speech, etc.). Their interpretation of testimony and confession provides a sound basis for the analysis of narratives whose main purpose is refusing understanding, for we are dealing precisely with stories that mostly dramatize impediment to communication. As Foster claimed about confessional narrative:

> The ultimate failure of even the most didactic narratives to deliver a clear, direct knowledge suggests a fundamental discontinuity between understanding (as a kind of mastery) and the knowledge being transmitted. And yet the failure to understand can mean one risks sin and pain. It is as if what narrative teaches is ignorance, every reader's lack of knowledge; it is a lesson that ensures *the struggle to understand will find no conclusion*. I am suggesting that this lesson of ignorance with its burden of passion is carried over to subsequent narratives. It helps explain why the story is so compelling. (Foster 7; emphasis added)

The same obstruction to knowledge is to be found in testimony writing. Against the belief that the essence of testimony literature is historical and political, its function to record and report certain events that enlarge a shared historical narrative with a healing goal, Felman, Laub, and other critics show that the act of bearing witness always points at the impracticability of speech. For example, "the imperative to tell the story of the Holocaust is inhabited by the impossibility of the telling" because what is there to be witnessed is a "cognitively dissonant" situation, a "situation with no cure" (Laub 78).[2] Testimony writing dramatizes the need to express through narrative that which thwarts any attempt at explanation or rationalization. The witness experiences a suspension, "a loss of connectedness" (Felman, "Education" 48–50); his or her testimony is a deviation of general perception because what has been seen breaks all logic and morality (Engdahl 8). The witness is invaded by strangeness and is alienated from the social arrangement we call reality.

Surprisingly, this "uninterpretability" of reality is considered in the same terms in theories of confession narratives. According to Foster, sin is experienced as an "uninterpretable strangeness" (15), as a loss of language and of truth, a discontinuity between understanding and the knowledge being transmitted (7). According to Engdahl, testimony "retains its alien and incomprehensible traits" (8). It revolves around acts that cannot be constructed as knowledge nor assimilated into full cognition. "[It] performs its own meaning in resisting our grasp" (Felman, "Education" 3).

Besides assumptions about the explicability of reality, another relevant factor to take into account is the emotional conditions in which stories are exchanged. Narrative or story as a soothing linguistic structure which generates intelligibility may not be sufficient to express experience and alleviate pain.[3] The witness or the confessant has confronted strangeness and horror or is consumed with guilt, and is trying to recover balance "through a narrative that re-structures the self as history and conclusions" (Foster 10). Both confession and testimony narrative are sequels of an *evil deed*, and the speaking or writing subject must perforce be unsettled, trapped between "incomprehension and the intoxication of speaking one's piece" (Al-Kassim 120). As Foster claims, there might be no "re-absorption in truth of a disturbing element" (11). While history "unravels the secrets of the past, neutralizes the conflicts, and absolves the faults" (qtd. in Engdahl 10), assuming, therefore, control and closure, confessional narratives and testimony writing hold the past as enigma, scandal, and interpellation. By doing so, they undermine the precautions that history has taken in the name of cause and event. They create the ever-present and annul the notion of progress by lingering on the unspeakable nature of a secret.

We may find an apparent paradox, however, between confession as a ritual and confession as a narrative strategy in literature. Confession as a ritual is a basic religious and non-religious practice aimed at achieving understanding, forgiveness, and redemption. It has a teleological sustenance as a mechanism for psychological survival. "The confessor hopes to regain his innocence by constructing a wholly comprehensible, coherent representation of himself" (Foster 16). However, confession narratives in literature just attest the desire and obligation to understand, what Smith calls "the demand to acquiesce before transcendental narrative" (Smith, preface); they do not imply an actual mastery of meaning or an agreement to submit to an imposed external precept. According to Foster, confessional narratives question the narrator's desire to master his story, his plan, and send characters on "a path that inevitably misses the encounter with truth" (4). The confessant's deviation into sin suggests his madness and the fragility of his grasp of knowledge. The lesson he or she experiences is encountering again and again a discontinuity between understanding and the knowledge being transmitted. "The struggle to understand will find no conclusion," as Foster claimed in a quotation above.

Thus, confession and testimony narratives inherently fight against external regulations and dramatize a conflict where all patterns of inquiry are nullified. The narrative becomes a battlefield between a desire to find control and transcendence and the need to affirm the undecipherable nature of scandalous experience. These opposed ideological forces are present in religious confession and in all other narratives outside that context because they all build up "story" upon the warring impulses of finality, on the one hand, and inconclusiveness or contradiction, on the other. The difference between other kinds of narrative and testimony and confession is that the latter openly reflect an aversion to history (see Smith 32; and Engdahl 10). As Engdahl puts it:

> Historical explanations are a kind of anodyne. Feelings aroused by human suffering are put to rest when what happened is seen as a logical sequence of cause and effect and therefore to some extent inevitable. The victim's reality is broken off from our own and posted to another region of being: the region of historical events.... Only testimony with its perpetual present tense and its direct touch can lift out of us this delusion and destroy the semblance of necessity, logical end and meaning. It does this not by clarifying: the witness talks of something that is incomprehensible in the hope that someone else will make it possible to understand and with the certainty that any explanation must be rejected as inadequate. In the revolt against explanations, testimony and literature are unified. (10)

Les W. Smith brings back Bakhtin's neglected notion of author-creator associated with dialogism in order to discuss the issue of characters' freedom from the author's perspective, that is, "the tensions between their [the author's and the characters'] perspectives, or their acts of perceiving, as fellow participants in the creative process" (Bakhtin qtd. in Smith 30). According to Smith, while our impressions of others in everyday life are random and incomplete, the author tends to consummate the characters. The author perceives characters through a "surplus of vision," as finished wholes: "When an author consummately achieves an outside, all-encompassing perspective on a hero, the novel becomes monologic" (Smith 30). A study of the internal tensions of narrative should therefore also include this challenge to the author's right to assume omniscient positioning.

The Collapse of Witnessing[4]

River Thieves shows a lack of acquiescence to external narrative and to any totalizable account of events. It does so by making all its plots subservient to rhetorical schemes that typify a flawed transmission of information in which the speaker is partly to blame. Ranting or abject speech, a kind of discourse similar to confession, also constitutes itself as a failed denunciation, "an impossible act of reproaching against the law" (Al-Kassim 121), and is produced when speech fails to authorize the speaker.

Within this general narrative ethos, which conspicuously conveys the weakness or indisciplinarity of the speaking subject or character, when it comes to the exchange of stories, we could speak of a certain progression from private and "unruly" narrative practices to public and transcendent narratives. This sequence would start in the journal as a narrative of present disarray, where there is yet no temporal and psychological distance between the writing subject and his or her past. It is a dialogue with one's self, a dialogue whose materiality, if unpublished, remains phantasmagoric. Then, confession would represent a second stage. With it, the re-establishment of order after the received or caused injury is carried out through narrative hindsight and the presence of a listener. A third stage would be testimony, where the witness testifies, that is, he or she performs an act of speech before an audience in the belief that it will guarantee truth. In addition, testimony demands a response from the human community (Engdahl 3). Only when this third stage has been achieved in history, an effective measure against oblivion and injustice has been taken.

In *River Thieves*, the journal and the confession are stifled because there is no assertion powerful enough to give credence to the perpetration of crimes before a community of listeners. The following descriptions will show how the novel engages in the models of narrative communication described above.

The core historical events in *River Thieves* are the attempts, on the part of British officers, to reconcile with the Indians in the colony of Newfoundland. The very first opening scene of the novel renders this contact.

It is told from the point of view of a Beothuk woman who sees a white man walking on a frozen lake, approaching her family. This encounter is narrated in hazy terms because, after being captured, the woman's face is pressed against the white man's shoulder and she can only hear shooting. However, she knows that all is lost to her. This is the first enigma in the story, which later on in the novel will keep surfacing in an incomplete fashion and will progressively acquire the quality of a scandal.[5] After this scene, the novel, for the most part, conveys the lack of communication generated in the home of two males and a female who are attempting to adjust to the idea of "family" as closely as possible. They are John Senior and his son John Peyton, masters and owners of a big portion of land in Newfoundland's Northern Peninsula. The woman is their attendant, Cassie Jure. They know what their roles should be in the household but their inability to perform them fills their everyday life with regret and confusion.

Cassie left her mother and father behind in England before becoming a housekeeper in John Senior's house. John Senior brought Cassie over to Newfoundland in the hope that, in time, she would become his son's wife. However, John Peyton thinks that Cassie is his father's lover. For John Senior, the question at stake continues to be whether Cassie should be his wife or his daughter, a question that remains unsolved until the very end. This uncertainty regarding parental and marital roles embitters their relationship. The stories about their past that the three characters share at different times with each other forms the substance of the novel.

Their conversations are arranged between two people; there is rarely a third person present. The audience that may have been present at the trials do not make it into the novel either. The reader is given the role of an overhearer; placed by the narrator in the midst of historical and journalistic details, the reader is compelled to recuperate a sense of finality by deciphering a set of recurring emotions and events kept secret. When reading *River Thieves* we may be struck by this fact: although the novel possesses a huge measure of chronicling—we are offered a detailed account of the policies of the British officers on the island and of the tasks of white settlers in the Bay of Exploits—the story is sustained by a thread of narrative made up mainly of conversations between two characters in the semi-darkness of a kitchen. Michael Crummey has carefully placed every conversation of relevance in this setting. The suspense develops on the basis of what is said and not said in these exchanges, occurring in the domestic space assigned to Cassie. Apart from the triangle of characters whose daily emotions form the network of narrative, their home occasionally hosts Lieutenant David Buchan, the English officer commissioned to find Red Indians and establish friendly contact with them.

On a failed expedition to the River of Exploits, an Indian man is murdered and there is a trial to uncover the truth of that clash. Before and after the trial there are a number of private confessions that trigger off one another: Cassie confesses to John Peyton that her father abused her when she was a child; John Senior confesses to Cassie that he once brutally killed an old Indian with a trap-bed; John Peyton confesses to Cassie that there were *two* murders at the lake; John Richmond confesses that he had once kidnapped and sold an Indian girl; Reilly confesses that he was a thief in London and was sentenced to the gallows. The captured Indian woman, Mary March, confesses to Cassie and Buchan—in broken words and with the help of a map—that her husband and brother had been killed in the skirmish.

As they unfold in the narrative, this string of confessions produces dizziness: the reader intuits that the encounter with the group of Beothuk turned out badly, but the evil deed, which has repercussions through the entire book, remains submerged under layers of other confessions. The truth, however, never reaches the jury. The emotional outbursts, full with narrative, will not reach testimony status because such declarations will remain in the realm of intimacy. Confession will be used only to illegitimately justify the behaviour of whites toward Indians and of men toward women, but the third next step, that of managing testimony, will not be taken. Testimony is not only a sequel of an evil deed, it also "requires an answer from the human community," as Engdahl claimed (3). By not assuming the solitary "burden of the witness" (Felman, "Education" 3), the responsibility in speech has been profaned. The vulnerable position of witnesses (women, servants, fugitives) makes any act of reproach against the law impossible; characters are barred from speaking the nature of their predicament. As Al-Kassim states: "each suffers that failure of naming as a perpetual repetition consigning [them] to the fate of 'piling sin upon sin' or 'going to pieces' again and again" (120).

All characters, including the Beothuk woman, become unsuccessful eye and *ear* witnesses, being imprisoned by the bonds of their own status. Cassie becomes the only innocent witness to the acts of brutality that male characters eventually confess to her. But she is imprisoned in her loyalty to her employers and is silenced by the rules of family and colonial power. She is also aware that clothing the gruesome reality in words and offering them to others may be fatal: "You are such a simpleton about the truth," she says to Buchan. "You think there is never anything to fear from it" (Crummey 299).

By accepting confession merely as a cleansing personal ritual and not testifying in court, the paths of inquiry become obstructed. Confession remains what Ian Craib calls "bad faith stories" or no-choice stories:

stories told in such a way that our agency does not have to be considered, they are not told as communication or as exploration but are attempts to close down on meaning and to deny agency. They are about what is done to *me* and what I am because these things have been done to me. They keep problems within a recognizable plot: "They are stories in which events have causes which lie in some previous external event or in the action of some original human mover that sets off a chain of connections that result in me being the sort of person I am, doing the sort of things I do. I make no contribution to this story, I am simply its conclusion" (Craib 68).

The characters in *River Thieves* equip themselves with certain narratives and they spend all their energy in maintaining their belief in these narratives. They are told to another person in secret to reduce anxiety, never to take responsibility for their acts. Acts and words will never transcend a circle of complicity (and proximity), they will never be chronicled—the words becoming only an "excitable utterance," as Judith Butler calls injurious speech acts: "In the law, 'excitable' utterances are those made under duress, usually confessions that cannot be used in court because they do not reflect the balanced mental state of the utterer" (Butler 15). Life will remain in disarray, the three-staged pattern of avowal unconsummated. The fact that *River Thieves* will eventually become a court deposition does not lend stability, order, or clarity to the facts. Only when the novel is well-advanced does the reader learn that an event kept in secret up till then prevented the plot from moving toward clarification. What we presumed to be the progressing overarching storyline—the killing of two Indians and the bringing of the criminals to justice—was in fact turning on this missing *hinge* all the time.

This confession, that Cassie had an abortion and that the child was Buchan's, makes reality look more out of kilter than ever. This is why: Cassie withholds this information for a very long time and only dares to disclose it by writing a few words in Buchan's journal: "*There was a child. Before I ended it, David. I was pregnant*" (Crummey 365). This was the same journal that attested to the crimes perpetrated by John Senior and John Peyton against the Beothuk and that Buchan was going to use in the trial. Cassie trespasses the privacy of a private journal that was going to become public proof, the final certification of evidence. Ironically, however, her inscription returns the journal to its role as personal diary. Cassie's confession destroys the official status of Buchan's investigations because, once the pregnancy has been written into his journal, its contents will not be able to come into the open—for the journal is stolen by Joseph Reilly, an accomplice of John Senior, and John Peyton reads Cassie's words. Now they can blackmail Buchan, who is a married man of high rank. They coerce him into silence before the trial because he does not want his adulterous affair to be revealed.

At this moment, Buchan suffers the unexpected consequences of what Butler called "the volatility of one's place in the community of speakers" (4). To be injured by speech means to lose context and authority: "'You didn't know about the child,' he said, 'did you, Captain.' Buchan looked up from Cassie's words in the journal and Peyton could see reflected in the officer's face a moment of sickening recognition, of bottomless panic. Dark sea pouring over the gunnels. Every seam leaking water" (Crummey 369).

Buchan had been interviewing the members of the expedition into Beothuk territory and his journal detailed how they had been involved in the murders. The unstable nature of the journal becomes evident here. Initially an intimate space, it has become a public document; the process has marred its validity. The power of a legally incriminatory text to accuse the perpetrators is undermined by the addition of a much smaller but embarrassing crime reported in just three sentences. Adultery in the end prevents justice for the Indians. John Senior's house becomes a site where carnal entanglements hide and complicate colonial policies on land and First Peoples. It is an opaque space where the mismanagement of intimacy (white intimacy) will force silence, however numerous the confessions inside its walls have been.

As we have seen, this exchange of narratives is not a freely performed act: it is determined by social and racial impositions as well as emotional liaisons. The novel includes all the ranks in the social structure of the colony. In hierarchical top-down order: English representatives of the crown, English officers, rich English merchants, household servants, poor whites, and Indians. This arrangement of power and possession ruled economy, sex, and also ethics; the colonies inherited the empire's structures. However, there were cracks in this taxonomy that opened narrow passages, illicit contacts that could never cross the barrier of the intimate into the open. The secret of Cassie's unborn child will be, against all prediction, inextricably related to the fate of the Indians. Their outrage will remain unaddressed from then on. With it, Michael Crummey has deliberately made two apparently unrelated facts interdependent: the slaughter of the Indians and an illicit affair between two whites. Significantly, Cassie is the most fictionalized character in the novel; Michael Crummey invented her sin and her silence, which eventually become the main obstructions to keeping the channels of communication flowing in that society.

John Peyton's trajectory is similar to that undergone by Buchan's diary because he retraces the steps taken in the attempt to assign responsibility to the murderers. Peyton initially confesses to his father's violence against the

Indians and wishes to make up for his father's lack of scruples by helping Lieutenant Buchan in his enquiries. But once his father's position becomes endangered—his role in the murder of the two Indians becomes clear in Mary March's account—he is not willing to testify any longer. Father, son, and servant eventually act for the sake of the family's interests. When confession is only private and the act of bearing witness is aborted, there is no ethical hold. If testimony—the last of the three ascending steps to a sharing of truth—is not realized, the road taken is a cul-de-sac: "a path that inevitably misses the encounter with truth," as quoted from Foster above.

Significantly, the two most far-reaching, cruel acts that the novel includes remain inscribed in a journal: the Beothuk woman's testimony of the murders and the confession that Cassie was pregnant. The stealing of the journal becomes yet another act of intimacy exposed and, in contrast to the public testimony of the court deposition, the journal renders the only true account of events in the novel, a truth for which there will be no effective witnessing. Furthermore, the journal shows the reader that this failed colonial encounter is not the only act that constitutes sin in the story. Before becoming settlers in Newfoundland, John Senior and his partners were already contaminated by disease: greed, corruption, lust, incest. Descriptions in the novel of John Senior's lifestyle in London and of Cassie's background provide many examples. The idea of original sin persecutes them (see Sugars). Precisely it is this permanence of original sin that makes the act of confession transcendent: "It gives meaning to what was 'disconcerting and scandalous' by transforming it into repetition of a mythic first sin" (Foster 16). The trope of sin is transformed into the idea of disease, a malady spread by colonizers into a land they covet.

It is important to mention, however, that there is a dimension to confession other than as a personal ritual where therapeutic narrative may restore the subject to self-possession. *River Thieves* shows the futility of this widely practised ritual by inscribing in its plot a social dimension, a community of speakers and listeners for which the notion of evidence would be crucial. Confession without testimony represents a crisis of evidence, the evil deeds (murder and rape) are presented as unwitnessed and therefore erased from record. If the ritual of confession terminates with an emptying out of sins, this liberation is only temporal and fatally spurred by self-interest.

The Disobedience to History's Dispositions

River Thieves cannot be understood only as a denunciation of the validity or implied completeness of historical accounts and official narratives. It also exposes the reader to a series of failed testimonies and therefore shows the incapacity or impossibility of history's participants to tell their stories, even when they could have undone history's flattening one-way account. Witnesses are constrained by networks of power and fear, and this intricate arrangement prevents them from making their experience "institutional," from putting it in the service of history. "It is a sad truth about the world, Cassie decided, that only a sense of mutual vulnerability promised any shelter at all" (Crummey 280). Her involvement with Buchan could only mean for her silenced complicity.

There is another reason why their attempt to utter the unspeakable fails. "What has been lived couldn't care less about writing," says Herta Müller in "Can Literature Bear Witness?" (29). Experience needs to be completely transformed before it can be reconciled with words. Rape, abortion, murder, these acts, as Felman said, "cannot be constructed as knowledge" ("Education" 5); they exceed our frames of reference. Felman speaks about a truth not available to its own speaker because what has been witnessed cannot be made whole and integrated into authoritative telling: "the scene of witnessing has lost the amplifying resonance of its communality. It is no longer a collective, but a solitary scene" (Felman, "Camus" 171). Precisely, and in the terms we have discussed in this paper, we find testimony going back to the status of private confession. And when the speech act has no historical weight, it has been just an encounter between the two solitudes of confession.

Moreover, when this happens, when denunciation fails, Felman recognizes that "the insignificance [also] claims the narrative, since it decenters and defocalizes the significance of all the rest" ("Camus" 171). These acts threaten intelligibility; they "leave residues," as the historian Dominick LaCapra has put it: they are "remainders that set limits to a history of meaning in that they cannot be fully mastered or integrated meaningfully into a historicized narrative or interpretive account" (161). While history is usually envisaged as a structuring grid that brings clarity and order to the past, some historians are aware that what they are really striving for is "to resist apocalypse" (LaCapra 160), trying to outmanoeuvre reality's chaotic manifestations with the aid of language and story. Michael Crummey's decision to imagine crucial moments of Newfoundland's cultural memory through moments of incomprehensible actions and confused intimate contacts shows an opposition to elevated objectivity. He wedges into a third-person omniscient master narrative stories that outrun commonly used grammars of finality. The emotional overflow of confession, only available to us in the words that an author uses in fiction, questions the historical enterprise but also the author's very impulse to present his or her narrative as conclusion or as transcendence. "The conflict between author and character in novelistic processes indeed resembles an inherent tension in narrative perspective that has always troubled the pure intention of a confessant 'to say the same thing' or 'agree in statement' (*homolegein*) with a transcendent perspective" (Smith 31). "Confession reflects a basic dissatisfaction with history" (32), Les Smith goes on to say, because it stays at the moment of perception coupled with incomprehension. It stays at a dimension where existence eludes intelligibility.

An example of this idea is one particular confession in *River Thieves* that conveys both the unspeakable horror of brutality and the refusal of the confessant to agree with the transcendent narrative of Christian repentance. Although in the following instance, John Senior makes a confession to Cassie, the voice of the third-person narrator takes over. On one of their jaunts up the River of Exploits, John Senior and his employees run into four mamateeks and start to fire at the Indians who disperse into the woods. They fire into the mamateeks and, inside one of the shelters, they find an old man who has been hit by a musket ball in the stomach and is unable to stand. He has a trap-bed in his hand that he had been working against a stone:

> John Senior stepped forward and bent to pick up the trap-bed. The Indian swung it then with a small fierce motion that caught the side of the white man's face and sliced into his ear. Miller stepped back and leveled his musket, but John Senior had already pulled the bed from the Indian's hand and was beating him about the head with it. The old man bent to the ground and raised a single arm uselessly against the blows until he lost consciousness, and John Senior continued striking with the sharp edge of the metal until he was too exhausted to lift it any longer. He stood catching his breath over the dead man. The battered skull showed through the long shearing wounds and tiny yellow flecks of bone had landed on John Senior's boots. [...]
>
> Miller stood in silence a few moments and then said, "That old fucker had all his teeth." He tongued the array of spaces in his mouth. They were like palings gone from a fence. "Did you see that John? That seems an unfair thing to my mind."
>
> "Shut up, Miller," he said. (Crummey 326)

This sadistic killing of a defenceless Beothuk man never became known, and it stands unrelated to the murder cases for the trial in the novel. Cassie's response to John Senior is silence; there is no need to ask her not to speak, as he had urged Miller. After this confession, John Senior is dismissive about Cassie's shock. However, throughout the novel, John Senior suffers from terrible nightmares: in his dreams, the *evil deed* keeps happening every night and it will never be settled. Furthermore, his account does not lead to a "transcendent narrative from outside the confessant's experience"

(Smith 31), as is mandatory in the ritual of confession. We only find the repeated re-enactment of this maddening experience in dreams, an experience that clashes with all common human and humane sense.

What characterizes *River Thieves* is thus a persistence to remain with sin as "uninterpretable strangeness" (Foster 15) and as loss of knowledge, a circumstance which causes "a loss of a sense of human relatedness" (79), as Laub claimed. The reader is trapped by the physicality of situations in which the underlying motives are not definable, where characters withdraw from ethical and ideological struggles (Engdahl 8). This experience of suspension halts the progress that history needs in its march toward the future.

Notes
1 See Mary Dalton for an analysis of the representations of the Beothuk in Newfoundland's poetry and fiction. Other more recently published novels could be added to Dalton's list, such as *Cloud of Bone* (2007) by Bernice Morgan.
2 Further on, Laub continues: "On the one hand, the process of the testimony does in fact hold out the promise of truth as the return to a sane, normal and connected world. On the other hand, because of its very commitment to truth, the testimony enforces at least a partial breach, failure and relinquishment of this promise" (91).
3 According to Felman, the experience of bearing witness to horror generates a "mode of truth's realization beyond what is available as statement" (15).
4 This expression has been quoted by Cynthia Sugars (150) from Cathy Caruth (10).
5 The Beothuk woman, we will learn later in the novel, is Mary March, who was taken to live in her captors' household (John Senior's). Mary March (Demasduit) and her niece Shawnadithit, the last Beothuk woman, were taken from the woods and lived with the whites. They took ill and died before they could return to their people. They are the only visible figures of the Beothuk (there is a well-known portrait of Demasduit and also drawings by Shawnadithit) and they haunt Newfoundland's historical memory.

Works Cited
Al-Kassim, Dina. *On Pain of Speech: Fantasies of the First Order and the Literary Rant*. Berkeley: U of California P, 2010.
Butler, Judith. *Excitable Speech: A Politics of the Performative*. New York: Routledge, 1997.
Caruth, Cathy, ed. *Trauma: Explorations in Memory*. Baltimore, MD: Johns Hopkins UP, 1995.
Chafe, Paul. "Lament for a Notion: Loss and the Beothuk in Michael Crummey's *River Thieves*." *Essays on Canadian Writing: The Literature of Newfoundland* 82 (2004): 93–117.

Craib, Ian. "Narratives As Bad Faith." *The Uses of Narrative: Explorations in Sociology, Psychology, and Cultural Studies*. Ed. Molly Andrews et al. New Brunswick, NJ: Transaction Publishers, 2000. 64–74.

Crummey, Michael. *River Thieves*. Toronto: Anchor Canada, 2001.

Dalton, Mary. "Shadow Indians: The Beothuk Motif in Newfoundland Literature." *Newfoundland Studies* 2 (1992): 135–46.

Engdahl, Horace. "Philomela's Tongue: Introductory Remarks on Witness Literature." *Witness Literature: Proceedings of the Nobel Centennial Symposium*. Ed. Horace Engdahl. River Edge, NJ: World Scientific, 2002. 1–14.

Felman, Shoshana. "Camus' *The Fall*, or the Betrayal of the Witness." *Testimony: Crises of Witnessing in Literature, Psychoanalysis, and History*. By Shoshana Felman and Dori Laub. New York: Routledge, 1992. 165–203.

Felman, Shoshana. "Education and Crisis, or the Vicissitudes of Teaching." *Testimony: Crises of Witnessing in Literature, Psychoanalysis, and History*. By Shoshana Felman and Dori Laub. New York: Routledge, 1992. 1–56.

Foster, Dennis A. *Confession and Complicity in Narrative*. Cambridge: Cambridge UP, 1987.

Freixas, Laura. "Auge del diario ¿íntimo? en España." *Revista de Occidente* 182–183 (1996): 5–14.

LaCapra, Dominick. "Resisting Apocalypse and Rethinking History." *Manifestoes for History*. Ed. Keith Jenkins, Sue Morgan, and Alun Munslow. London: Routledge, 2007. 160–78.

Laub, Dori. "An Event without a Witness: Truth, Testimony and Survival." *Testimony: Crises of Witnessing in Literature, Psychoanalysis, and History*. By Shoshana Felman and Dori Laub. New York: Routledge, 1992. 75–92.

Lejeunne, Philippe. "La práctica del diario personal." *El diario íntimo: Fragmentos de diarios Españoles*. *Revista de Occidente* 182–183 (1996): 56–86.

Miller, J. Hillis. *The Form of Victorian Fiction*. Cleveland, OH: Arete, 1979.

Morgan, Bernice. *Cloud of Bone*. Toronto: Knopf Canada, 2007.

Müller, Herta. "When We Don't Speak, We Become Unbearable, and When We Do, We Make Fools of Ourselves. Can Literature Bear Witness?" *Witness Literature: Proceedings of the Nobel Centennial Symposium*. Ed. Horace Engdahl. River Edge, NJ: World Scientific, 2002. 15–32.

Smith, Les W. *Confession in the Novel: Bakhtin's Author Revisited*. Madison, NJ: Fairleigh Dickinson UP, 1996.

Sugars, Cynthia. "Original Sin, or, The Last of the First Ancestors: Michael Crummey's *River Thieves*." *English Studies in Canada* 31.4 (2005): 147–75.

Tacussel, Patrick. "Las leyes de lo no dicho: notas para una sociología del silencio." *Revista de Occidente* 154 (1996): 67–86.

EIGHT

Indigenous Criticism and Indigenous Literature in the 1990s: Critical Intimacy

Michèle Lacombe

This essay focuses on literary history, criticism, and fiction by Indigenous writers in the 1990s. It takes for granted Sami scholar Rauna Kuokkanen's belief, citing Thomas King's short story "Borders" in her 2007 book *Reshaping the University: Responsibility, Indigenous Epistemes, and the Logic of the Gift*, that in their capacity as "metaphors for multiple, complicated identities, borders between worlds—be they geographical, physical, political and/or colonial, racial, cultural, or any of these in combination," are sometimes also "concrete, lived *experiences*" (Kuokkanen x). She uses the term "critical intimacy"[1] for her understanding of the exclusions and silences in narratives, as well as for some of the ways in which our sense of scholarly distance is challenged. Her analysis stresses the university as a whole when she reminds us of Jacques Derrida's emphasis on how criticism addresses the ethics of not speaking "in a language that is extraneous to what it seeks to contest" (Kuokkanen xiv).[2] Jennifer Kelly, in a recent essay on using Indigenous literature in the university classroom, asks us to consider how "our adherence to notions of 'objectivity' reassert[s] itself through our failure to explore... culturally and nationally specific perspectives on the roles and *responsibilities* of listeners/ readers of indigenous literatures" (Kelly 118). Kuokkanen's own preface comments on her relation to the Deatnu River, now on the border between Norway and Finland, a river experienced as a border but also as "a bond that connects the families who live on its banks." For Kuokkanen, now living in Canada, this becomes a metaphor for the complexities of postmodern situatedness: "Before roads were built along both its banks, the Deatnu was the main *johtolat*—a Sami word signifying passage, way, route, channel, connection—for people, news, provisions, mail, building materials, and so on.... Besides being a significant salmon river, the Deatnu has been a source of physical and spiritual sustenance for generations" (Kuokkanen ix).

Kuokkanen adds that "had the vagaries of history, such as the drawing of the border between present-day Norway and Finland, taken place, say, ten or twenty years earlier or later, my family might have been living on the bank of the river that became Norway, and I might today be carrying a Norwegian passport rather than a Finnish one" (Kuokkanen xi). I am reminded of how some of my own French and Maliseet/Métis ancestors lived on both sides of the Saint John River before lumber interests and the 1842 Webster-Ashburton Treaty, in the wake of the bloodless Aroostook War, arbitrarily drew the border in its current location in New Brunswick; some of my relatives are now Canadian citizens, others American.[3] Migration and mobility, as well as rootedness, have long been physical and intellectual realities in the lives of Native people; many of their stories remain untold.

While I do not by any means agree with everything said by Kuokkanen or indeed by any other critic cited in this essay, I believe that Indigenous scholars have important insights to offer, approaches that are under-represented and sometimes contested in our discipline and in the academy, and that merit greater attention. My comments should not in any way be taken as undervaluing the very important contributions of other scholars who have written sensitively about Native literature in ways that acknowledge their own situatedness.[4] Rather, my contribution aims to restore the balance of Native and non-Native voices in critical debate, leaving ample room for both. My choice of literary texts is also necessarily selective; while I focus on two well-known "university educated writers," to use Lally Grauer and Armand Ruffo's term (507), it is important to acknowledge the richly diverse aspects of contemporary oral and written Native literature—literature that tends to be defined communally rather than as single author studies. Concerned primarily with Indigenous criticism, this essay very briefly makes use of two realist stories and two "meta-fictional" stories—for lack of a better word—from Thomas King's and Eden Robinson's collections *One Good Story, That One* (1993) and *Traplines* (1997) respectively. For me, these stories are a form of theory (and vice versa), and I use them in the classroom alongside more explicitly theoretical work in my upper-year courses on Canadian literature, Indigenous literature, and critical theory as it relates to Indigenous studies. Intertextuality between

King's "Trap Lines" and Robinson's "Traplines" opens up questions of family life, community, and especially of the place of education in the lives of contemporary youth. King's "How Corporal Colin Sterling Saved Blossom, Alberta, and Most of the Rest of the World as Well" and Robinson's "Dogs in Winter," for their part, play with popular genres and conventions to satirize stereotypical notions of "the Indian."

As Christina Fagan reminds us in her introduction to *Troubling Tricksters*, "there is always a danger in focussing on cultural symbols of difference ... those cultural symbols can easily become labels, commodities, and stereotypes, ways of explaining and controlling that which is unfamiliar" (5). But pan-Indianism, whether deployed in Canadian or Indigenous cultural contexts, also carries risks. Niigonwedom Sinclair, in a contribution to *Troubling Tricksters*, sees stories as "the predominant vessels in which *Anishinaabeg* knowledge is carried" (22; emphasis added). For him, the continuum of oral and written stories of different kinds that are part of the legacy of his father (Justice Murray Sinclair, current chair of the national Truth and Reconciliation Commission) is "the modern-day continuance of a very old Anishinaabeg intellectual tradition—storytelling" (22). For some Native writers, the interplay of English and First Nations languages is one of the points of reference in their complex relation to story. Marie Battiste reminds us that "Western education has much to gain by viewing the world through the eyes and languages of Aboriginal peoples," and that "Aboriginal languages are irreplaceable resourses that require protection and support" (202–3). In different ways, King's and Robinson's stories can be read as consistent with both Fagan's and Sinclair's views of literary criticism as well as with Battiste's understanding of education. "Trap Lines" and "Traplines" suggest the marginalization of traditional beliefs and economies, invoke the appeal of modernity, and hint at counter-narratives. "Sterling" and "Dogs" use trickster motifs in ways that typically blur some of the boundaries between past and present, as well as between Indigenous and Canadian realities, although trickster discourse represents only one of a number of approaches for interpreting these stories' satire. I am interested in how King's and Robinson's texts reveal intertextual dialogue with some of the critical discourses I invoke, as well as with each other's work and that of other writers.

Indigenous Challenges to Canadian Nationalism

Let me begin with a few observations about Indigenous responses to Canadian nationalism in the 1960s before commenting on Native literary critics' representation of their own literary history since that decade. The Expo 67 world's fair in Montreal offers a useful focus for encapsulating

Canadian nationalism at the time. In *Canada's 1960s: The Ironies of Identity in a Rebellious Era*, Canadian historian Bryan Palmer explores Indigenous challenges to the Canadian state in a chapter entitled "The 'Discovery' of the 'Indian.'" He documents the controversy around exhibits mounted in the Indians of Canada Pavilion at Expo 67, exhibits that—while critical of the federal Department of Indian Affairs—were if anything relatively muted in their condemnations of the colonial legacy. Eva Marie Kröller notes dissenting voices such as that of the socialist author and constitutional lawyer F.R. Scott in his poem "The Indians Speak at Expo '67." Citing popular historian Pierre Berton, she observes that Expo 67 did re-educate some visitors on Native issues:

> [In] imitation of the Confederation Train and Caravans that took exhibitions of Canadian historical artifacts across the country, Native artists and activists created the "Indian Traveling College" to spread the message of the Pavilion further abroad. Several of the activities organized by Aboriginal people parodied or reversed official versions that left them out or involved them insufficiently. Fourteen Nova Scotia Mi'kmaqs [sic], for example, paddled "from Cape Breton to Montreal to relive an 1894 treaty signing between their people and the Quebec Iroquois," that is, not with the purpose of commemorating the Centennial of Confederation, and they proceeded in the opposite direction to the celebrated Centennial Canoe Pageant retracing the traditional *voyageur* routes. (Kröller 319)

Palmer comments on the government's awkward realization at the time that attempts by the minister in charge to shut down the pavilion's exhibits would likely lead to greater embarrassment than allowing open access to the pavilion and its contents (Palmer 391–92). In relation to images reflected in the centennial celebrations of 1967, Teresa Gibert notes that Canadian artists began to view the beginnings of their country critically rather than nostalgically at this time; she uses Newfoundland writer Wayne Johnston's term "ghost history" to signal the post-1960s "symbolic representation of those elements of the country's society that were previously barred from consciousness" (Gibert 478).

Palmer's own focus is on the emergence of Red Power in the 1960s, a movement spinning off from radical African American groups such as the Black Panthers. By way of background, he looks to the Indian Act and residential schools as assimilative acts, and anticipates occupations such as the Oka Crisis in Quebec and the incidents at Ipperwash in Ontario. While he includes chapters on topics such as youth radicalism, Palmer does not address the emergence of second-wave feminism and the critiques surrounding the 1967 Royal Commission on the Status of Women, for instance. If the 1951 revisions to the 1876 Indian Act governing the legal status of "Indians" in Canada lightened a few of the many legal restrictions placed on First Nations individuals and strengthened others, regulations concerning women's loss of Indian status when they married non-Native men were reinforced. This situation would not be rectified until Bill C-31 in 1985, following legal challenges by Jeannette Courbiere Lavell, currently President of the Native Women's Association of Canada, alongside some of her Native sisters from Six Nations and Maliseet women from Tobique First Nation in New Brunswick.[5] Anticipating findings and recommendations in the 1996 report of the long-overdue Royal Commission on Aboriginal Peoples, however, Palmer notes the failure of liberal policy documents such as the Hawthorne Report (1966–1967), which viewed and advocated for "Indians" as "citizens plus," and the federal government's White Paper (1969), which considered "the problem of the Indian" as something that would be solved by abolition of "special status." Native people lost no time objecting to these documents' constructions of "the Indian" on a number of fronts. Some time before Bill C-31 was enacted, Kathleen Jamieson, for instance, ironically described the status of Native women as "citizens minus" (see Jamieson). Palmer concludes that "it was centuries of subordination and generations of abuse, 'discovered' in the changed climate of radicalism that was 1967–8, which really ushered Red Power into being," at the same time that the White Paper's "arrogant and arbitrary expression of the state's resurgent program of repressive acculturation" focused the movement's energies and inspired it to action (402).

Numbers of new Native writers emerged in the 1970s on the heels of these protests and the growing awareness on the part of some Canadians. Grauer and Ruffo note that Pierre Trudeau's White Paper "proposing an end to Indian status, purportedly in the interests of a 'just society,' sparked a protest movement of pan-Indian nationalism fuelled by Cree organizer Harold Cardinal's dissection of 'extermination through assimilation' in *The Unjust Society* (1969)" (Grauer and Ruffo 500). Cree/Métis author Maria Campbell's *Halfbreed* (1973) and the *Poems of Rita Joe* (1978) are only two of many books that he mentions as growing out of grassroots education in the sixties (Grauer and Ruffo 502). Many other Indigenous writers responded to the Canadian federal government's White Paper with their own forms of resistance writing. Palmer mentions Maria Campbell's *Halfbreed* (1973), Lee Maracle's *Bobbie Lee: Indian Rebel* (1975), and Jeannette Armstrong's *Slash* (1985), as well as serial publications such as *Akwesasne Notes*, which—following protests and blockades in response to the imposition of custom duties in "cross-border" reserves—became a focus for "Red Power" writing, some of it by jailed writers (Palmer 403). When

Armand Ruffo visited my graduate class a few years ago, he noted that "local" papers and magazines also served as outlets for prison writing as well as other kinds of work in the 1970s and beyond. In "Why Native Literature?" Ruffo identifies two tendencies or "branches" in Native writing, "a body of work that differs remarkably from that of Non-native people": the mythic/sacred and the historical/secular (which I take to include more overtly political as well as autobiographical writing, fiction, etc.), arguing that these two branches are not mutually exclusive (119). If Canadian society is posited, like most Western liberal democracies, on the separation of church and state, many Indigenous theorists, from Vine Deloria Jr. in the United States to Taiaiake Alfred in Canada, link politics and spirituality—for them, the latter is not to be confused with the institutions of religion. Even those Indigenous writers and critics who self-identify as largely secular would agree with Ruffo that much "Native literature, while grounded in a traditional, spiritually based worldview, is no less a call for liberation, survival and beyond to affirmation" ("Why Native" 110).

Indigenous Literary Criticism
In *Reasoning Together: The Native Critics Collective*, Christopher Teuton (Cherokee) offers an overview of modern American Indian literary studies, its main modes of interpretation, and its periodization, which partly overlaps with the frameworks developed in Native Canadian literary studies. Beginning with a creation story from his own tribe, which he proceeds to analyse, he underscores the timelessness of what Ruffo refers to as the mythic/sacred. He then goes on to identify three modes that have occupied a prominent place in criticism since the mid-1970s, and that "may be differentiated not just by the central questions they ask, but by the ethical positions they define in relation to the social contexts they engage" (Teuton 200). Anthropological and ethnographic discourse, associated with the first mode, is concerned with cultural authenticity and identity. Mode two "attempts to correct the misrepresentation of Native peoples and cultures," critiquing (in Robert Warrior's words) "appeals to idealism and/or essentialism," hoping to provide a "strong counternarrative to received academic and popular understandings of American Indian people and cultures" (Teuton 200–1). Mode three "bypasses questions of representation to theorize how academic work can be made accountable and put in dialogue with Native people, communities and nations" (201). He argues that "the progression of the modes marks a gradual shift from non-Native centred to Native-centred epistemologies employed in the analysis of Native literature" (200). Implicitly, for Teuton, mode one asks "Who and what is an Indian?"; mode two asks "Who can say who and what is an Indian but

an Indian?"; and mode three asks "How are we Native people and nations to become who we want to become?" (201). While these modes are parallel and continuous in critical discourse, they also tend to be sequential in some ways and in other ways to overlap. Teuton concludes that "a definition of 'theory' may be a little late in coming for Native American literary studies, since scholars of Native literature have surely been theorizing, creating concepts, and defining terms for years" (209). In reference to Jonathan Culler's "mainstream" definition of theory as interdisciplinary, analytical and speculative, critiquing common sense, and engaging in reflexive thinking about thinking, Teuton adds a crucial, missing dimension that might make that definition less inappropriate: "theory arises out of the dialectical relationship among artists, arts, critics, and Native communities" (209).

In this sense, many Native critics place the emphasis on synthesis even more than analysis. My own essay making use of Eden Robinson's novel *Monkey Beach* to discuss some of these issues, reads that book in relation to two "American" schools of thought that have occupied prominent places in critical debates since 2000: Indigenous nationalism, with which Teuton is sometimes associated, and trickster studies, representing a range of approaches of which the most prominent contributor has been the "American" Chippewa author and theorist Gerald Vizenor (Lacombe "On Critical"). These two tendencies, far from mutually exclusive, do not encompass the breadth of questions and approaches in contemporary criticism. Feminist literary theory and questions of ethics each would merit an essay in itself, for instance, in the history of Indigenous literary criticism in Canada. Like feminism, post-colonial studies, trauma studies, tricksterism, and resurgence represent only a few of several recurring approaches, sometimes blurring generic boundaries between autobiography, fiction, poetry, and theory.[6]

Vizenor's own approach, to the extent that he defines anything in essays that resist such classifications, is to counteract what he views as misapprehensions of Native writing:

> There are at least four postmodern conditions in the critical responses to Native American Indian and postindian literatures: the first is heard in aural performances; the second is unbodied in translations; the third is the trickster hermeneutics of liberation, the uncertain humor and shimmer of survivance that denies the obscure maneuvers of manifest manners, tragic transvaluations, and the incoherence of cultural representations; the fourth is narrative chance, the counter causes in language games, consumer simulations, and the histories of publications since the removal of tribal communities to federal enclaves or reservations. (Vizenor 66)

If King's and Robinson's stories can be said to engage some of Vizenor's categories of postmodern responses, his work on tricksterism, like trickster approaches more generally, represents the tip of the iceberg when it comes to the myriad ways of reading contemporary Indigenous writing. The proliferation of critical models, extensive as it is, has emerged in the relatively recent past, although Indigenous literature has of course offered a commentary on a number of issues long before the advent of modern literary theory in the academy.

Based in Manitoba, poet and scholar Emma LaRocque (Cree/Métis), one of the first to teach Native literature and Native Studies in Canada, has been producing critical analyses for many years; her recently released book *When the Other Is Me: Native Resistance Discourse, 1850–1990* is only the latest of her many contributions to the field over the years. From early work such as *Defeathering the Indian* (1975), her handbook for primary school educators of Native students, which speaks to the problematic legacy of the Euro-Canadian system and its curriculum, to more recent publications such as her essay "Teaching Aboriginal Literature: The Discourse of Margins and Mainstreams" (2002), focused on the university curriculum and its methods, she has defended the validity and argued for the necessity of a Native literary criticism centred on both Canadian and Indigenous writing. LaRocque speaks of the relative absence of dialogue between Native Studies and English departments, and to the underemployment of Indigenous graduate students trained in literary analysis, a situation alarmingly similar to what she encountered forty years ago: "In the 1970s and much of the 80s, Native Studies was largely treated as a cultural sensitivity, remedial program, not as a serious scholarly field. Critical intellectual work was often misunderstood or dismissed as 'biased,' and the barely emerging handful of Native scholars had not yet developed methodological tools or languages by which to articulate what we, in praxis, were modeling, namely, Indigeneity and post-coloniality" (LaRocque, "Teaching" 212). She adds that "cultural differences notwithstanding, both Native and non-Native students continue to arrive in universities with a disturbing combination of absence of basic knowledge *and* misinformation about Aboriginal peoples and issues" (212). Here is how she summarizes her view of this situation in a 1990 interview with Hartmut Lutz:

> The dilemma now is in the loneliness of not being taken seriously, and the loneliness of not being understood simply because white Canadians are dismally ignorant of Aboriginal peoples. I don't mean this as an insult, I mean it as a historical fact [...] you are forever forced to explain before you can even begin to dialogue. A lot of energy is being derailed and drained that way [...] we can grow only if we dialogue with both the white and the

Native intellectual communities, but as I have pointed out many times, dialogue is a two-way street. (LaRocque, "Interview" 186–87)

In a comment frequently echoed by other scholars, she reminds us that "classically colonial archival and academic descriptions and data about Natives' tools, physical features, 'rituals,' or geography have been equated with objectivity, while Native-based data has been subsumed under subjectivity" (LaRocque, "The Colonization" 12). She stresses the work of Indigenous women writers who are translating "the Aboriginal achievements, world views, and colonial challenges into meaningful and compelling art" (LaRocque, "Reflections" 149).

As late as 1987, Thomas King, in his introduction to the critical anthology *The Native in Literature*, still had to contend with a similar situation; he comments that it is only in the last third of the book that analysis of Euro-Canadian views gives way to a critical focus on writing by Indigenous authors, although many Native writers had been publishing for some time. In addressing representations of Native characters by Euro-Canadian writers, King singles out Wayland Drew's 1973 novel *The Wabeno Feast*, foregrounding an environmental ethic, as embodying some of the prevailing stereotypes—from the noble savage to the helpless victim by way of the drunken Indian.[7] Similarly, Armand Ruffo found it necessary to address the legacy of Northrop Frye's conclusion to the *Literary History of Canada*, edited by Carl Klinck in 1965, and of Frye's collected essays in *The Bush Garden* (1971):[8]

> It goes without saying that where Native people figure in Frye's Canadian landscape they are inevitably connected to the land, and, as the land is considered terrifying, the embodiment of a denial of Western cultural values, so too do Native people symbolize this perception.... Accordingly, as it has been illustrated by Daniel Francis in *The Imaginary Indian: The Image of the Indian in Canadian Culture* and Leslie Monkman in *A Native Heritage: Images of the Indian in English-Canadian Literature*, these imaginings run a gamut of variations from the noble savage embodying spirituality to the savage lacking spirituality with a myriad of versions of the degraded and doomed. In the American context, Robert Berkhofer picks up a similar theme. He writes that "[o]nly civilization had history and dynamics in this view, so therefore Indians must be conceived of as ahistorical and static." (Ruffo, "Why Native" 111)

Other critics note that, in the *Literary History of Canada*, Native literature merits a brief mention in the chapter on children's literature; LaRocque, for instance, comments on how colleagues in the English department at her university "assumed Native literature consisted mostly of 'folktales' and 'children's literature'" ("Teaching" 210). She notes that these are "honourable subjects but the assumptions revealed ignorance about the scope of study available in Native literatures" (210). Volume 4 of the *Literary History* (1990), which appeared at a much later date, also does not include a chapter on Native writing. Instead, the new format and approach for this volume include, along with essays on neglected and emerging genres of Canadian writing, a chapter on anthropological writing. Although some anthropologists support Indigenous ethical protocols and political concerns, many remain uneasy about the discipline's mixed legacy, which is sometimes associated with orientalism as described by Edward Said, a theorist highly respected by Native scholars.[9] To my knowledge, few comprehensive entries on Indigenous literature, and virtually none by Indigenous scholars, appeared before the 2009 publication of *The Cambridge History of Canadian Literature*, edited by Coral Ann Howells and Eva-Marie Kröller.

Since the 1980s, and parallel with the emergence of questions of hybridity in post-colonial studies, scholarly books and articles by Indigenous writers and academics have generated considerable discussion about how Western genres and traditions relate to Native literature. LaRoque's experiences provide one context for the emergence of Indigenous nationalism in Canada, although here it does not occupy the prominence it does in the United States; debates about international boundaries and different historical contexts for anti-colonialist work in North American former colonies further complicate this question of boundaries and comparative approaches. Victoria-based Kahnawake Mohawk scholar Taiaiake Alfred, for instance, unpacks the term "nationalism" as linked to European contexts for engaging in political and cultural studies in books such as *Peace, Power, Righteousness* (1999) and *Wasáse* (2005). Cherokee scholar and fiction writer Daniel Heath Justice, for his part, co-edits the Nebraska-based journal *Studies in American Indian Literature*, while at the same time teaching Indigenous literature at the University of Toronto.

Indigenous literary nationalism, which encompasses several overlapping generations of scholars and methods, possesses its own vocabulary indebted to Native Studies, ranging from Robert Warrior's "intellectual sovereignty" to Daniel Heath Justice's "kinship," to Craig Womack's "code talk," "talking stick," and "call and response" approaches, to Lisa Brooks's "gathering place," among others. Some of these scholars collaborated on the 2006 book *American Indian Literary Nationalism*, which pays homage to Acoma Pueblo poet Simon Ortiz's 1981 essay "Towards a National Indian Literature: Cultural Authenticity in Nationalism." Ortiz, for his part, spent several years as a visiting scholar at the University of Toronto.

In short, scholars working in both countries challenge the colonial border, although at times Indigenous scholars from the United States seem more visible than their counterparts from Canada. Kristina Fagan and Sam McKegney, in "Circling the Question of Nationalism in Native Canadian Literature and Its Study," discuss the limits as well as the usefulness of the "American" school of Indigenous nationalists for talking about Indigenous writing in Canada. They observe that not all Indigenous writers are interested in foregrounding questions of spirituality, or even in speaking openly or exclusively as Native writers on Native topics (however these might be defined). They mention (as does Ruffo) that Eden Robinson's short stories, like her most recent novel *Blood Sports*, do not identify the characters as belonging to any cultural community.

In his introduction to *All My Relations: An Anthology of Contemporary Native Canadian Fiction* (1990), not unlike Drew Taylor in his 1997 book of essays *Funny, You Don't Look Like One*, Thomas King humorously critiques tendencies to racialize and otherwise categorize "membership," including membership in the writers' community: "In our discussions of Native literature, we try to imagine that there is a racial denominator which full-bloods raised in cities, half-bloods raised on farms, quarter-bloods raised on reservations, Indians adopted and raised by white families, Indians who speak their tribal language, Indians who speak only English, traditionally educated Indians, university-trained Indians, Indians with little education, and the like all share. We know, of course that there is not" (King, Introduction x–xi). Nevertheless, he argued that "if we wait long enough, the sheer bulk of this collection [of literary works by Native authors], when it reaches some sort of critical mass, will present us with a matrix within which a variety of patterns can be discerned" (x). King's widely anthologized essay "Godzilla vs Post-Colonial," which first appeared in 1990, three years before Vizenor's own formulation of Indigenous theory in *Manifest Manners*, offers one such matrix at the same time that it too uses humour to tease out some of the creative tensions identified by critics such as LaRocque. King suggests that while the term post-colonial "strives to escape to find new centres, it remains, in the end, a hostage to nationalism" ("Godzilla" 243). Reminding us that there are many kinds and traditions of Native writing and that "assumptions are a dangerous thing" (241), in characteristic tongue-in-cheek fashion, King, not unlike Vizenor, tends to qualify most of his own statements.

Thomas King's CBC Massey lectures *The Truth about Stories: A Native Narrative* (2003) extends his earlier statements about the types of Indigenous literature to offer some comments about the effects of the colonialist legacy on Native people; he turns to stories (including autobiography) as a way of addressing this impact. King offers his own formulation of contextual frameworks for making sense of different kinds of Indigenous literature in "Godzilla." He divides that literature into four categories: tribal (oral, taking place in First Nations languages, and circulating within specific "tribes" or Nations); polemical (about contact and conflict between Europeans and First Nations, and addressed to a broader audience); interfusional (self-consciously hybrid forms of writing that play with oral traditions as well as with Western genres); and associational (including a wide range of forms and genres, not restricted to a specifically Indigenous thematic, and taking for granted a Native world view). These four categories are not necessarily sequential, to the extent that all four coexist in the contemporary period. The reader is never quite sure of the extent to which King's essay parodies the structuralist legacy of Northrop Frye's four-fold mythical structure in *The Anatomy of Criticism* (1957), which is indebted to a long tradition of Christian hermeneutics, and which makes use of the seasons to talk about different literary modes. Nor can we ascertain whether King alludes to the four directions of the medicine wheel associated with traditional knowledge in Algonquian cultures. Medicine wheel teachings, as Maliseet scholar Andrea Bear Nicholas reminds us, have been adopted, travestied, and invented by New Age gurus and subsequently applied to a number of First Nations who traditionally did not make use of the wheel (Bear Nicholas 26). Marie Battiste, for her part, reminds us that "rituals and ceremonies that cleanse and heal, maintaining the balances, must be respected and honoured" (202). The appropriation, misuse, and commodification of Indigenous stories, ceremonial objects, and traditional knowledge frameworks in academic contexts, like the more generalized stereotypical images of Native people in the culture at large, are ripe for sly satirical treatment by humorists such as King. The mainstreaming of Indigenous literature, which I address elsewhere (see "On Critical"), like the more insidious problem of co-option, sometimes leads Native authors to engage in polemics, a genre that—as King recognizes—has a long and honourable tradition. Nationalism, sometimes read in purely ideological terms, is one such rhetorical mode. Language revitalization programmes, and the recognition that contemporary Indigenous literature continues to make use of Indigenous languages as well as English, are linked to indigenist perspectives and to the theme of resurgence in recent anthologies of essays by authors and scholars such as Kim Anderson, Bonita Lawrence, and Leanne Simpson. No matter what theoretical model we invoke, including postmodernism, "it's turtles all the way down," as King puts it in *The Truth about Stories* (2)—which I take to mean that there is no end to Indigenous creation.

King's reservations about post-colonial theory help bridge the gap between different, Canadian understandings of this term: in making "a rather simplistic comparison between pre-colonial and post-colonial, I left out one of the players, rather like talking about pre-pubescence and post-pubescence without mentioning puberty" ("Godzilla" 242). Questions of periodization are affected by point of view: in Native critical circles, Indigenous cultures—which pre- and post-date the moment of "contact" with European "civilization"—do not necessarily use that moment as their central point of reference. In post-colonial critical circles, the term has a different meaning, often referring to the articulation of culture and politics in the period since India's independence from Britain, for example. King's ongoing concern with the appropriation of lands, lack of recognition for aboriginal rights, and ongoing ignorance of Indigenous cultures is evident in his most recent collection of stories *A Short History of Indians in Canada* (2005). His commitment to social justice emerged clearly and eloquently in a keynote address at the tenth anniversary of the Ph.D. in Canadian Studies at Trent University in 2011, entitled "Home and Native Land: First Nations and the Politics of Property."

The many consequences of broken treaties and the legacy of residential schools mentioned by so many critics include disproportionately low numbers of Indigenous students who finish high school and the incarceration of disenfranchised youth in Canada's prison system. Less quantifiable effects on the well-being of intergenerational survivors, many of whom experience severe poverty in both rural and urban contexts, are also addressed by native critics. Cree/Métis scholar Jo-Ann Episkenew, who co-authored the critical anthology *Creating Community: A Roundtable on Canadian Aboriginal Literature* with Renate Eigenbrod in 2002, speaks to some of these concerns in *Taking Back Our Spirits: Indigenous Literature, Public Policy, and Healing*. Episkenew's book revisits the legacy of the 1960s and its aftermath with reference to the failure of social policy to redress systemic racism:

> Following the awakening of social consciousness in the 1960s and 1970s and supported by subsequent human rights legislation, racism in its overt forms has become a cultural *faux pas* among White people who consider themselves educated and enlightened. That is not to say that blatant racism does not exist in Canada. It does, and to remedy blatant racism, "cultural awareness training" proliferates. The basic premise of cultural awareness training is that if White people could only learn to understand Indigenous people's strange and exotic ways, they would come to appreciate us and put an end to their racist behaviours. However, cultural awareness training does not acknowledge the more subtle forms of racism—the racism of structures and systems—that are founded on and support "White privilege." (Episkenew 7)

For Episkenew, "contemporary Indigenous literature cannot be divorced from its contextual framework" (186). Because stories have sometimes contributed to racist attitudes, stories are also needed to heal, functioning as medicine alongside other healing rituals in the Indigenous community. Transformational stories play an important role in the Indigenous community of writers and readers (Episkenew 13).

Trap/lines

Thomas King's "Trap Lines" and Eden Robinson's "Traplines" are both concerned with young men who, at the beginning of the stories, might or might not be university bound. These characters contend with peer pressure from friends, and with parents whose past experience differs from theirs. The difficulty of communication between the generations and between couples in these stories is compounded by silences about feelings and memories that seem impossible to articulate. While the violence of loss and betrayal is more viscerally evident in Robinson's story, it is palpable in King's as well. While nostalgia and its inventions are gently called into question, both stories make use of specific references to activities "on the land"—trapping (in both stories), recreational fishing with the grandfather in King's story, and an incident based on visiting the father's trapline in Robinson's—to suggest the emotional fault lines of human relationships. The young man's parents in King's story have their differences of opinion about whether it is preferable to live on the reservation or in the city, but are represented as a loving, close-knit family unit. As the adolescent leaves home for the first time at the end of each story, the outcome is not clear. There the resemblance between the two plots ends. The boy's economic circumstances seem more promising in King's story than in Robinson's, as do family relationships. Exposition and narrative techniques, including the treatment of time and point of view, are very different.

When I first taught these stories, I was surprised by my students' responses. They did not react to the "realist" humour of King's "Trap Lines" story as much as to the humour associated with what they saw as a subversive use of magic realism in the collection's coyote stories. I suspect this is partly because "Trap Lines" represents the generation gap from the parents' rather than the youth's point of view. By contrast, they were fully absorbed by Robinson's story, which seemed to resonate more than the other stories in her volume *Traplines* for them. Again, I suspect this is because the narrator adopts the youth's point of view. But there are other reasons having to do with how my students read based on where they are coming from. While it is impossible to generalize and while exceptions do occur, among those students who chose to identify their backgrounds and who are Native, those who left the reserve for post-secondary education empathized with the characters' choices and situation, even when these were different from their own, while non-Native students from middle-class, small-town Ontario backgrounds had greater difficulty understanding his choices and circumstances. Specifically, the boy's experience of inner conflict relative to the feelings about his family and about the couple who want to adopt him, together with the importance of being accepted by one's peers, resonated deeply for all, but in very different ways based on the students' own positions as members, outsiders, or partial outsiders to the kind of village life described by Robinson. At the risk of being reductive, I would suggest that in my experience, for "Canadian" students, Robinson's story is an eye-opener, while for Indigenous students, it offers a sense of recognition—at the same time that everyone liked the fact that the characters "ethnic" or cultural identity, unlike their socio-economic background, remains unstated in the story.

Thomas King's "Trap Lines" is similar to his other stories to the extent that the reader is not always sure who is speaking or which timeline we are in. The father whose son Christopher is leaving for university remembers a time before his own family moved to the city. A contrast is created between life in a government house on the reservation near Medicine River and life in the city, at the same time that both his father and his grandfather (Christopher's great-grandfather) were seasonally employed as trappers and as car mechanics. The idea of sport fishing appealed to these prairie boys from an earlier generation. For Christopher, the stories associated with their lives blur and seem immaterial, although he evinces some interest in how they lived. The usefulness, and luxury, of being able to access two bathrooms in their somewhat constipated household is contrasted to memories of the outhouse "on the rez." In a conversation with his friend Jerry, overheard by his father, Christopher states that his father wants him to be a trapper; the reader knows that in fact it is his mother, and not his father, who would rather live on the reserve where she grew up. For his part, Christopher's friend Jerry, whose own background is never identified and whose father sells cars, assumes that he is expected to follow in his own father's footsteps. While neither boy is interested in these occupations, trapping clearly is considered "weird" in comparison with selling cars or working with computers—where "weird" variously means both "cool" and "bizarre" in the boys' usage of the term (King, *One Good* 40). When, just before they leave home, Jerry's father gives him the red metal toolbox that had belonged to his own father, Christopher retrieves from the back of a closet his grandfather's green metal fishing tackle box. When they depart, presumably to attend university as planned, different interpretations of the fishing tackle box story are put forward in playfully affectionate teasing between Christopher's parents. Gendered and generational relationships with language and silence are evoked and sometimes explicitly commented on by the introspective narrator, Christopher's father. King ends his story more or less randomly, with Christopher's mother Alberta going grocery shopping and his father meditating on a rare fishing trip with his own dad: "I sat in the bathroom and imagined what my father had been going to say just before the wind took his hat, something important I guessed, something I could have shared with my son" (*One Good* 46). While the story easily could be read as a "universal" narrative about love and loss, its focus on the "price of life" for Native people in "modern times" is evident, as is King's critique of commodity capitalism. At the same time, possibilities remain for the next generation to renegotiate and renew, in their own way, their relationship to Indigenous community and identity as well as to the global village that is Canada.

In some ways, "Traplines," the title story of Robinson's collection, picks up where King's short story ends. Robinson's story opens with a father and son out on the family trapline, where among different furs with different dollar values depending on the nature of the animal and they way in which it interacted with the trap, they find a valuable, flawless white marten. The father is pleased at the prospect of the Christmas money that this perfect specimen represents. This family, however, is deeply scarred by the legacy of residential school and by the intergenerational trauma and violence that continue to play out even after the demise of these schools. Their dealings with one another are characterized by a different set of emotional traplines and fault lines than those dramatized in King's stories, despite the continuing love bonds that link the parents and their children. Often, roles are reversed, as children are protective of their parents' dignity and concerned to meet their physical needs. In this story the violence manifests most destructively in the relationship between two sons: Eric revisits the beatings he experiences at the hands of his drunken father by inflicting them, in a drug-addled state, upon his brother Will, from whose point of view the story is told. In a parallel plot line, emotional abuse is heaped upon another boy in the village who, as part of a dare issued by their circle of "friends," is tricked by a young woman he thinks of as his girlfriend. Will, gifted and academically motivated, is briefly "rescued" by his high school English teacher, Mrs. Smythe, and her husband.

Accepting the offer to live with them and (it is suggested) to be adopted by them, which would represent the road to success, poses as many problems for Will as refusing the offer—something that not all of my students pick up on, and that others want to raise as a topic for debate.

Will's dilemma captures some of the feelings of some Native students who leave home to attend university, even if they do not come from such an unhealthy family. Will feels pressure on a number of fronts. The peer pressure of the town's youth, whose gang-like behaviour defines social norms, cannot be ignored if he is to survive in his community. His loyalty and love for his family, however dysfunctional that family may be, and his fear that in pursuing his educational goals he would be cutting himself off, vie with his need to find physical and emotional safety. There is also the hint, in an earlier photograph of Mr. Smythe with an absent young boy whose relationship to him is never clarified, of a tragic if not a sinister repressed history of earlier parental relations of some sort. Will's decision not to live with the Smythes, however, makes it that much harder for him to keep up with the school work that he otherwise would experience more positively.

The urge to reach out to those who offer a healthier way of life comes with its own costs, as indeed does the choice of remaining with those who, like his friends and family, are caught up in substance abuse and other addictions. Mr. and Mrs. Smythe, for all their kind and well-intentioned ways, do not entirely understand these dilemmas. In the end, Will and his friend decide to hitchhike to Vancouver for Christmas, mostly to escape from Will's brother, who had been picked up by the police but was about to return home. The bitter cold and significant distance between the city and their northern coastal community renders this a somewhat risky move, one that for me ironically contrasts with the more treacherous but necessary decisions of even younger children, at other times and in other contexts, to run away from residential school. Here, the boys would have to "hitch to town, hitch to Smithers, then down to Prince George" before eventually hitching to Vancouver (Robinson 34). Such a move has the advantage of allowing Will to escape unacceptable alternatives, while generating new and no less problematic ones on the road and in the city. If nothing else, Will feels that "*anything*'ll be better than sitting around" (35; emphasis added). In an unresolved, open ending characteristic of Eden Robinson's narrative structures, the reader can only speculate about the outcome. While this is a less auspicious if not more ominous situation than that which the son faces in Thomas King's "Trap Lines," one cannot but hope that Will resurfaces alive and well. While limited in his options, for the moment at least he still possesses a measure of agency, of "free will," so to speak, although the outcome is far from clear. If King's character Christopher blithely sails into his future life with few apparent worries after leaving home, presumably bringing with him the possibility of return, Will knows full well that whether he stays or whether he goes, he may have to foreclose on his dream of being a poet. But his story as told by Robinson suggests that it is now possible for the narrator to write a new kind of story, where Will's story, fully immersed in the present moment, must bide its time.

Post-Indian Narratives

King's "How Corporal Sterling Saved Blossom, Alberta, and Most of the Rest of the World as Well" and Robinson's "Dogs in Winter" turn to crime fiction and true confession stories on the one hand, and to science fiction and the Western on the other, to trouble received notions of the moral majority, small town family values, authority figures, and literary conventions. King introduces his story with a motel owner name Ralph, whose wife awakens him by drawing to his attention some noisy Indians, which he claims are just coyotes. The story then morphs into a community's invasion by blue coyotes from outer space, who make off with the petrified Indians that the mayor, doctor, local policeman, and other officials and dignitaries insist on rescuing in a thinly veiled parable of the Indian Act. Robinson opens her story with Aunt Genna, a spinster who seems to be an amalgam of the British Columbia artist Emily Carr, Agatha Christie's detective Miss Marple, and the murderous sisters in Frank Capra's 1944 film *Arsenic and Old Lace*. A Victorian lady from British Columbia, although "she was born in Bended River Manitoba, she liked to believe she was an English lady" (Robinson 42). Robinson is known for "campy" references to popular culture and film in her fiction. Here, in addition to Capra, she may also be playing with Agatha Christie's best-selling first novel *Ten Little Niggers* (1939), originally entitled *And Then There Were None* (1939) and subsequently filmed as *Ten Little Indians*. Its female characters, all morally suspect, could serve as models for the maiden aunt, the adoptive mother, and the birth mother in *Dogs*. While this story's affectionate satire extends to Emily Carr, known for her menagerie of exotic pets and her painterly depictions of totem poles and forest landscapes influenced by a mixture of Indigenous, Western, and oriental spirituality, I believe the story's many ironic reversals serve to underscore the toxic effects of misrepresentations of aboriginal cultures as "barbaric." Here it is the narrator's birth mother who is a mass murderer, killing the sweet little old lady, and her adoptive parents Paul and Janet, who seem terminally normal.

The innocuous Paul and Janet in "Dogs in Winter" remind me of Mr. and Mrs. Smythe from "Traplines." Initially, we are told that they are "the parents I've always wanted," something Disneylike, out of a storybook or a TV set (Robinson 41). Janet's blonde hair is neatly tucked behind her ears, she wears a demure navy dress, a white Peter Pan collar, pearls, and matching white shoes—at the same time that she enjoys "weird art movies" such as *Street Angel* (41–42). The narrator's birth mother, on the other hand, seems indiscriminate in her choice of murder victims, but her crimes take place in ubiquitous locales, such as the local curling club. Following her jailbreak, mother and daughter spend some years on the road, moving from town to town and camping out in quintessentially Canadian places such as Banff National Park. The opening sequence of Robinson's story, in which the poodle Picnic attacks police officer Wilkinson, humping the wrong leg, suggests the kind of tale associated with coyote in King's work, although it is Raven who is the Haisla trickster figure. The story mentions Aunt Genna's lace collars, the lace curtains and Persian carpets in the house of Lisa's friend Amanda, and "plastic" porcelain tea parties featuring lemonade and grape juice. There are references to Paul and Janet attending a business conference in Masset on the Queen Charlotte Islands when not watching videos that resemble Louis Buñuel and Salvador Dalí's *Un Chien Andanou*. Yet Janet is horrified by a print of a moose giving birth to a human baby that the narrator finds in a tourist shop featuring "nature pictures and small portraits of sad-eyed Indian children" (Robinson 17). The story mentions the moose-hunting habits of the narrator's mother as part of her daughter's unusual puberty initiation rites, but does not explicitly locate any of these characters and events within any particular ethnocultural context. As with the "medium-sized light-blue things" that emerge from a spaceship in King's story and that are variously taken to be coyotes or the alien's pets (King, *One Good* 57), Aunt Genna's dogs Jenjen, Coco, Ginger, and Picnic also resemble tricksters. When Mama, identified as Moreen Lisa Rudford, kills off the narrator Lisa's beloved aunt Genna, the reader does not know whether to laugh or cry. Different ages are given for different time sequences in Lisa's story, reinforcing the impression that she is, on one level, an unreliable narrator. In a story that also features almost-murders by young men and almost-suicides by young women, the shape-shifting narrative seems to position the female parent as the criminal and her child as her victim, although as many critics have noted, Robinson is intent on debunking gendered and racialized stereotypes. "I can betray, but I can't kill. Mama would say that betrayal is worse" (Robinson 67).

King's story "Sterling" uses a different kind of humour to make its own satirical point. In this science-fictional, spaghetti-western pulp fiction narrative, urban prairie settlers, including the North-West Mounted Police, are unable to decipher what is happening to a group of "stiff" Indians following a party at a local motel. Medical experts cannot understand how they come to be encased in a sticky, impermeable membrane. Villagers cannot understand where the constant coyote howls are coming from. Unsure of how to deal with the situation, the Mounties, under Sterling's leadership, place the hardened Indians in storage, neatly stacking them up like cordwood in local warehouses when they start to run out of other places in which to store them. They claim that this is for the Indians' own protection, although they also fear that the Indians, who are excreting and/or are covered with a sticky, impermeable, resin-like substance that confers a wooden texture upon them, might carry some sort of previously unknown contagious disease. Eventually, what Corporal Sterling describes as "aliens disguised as blue coyotes" (*One Good* 60) descend on Blossom in a spaceship and carry away the well-seasoned local "Indians"; the same thing seems to be happening all over the world—including Germany, where "almost fifty Indians" on vacation are picked up by the blue coyotes. The coyotes are able to walk through padlocked doors, while Sterling's bullets bounce off the transparent glass wall that protects the spaceship and its doorway. Unable to stop these "aliens" despite firing their weapons at the departing spaceship, Corporal Sterling concludes that the town's officers have at least managed to save themselves, although they regret not being able to save the "kidnapped Canadian citizens" (62). Upon discovering that one Indian in the motel, who appears to be singing, was in fact asking "what took you so long?" this reader could not help but think of the famous "camp" line from the Star Trek science fiction television series, "Beam me up, Scotty, there's no intelligent life down here."

I am also reminded of Gerald Vizenor's comment that Indians "must be the simulations of the 'absolute fakes' in the ruins of representation, or the victims in the literary annihilation" (9). King, like Vizenor, would seem to replace prevalent images of Indians with that of the post-Indian warrior. According to Vizenor, the trickster's creative, liberatory moves, in which "the animals laughed," are in fact "the translation of liberation" (15). Reading King, Vizenor cites Linda Hutcheon's *The Politics of Postmodernism* in his pastiche of theoretical texts, to the effect that the "representation of history becomes the history of representation" (Vizenor 62). For him, "nominal tricksters are silhouettes in most commercial literature, the concoctions of the other" (173). It would be easy to apply some of his comments to "Sterling" and especially to "Dogs" when he talks about "postindian narratives" as "suspended shadows": "these are not the binaries of savagism and civilization, rather, the paradoxes of narrative fear, the suspension of domination, and survivance hermeneutics" (169–70). They revisit the ghost histories discussed by Gibert above. Despite the weight of oppression that affects many of her characters and the "gothic" effects identified by many of her critics, for me Eden Robinson's stories and novels are characterized by resilience and delightfully dark humour. While the richness of her open-ended narratives is precisely that they can be interpreted in ways that are consistent with both Western and Indigenous frames of reference, I believe that Haisla myth percolates through all of her fiction, including her dark fantasy *Blood Sports*.

Robinson's trick of making the female the hunter, and of turning her into a blonde mass murderer, challenges readerly expectations on a number of fronts, deconstructing images of "the barbaric/noble savage" and poking fun at a few middle-class Anglo-Canadian viewpoints. When Lisa finds the picture of the moose, I am reminded of Canadian artist Charles Pachter's 1970s moose paintings and of Margaret Atwood's representation of Group of Seven paintings in "Wilderness Tips," as much as of the Woodlands School of Anishinaabe art, with its animals and mythical creatures linked by spirit lines. It is the juxtaposition of female moose and human baby that specifically horrifies Lisa's adoptive mother Janet, we are told. While her hysterical response could suggest that she is privy to Lisa's prior history, including the mother's ritual initiation of Lisa into puberty—involving the killing of a moose—it is more likely that Janet is squeamish about art that blurs the boundaries between humans, animals, and spirit beings, boundaries that typically are much more fluid in Indigenous than in Western art. And as with her novel *Monkey Beach*, Robinson subtly weaves elements derived from Haisla potlatch dances such as the dog dance into her narrative. If she begins her story *in medias res* with Aunt Genna's Picnic, she ends it, also *in medias res*, with an unforgettably haunting portrait of Lisa's mother. In the story's closing lines, Moreen leaves Lisa behind in her house for what she claims will only be a little while, alone with a freezer-full of thawing human remains: "I watch her bounce down the walkway to the car, wave once, and drive away, smiling and happy and lethal" (Robinson 70). The reader, like Lisa, is left in an indeterminate space, unsure of her feelings in a story whose *mise-en-abyme* of the boundaries between worlds remains disconcerting, at once hilarious and chilling.

The Web of Relationships
While the stories of Thomas King and Eden Robinson, like those of many other Native Canadian writers, do not necessarily dwell on the recent colonial past, their perspectives on contemporary Indigenous culture have had to contend with that past, at the same time that they also refuse to be defined or constrained by it. Their narratives also engage Indigenous literary theory in an intertextual dialogue with a number of authors; my own readerly strategy has been to stress their dialogue with critical debates and artistic practices, whether or not Indigenous perspectives are explicitly alluded to in such work. These authors articulate a range of strategies for communicating and celebrating a collective sense of Indigenous identity

that resonates with a wide variety of readers, both Native and non-Native, in academic and other contexts.

As a professor of English Studies, Emma LaRocque sees no contradiction between recognizing Native cultural diversity, addressing the colonial experience, and acknowledging the continuity of shared aspects of Indigenous ethics, culture, and knowledge systems that differ from Western perspectives ("Teaching" 214, 217, 223). At the same time, she is also critical of the "tremendous pressure today for all Native artists and intellectuals to produce works expressly and manifestly different from the dominant culture" (LaRocque, *When the Other* 135). LaRocque asserts that Indigenous scholars "provide new directions and fresh methodologies to cross-cultural research," broadening "the empirical and theoretical bases of numerous disciplines" and posing "new questions to old and tired traditions" ("The Colonization" 12). Yet such "research, critical constructions, interrogations and ideas" are "only beginning to be discovered, not discerned" in Canadian and international contexts (*When the Other* 165). Despite the advent of interdisciplinary post-colonial studies, it is still the case that from an Indigenous standpoint "Canada is centrally a colonial project" in need of unpacking (LaRocque, "Teaching" 215).

Like LaRocque, Rauna Kuokkanen borrows from both Western and Indigenous theory, specifically theories concerning hospitality and the notion of the gift, to comment on how Canadian academia reproduces colonialist structures and attitudes, and how Native people resist such moves. For her, as for so many Indigenous scholars and writers, the concepts of *relationality* and reciprocity, as informed by but not limited to Indigenous spirituality, remain vital to and central aspects of "an infinite *web of relationships*" (Kuokkanen 32; emphasis added). As part of that infinite web, "gift relations at the epistemic level are predominantly about transforming colonial, patriarchal, and supremacist mindsets, paradigms, and values" (Kuokkanen 163). Kuokkanen analyses the concept of hospitality as discussed by Derrida and Levinas from an ethical stance grounded in Indigenous epistemology to unveil the ambiguity that characterizes the academy's assumption of the host role, in that the systematic erasure of Indigenous people's hospitality and understanding of what it entails reproduces colonial power relations. For her, revisiting "the hospitality of the academy" as an Indigenous theorist entails several "critical components." One is "a welcome of the 'other' without conditions (such as translations or definitions)" into Western theoretical formulations; another is an "openness to learning about the logic of the gift and indigenous epistemes" in ways not "violated by demands that they be transcoded into the language of the [European] host" (Kuokkanen 132). Objecting to the undervaluing of Indigenous culture, she challenges our society and our universities' complicity in what Marie Battiste terms "cognitive imperialism" (194). The university has a crucial role to play in that complex process of epistemological transformation.

Notes

1. See Amy Hinterberger's "Feminism and the Politics of Representation" (2007) for an accessible overview of related terminology from post-colonial theorists such as Gayatri Spivak.
2. In this, the context for her brief comment about King's short story "Borders" is somewhat different from the more elaborate reading offered by Davidson, Walton, and Andrews in *Border Crossings: Thomas King's Cultural Inversions* (2003). No less political, their own deconstructive reading addresses an English-discipline-based academic audience.
3. American interpretations of the 1794 Jay's Treaty recognize the rights of Canadian-born members of First Nations to cross the border to work and engage in other activities; as I understand it, since 1928, Métis people must have a fifty percent blood quantum in order to qualify—although many are troubled by the use of a blood quantum as a marker of cultural identity and legal status in *any* context.
4. Helen Hoy's *How Should I Read These? Native Women Writers in Canada* (2001) and Renate Eigenbrod's *Travelling Knowledges: Positioning the Im/migrant Reader of Aboriginal Literatures in Canada* (2005), for instance, build the critics' subject positions into their theoretical frameworks in highly productive ways.
5. See *Enough Is Enough: Aboriginal Women Speak Out*, as told to Janet Silman (1987). Even now, the Indian Act's gender biases and ensuing impact on some Native women's children continue to be felt when it comes to the question of legal status.
6. See my essay "La critique littéraire autochtone en amérique du nord: approches canadiennes anglophones mises en contexte" (2010) for an earlier and more cursory overview.
7. King's comment about Drew's book reminds me of LaRocque's comments about Margaret Laurence's *The Diviners* (1974) when her interviewer suggests that she is too hard on Laurence: "I think she is probably the most perceptive writer Canada has... and she perceived a lot about the place of Métis people in Canadian society. I especially like how, with each novel, the marginalized Tonnerre family moved in closer and closer to white society. Literally and metaphorically, they moved in from the outskirts of town *to* town, finally, even *into* Morag, sexually speaking. But even Margaret Laurence, for all her perceptiveness, plays into some big stereotypes. The Métis are presented as noble, even if a little wild. Jules Tonnerre doesn't like fences and is lusty, mysterious, and of course, dies with nobility. But the larger point I was making [in her article on 'The Métis in Canadian English Literature'] was that we have yet to be treated to a great novel by a Native writer, one that would catch the ethos of being Métis" (LaRocque, "Interview" 187).

8 Anansi, the publisher of Drew's novel and of Frye's book, was prominent among alternative Canadian publishers associated with the nationalist period of the 1970s. Anansi derives its name from the African trickster figure whose shape-shifting included the middle passage from Africa to the Americas in the context of the slave trade. Given that Indigenous studies (including literary studies) extends its understanding of these cultures to include all tribal peoples, the fact that Native Canadian authors and their perspectives have until recently been marginalized and excluded from countercultural publishers such as Anansi is ironic.

9 See, for instance, Robert Warrior's "Native Critics and the World: Edward Said and Nationalism" (2006).

Works Cited

Battiste, Marie. "Maintaining Aboriginal Identity, Language, and Culture in Modern Society." *Reclaiming Indigenous Voice and Vision*. Ed. Marie Battiste. Vancouver: U of British Columbia P, 2000. 192–208.

Bear Nicholas, Andrea. "The Assault on Aboriginal Oral Traditions: Past and Present." *Aboriginal Oral Traditions: Theory, Practice, Ethics*. Ed. Renate Eigenbrod and Renée Hulan. Black Point, NS: Fernwood, 2008. 13–44.

Davidson, Arnold E., Priscilla L. Walton, and Jennifer Andrews. *Border Crossings: Thomas King's Cultural Inversions*. Toronto: U of Toronto P, 2003.

Eigenbrod, Renate. *Travelling Knowledges: Positioning the Im/migrant Reader of Aboriginal Literatures in Canada*. Winnipeg: U of Manitoba P, 2005.

Episkenew, Jo-Ann. *Taking Back Our Spirits: Indigenous Literature, Public Policy, and Healing*. Winnipeg: U of Manitoba P, 2009.

Fagan, Kristina. "What's the Trouble with the Trickster? An Introduction." *Troubling Tricksters: Revisioning Critical Conversations*. Ed. Deanna Reder and Linda Morra. Waterloo, ON: Wilfrid Laurier UP, 2010. 3–20.

Fagan, Kristina, and Sam McKegney. "Circling the Question of Nationalism in Native Canadian Literature and Its Study." *Review: Literature and Arts of the Americas* 41.1 (2008): 31–42.

Grauer, Lally, and Armand Ruffo. "Indigenous Writing: Poetry and Prose." *The Cambridge History of Canadian Literature*. Ed. Coral Ann Howells and Eva-Marie Kröller. Cambridge: Cambridge UP, 2009. 499–517.

Gibert, Teresa. "Ghost Stories: Fictions of History and Myth." *The Cambridge History of Canadian Literature*. Ed. Coral Ann Howells and Eva-Marie Kröller. Cambridge: Cambridge UP, 2009. 478–98.

Hinterberger, Amy. "Feminism and the Politics of Representation: Towards a Critical and Ethical Encounter with 'Others.'" *Journal of International Women's Studies* 8.2 (2007): 74–83.

Howells, Coral Ann, and Eva-Marie Kröller, eds. *The Cambridge History of Canadian Literature*. Cambridge: Cambridge UP, 2009.

Hoy, Helen. *How Should I Read These? Native Women Writers in Canada*. Toronto: U of Toronto P, 2001.

Jamieson, Kathleen Hall. *Indian Women and the Law in Canada: Citizens Minus*. Ottawa: Advisory Committee on the Status of Women, 1980.

Kelly, Jennifer. "Gasps, Snickers, Narrative Tricks, and Deceptive Dominant Ideologies: The Transformative Energies of Richard Van Camp's 'Why Ravens Smile to Little Old Ladies as They Walk By ...' and/in the Classroom." *Troubling Tricksters: Revisioning Critical Conversations*. Ed. Deanna Reder and Linda Morra. Waterloo, ON: Wilfrid Laurier UP, 2010: 99–123.

King, Thomas. "Godzilla vs. Post-Colonial." *New Contexts of Canadian Criticism*. Ed. Ajay Heble, Donna Palmateer Pennee, and J.R. (Tim) Struthers. Peterborough, ON: Broadview, 1997. 241–48.

King, Thomas. Introduction. *All My Relations: An Anthology of Contemporary Canadian Native Fiction*. Ed. Thomas King. Toronto: McClelland and Stewart, 1990. ix–xvi.

King, Thomas. Introduction. *The Native in Literature*. Ed. Thomas King, Cheryl Dawnan Calver, and Helen Hoy. Toronto: ECW, 1987. 7–14.

King, Thomas. *One Good Story, That One*. Toronto: Harper Perennial, 1993.

King, Thomas. *The Truth about Stories: A Native Narrative*. Toronto: Anansi, 2003.

Kröller, Eva-Marie. "The Centennial." *The Cambridge History of Canadian Literature*. Ed. Coral Ann Howells and Eva-Marie Kröller. Cambridge: Cambridge UP, 2009. 312–34.

Kuokkanen, Rauna. *Reshaping the University: Responsibility, Indigenous Epistemes, and the Logic of the Gift*. Vancouver: U of British Columbia P, 2007.

Lacombe, Michèle. "La critique littéraire autochtone en amérique du nord: approches canadiennes anglophones mises en contexte." *Littératures autochtones émergentes: Canada, Afrique du Nord, Océanie francophone*. Ed. Louis-Jacques Dorais and Maurizio Gatti. Montreal: Mémoire d'encrier, 2010.

Lacombe, Michèle. "On Critical Frameworks for Analyzing Indigenous Literature: The Case of *Monkey Beach*." *International Journal of Canadian Studies / Revue internationale d'études canadiennes* 41.1 (2010): 253–78.

LaRocque, Emma. "The Colonization of a Native Woman Scholar." *Women of the First Nations: Power, Wisdom and Strength*. Ed. Christine Miller and Patricia Chuchryk, with Marie Smallface Marule, Brenda Manyfingers, and Cheryl Deering. Winnipeg: U of Manitoba P, 1996. 11–18.

LaRocque, Emma. "Interview." *Contemporary Challenges: Conversations with Canadian Native Authors*. Ed. Hartmut Lutz. Saskatoon, SK: Fifth House, 1991. 181–202.

LaRocque, Emma. "The Métis in English Canadian Literature." *The Canadian Journal of Native Studies* 3.1 (1983): 85–94.

LaRocque, Emma. "Reflections on Cultural Continuity through Aboriginal Women's Writings." *Restoring the Balance: First Nations Women, Community, and Culture*. Ed. Gail Guthrie Valaskakis, Madeleine Dion Stout, and Eric Guimond. Winnipeg: U of Manitoba P, 2009. 149–74.

LaRocque, Emma. "Teaching Aboriginal Literature: The Discourse of Margins and Mainstreams." *Creating Community: A Roundtable on Canadian Aboriginal Literature*. Ed. Renate Eigenbrod and Jo-Ann Episkenew. Penticton, BC: Theytus Books, 2002. 209–34.

LaRocque, Emma. *When the Other Is Me: Native Resistance Discourse 1850–1990*. Winnipeg: U of Manitoba P, 2010.

Palmer, Bryan. *Canada's 1960s: The Ironies of Identity in a Rebellious Era.* Toronto: U of Toronto P, 2009.

Robinson, Eden. *Traplines.* Toronto: Knopf, 1996.

Ruffo, Armand. Introduction. *(Ad)dressing Our Words: Aboriginal Perspectives on Aboriginal Literatures.* Ed. Armand Ruffo. Penticton, BC: Theytus, 2001. 5–16.

Ruffo, Armand. "Why Native Literature?" *Native North America: Critical and Cultural Perspectives.* Ed. Renée Hulan. Toronto: ECW, 1999. 109–21.

Silman, Janet, ed. *Enough Is Enough: Aboriginal Women Speak Out.* Toronto: Women's Press, 1987.

Sinclair, Niigonwedom James. "Trickster Reflections Part I." *Troubling Tricksters: Revisioning Critical Conversations.* Ed. Deanna Reder and Linda Morra. Waterloo, ON: Wilfrid Laurier UP, 2010. 21–58.

Teuton, Christopher B. "Theorizing American Indian Literature: Applying Oral Concepts to Written Traditions." *Reasoning Together: The Native Critics Collective.* Ed. Craig S. Womack, Daniel Heath Justice and Christopher B. Teuton. Norman, OK: U of Oklahoma P, 2008. 193–215.

Vizenor, Gerald. *Manifest Manners: Narratives on Postindian Survivance.* Lincoln, NE: U of Nebraska P, 1994.

Warrior, Robert. "Native Critics and the World: Edward Said and Nationalism." *American Indian Literary Nationalism.* Ed. Jace Weaver, Craig S. Womack, and Robert Warrior. Albuquerque, NM: U of New Mexico P, 2006. 179–224.

Weaver, Jace, Craig S. Womack, and Robert Warrior. *American Indian Literary Nationalism.* Foreword by Simon J. Ortiz; Afterword by Lisa Brooks. Albuquerque, NM: U of New Mexico P, 2006.

Contributors

Richard Cavell is Professor of English at the University of British Columbia and the author of *McLuhan in Space: A Cultural Geography*; the editor of *Love, Hate and Fear in Canada's Cold War*; and the co-editor, with Peter Dickinson, of *Sexing the Maple: A Canadian Sourcebook*; as well as more than seventy chapters, articles, and reviews.

Eva Darias-Beautell is Associate Professor of American and Canadian literatures at the University of La Laguna, Spain. Her books include *Shifting Sands: Literary Theory and Contemporary Canadian Fiction* and *Graphies and Grafts: (Con)Texts and (Inter)Texts in the Fictions of Four Canadian Women Writers*, which was chosen by the International Council for Canadian Studies as one of the "30 most notable books in Canadian Studies." She is the co-editor, with María Jesús Hernáez Lerena, of *Canon Disorders: Gendered Perspectives on Literature and Film in Canada and the United States*, and is currently directing the research project "The City, Urban Cultures and Sustainable Literatures: Representations of the Anglo-Canadian Post-Metropolis," with the participation of scholars from Canada, the UK, and Spain.

Ana María Fraile-Marcos is Associate Professor of English at the University of Salamanca, Spain, where she teaches Canadian Literature. Among her current research interests are the interconnections between racialization and the urban milieu in Canadian literature. Forthcoming is the collection of essays *The Glocal City in Canadian Literature* (Routledge). Other recent publications include the books *Richard Wright's Native Son* (2007) and *Planteamientos estéticos y políticos en la obra de Zora Neale Hurston* (2003), as well as articles about African American and African Canadian writing.

María Jesús Hernáez Lerena is Associate Professor of American and Canadian literatures at the University of La Rioja, Spain. She is author of the books *Exploración de un Género Literario: Los Relatos Breves de Alice Munro* (1998), *Short Story World: The Nineteenth-Century American Masters* (2003), and co-author of *Story Time: Exercises in the Study of American Literature for Advanced Students of English* (1999). She co-edited the volume *Canon Disorders: Gendered Perspectives on Literature and Film in Canada and the United States* (2007) with Eva Darias-Beautell. She is currently at work on a book on the literature of Newfoundland and Labrador.

Coral Ann Howells is Professor Emerita of English and Canadian Literature, University of Reading, England, and Senior Research Fellow, Institute of English Studies, University of London. She has lectured and published extensively on contemporary Canadian women's fiction in English. Her books include *Margaret Atwood* (1997; second edition 2005), *Alice Munro* (1998), and *Contemporary Canadian Women's Fiction* (2003). She is editor of the *Cambridge Companion to Margaret Atwood* (2006), and co-editor with Eva-Marie Kroller of the *Cambridge History of Canadian Literature* (2009). She is a Fellow of the Royal Society of Canada and is currently co-editing a volume of the *Oxford History of the Novel in English*.

Smaro Kamboureli is Professor and Canada Research Chair Tier 1 at the School of English and Theatre Studies at the University of Guelph. Her publications include *Scandalous Bodies: Diasporic Literature in English Canada*, and her co-edited volumes, *Trans.Can.Lit: Resituating the Study of Canadian Literature*, *Shifting the Ground of Canadian Literary Studies*, and *Retooling the Humanities: The Culture of Research in Canadian Universities*. She is the founder and Director of TransCanada Institute.

Michèle Lacombe is Associate Professor in the Canadian Studies and Indigenous Studies Departments at Trent University in Peterborough, Ontario. Relevant recent work addresses Indigenous literary criticism, in *Littératures autochtones*, edited by Maurizio Gatti and Louis-Jacques Dorais (2010); Haisla fiction writer Eden Robinson, in *International Journal of Canadian Studies* 41.1 (2010); and Huron-Wendat dramatist Yves Sioui Durand, in *Indigeneity in Dialogue: Indigenous Literary Expression Across the Linguistic Divides*. She co-edited a special section of *Studies in Canadian Literature* (35.2, 2010), with Heather MacFarlane and Jennifer Andrews, and addressed Acadian misapprehensions of Mi'kmaw culture in *Open Letter: A Canadian Journal of Writing and Theory* 14: 6 (2011).

Belén Martín-Lucas teaches Postcolonial, Diasporic, and Gender Studies at the University of Vigo, Spain. She has co-edited several volumes on globalization and nationalisms from post-colonial perspectives. Her recent publications include *Transnational Poetics. Asian Canadian Women's Fiction of the 90s*, with Pilar Cuder Domínguez and Sonia Villegas López (Toronto: TSAR, 2011), and the collective volume *Violencias (In)visibles: intervenciones feministas frente a la violencia patriarcal* (Barcelona: Icaria, 2010). She is currently director of the international research project "Globalized Cultural Markets: the Production, Circulation and Reception of Difference," involving eleven universities from Europe, Canada, and Australia.

Index

abjection, 111; women's, 121
abnormality, 110, 120, 121; physical, 111
Aboriginal literary history: Klinck, 22, 23; New, 26, 27. *See also* Aboriginal writing; Indigenous literary criticism; Indigenous literature
Aboriginal peoples, 32, 160, 201, 206; background, 143; communities, 149; cultural genocide of, 160; cultural misrepresentations of, 216; languages, 201; place, 145; theatre, 38. *See also* Indigenous; Native
Aboriginal writing, 19, 20, 29, 34, 37; implied absence of, 24. *See also* Aboriginal literary history; Indigenous literature
Adderson, Caroline, 158. *See also History of Forgetting*
The Aeneid (Virgil), 164, 165
affected cynicism, 168
affective: bond, 166; identification, 165; space, 141
affective memory, 163, 166. *See also* memory
African Canadian: adherence to Canadian soil, 78; culture as international, 78; ethnicity, 83; literature, 11. *See also* Afro-Caribbean; *Any Known Blood*; black; George Elliot Clarke; *Kameleon Man;* mixed race
African diaspora. *See under* diaspora
Afro-Caribbean folklore, 115, 116. *See also* Nalo Hopkinson
After the Fire (Rule), 167, 172
alienation, 99, 118, 152
alieNation, 112, 118, 119
alienness, 120
The Amalgamation Waltz: Race, Performance, and the Ruses of Memory (Nyong'o), 93
ambivalence, 13; Asian Canadian studies and, 45, 52, 56, 57; belatedness and, 67
American Indian Literary Nationalism, 208
The Anatomy of Criticism (Frye): parody of structuralist legacy in, 210. *See also* Thomas King
anthropological space, 144
antiglobalization, 132
Any Known Blood, 77, 81–83, 93, 97, 100; as Künstlerroman, 89; miscegenation in, 93, 94. *See also* African

Canadian ethnicity; Langston Cane the Fifth; miscegenation; mixed race
apostrophe, 45, 58. *See also* Asian Canadian studies
Appadurai, Arjun, 131, 132
Arachne, 6. *See No Fixed Address*
An Archive of Feelings (Cvetkovich), 166
area studies, 46–52. *See also* canonization; curriculum development
Armstrong, Jeannette, 25, 26
Asian American studies, 44, 58–63, 68, 69. *See also* Asian Canadian studies
Asian Canadian, 10; as sign, 43, 62; as term, 44, 45; Vancouver, 152; West Coast communities, 137
Asian Canadian literary studies, 44, 45, 53, 61; institutionalization of, 57, 58, 59, 62; wilderness, in, 67. *See also* curriculum development
Asian Canadian literature, 26, 45, 54–56, 60, 64, 68; fiction, 137; institutionalization of, 67, 70; institutional space for, 71n7; paradigm shifts in, 10; questions raised by, 43; state of, 59, 62; systematic approach to, 63; Vancouver-based, 137. *See also* Asian American studies; Asian Canadian studies; Asian Canadian literary studies; Guy Beauregard; belatedness; Donald Goellnicht
Asian Canadian studies, 43–70; ambivalence and, 45, 52, 56, 57; birth of, 63; calls for institutionalization, 10, 45, 46, 57, 62. *See also* apostrophe; Asian American studies; Asian Canadian literary studies; Asian Canadian literature; Guy Beauregard; Donald Goellnicht
"Asian Canadian Studies: Unfinished Projects" (Beauregard), 10, 44, 45
"Asiancy: Making Space for Asian Canadian Writing" (Roy), 58, 59
Asian diaspora. *See* diaspora

"Asian Kanadian, eh?" (Goellnicht), 10, 45, 64–67
The Assassin's Song (Vassanji), 158
Atwood, Margaret, 20, 29, 39, 59; Centennial Poetry Competition, 23; editorial work, 25, 26; fiction, 30, 219; literary criticism, 3, 19, 21–24. *See also The Oxford Book of Canadian Short Stories in English; The Penelopiad; The Robber Bride; Survival; Wilderness Tips*

Bakhtin, Mikhail, 188
Bannerji, Himani, 30, 109
Barootes, Ben, 121, 122
Baudrillard, Jean, 135
Beauregard, Guy, 10, 45, 53–57, 63, 67; Kogawa criticism, 55, 56. *See also* area studies; "Asian Canadian Studies: Unfinished Projects"; Asian Canadian literary studies; canonization; curriculum development
belatedness: ambivalence and, 67; Asian Canadian literature's, 45, 51, 57, 64, 67–69; cultural inauthenticity and, 14; in literary history, 27; national, 15, 79
Belmore, Rebecca, 132, 137, 143, 152; ethics of otherness, 144; own body in art, 145. *See also* "Vigil"
Beothuk, 183, 184, 190–97; crimes against, 192, 196; extinction of, 184; last, 183. *See also River Thieves*
biotechnology, 115
Bissoondath, Neil, 26, 79
black: Canadian, 23; culture, 92; experience, 88, 89, 92, 101; history, 27, 38, 100; identity, 87; nationalism, 77, 100; subjectivity, 78; writing, 19, 21, 37, 38; West Indian origins, 23. *See also* African Canadian; Afro-Caribbean; mixed race
black diaspora. *See* diaspora

black masculinity, 83, 92, 93, 96; as sexual threat, 93, 96, 97; urban masculinity, 93. *See also* race and gender
blackness, 82, 83, 87, 92; in Canada, 78; commodification of, 90
black resistance, 94; neutralization of, 95; oppression, 100; struggle for liberation, 100
The Blind Assassin (Atwood), 30
Blodgett, E.D., 31, 32
The Book of Negroes (Hill), 158
borders, 199, 200; colonial, 209. *See also* boundaries
"Borders" (King), 199, 221
boundaries, 82, 97. *See also* borders
boutique multiculturalism, 84
Bowering, George, 132, 141–43, 144, 145. *See also* "Standing on Richards"; "Vancouver"
Brand, Dionne. 26, 158. *See also In Another Place, Not Here*, 158
Brant, Beth, 26
Brunhuber, 85, 89, 92, 95, 100; debut novel, 81; dehistoricizing move, 101; focus on race/racialization, 81, 82; history of racialization, 89; mixed-race protagonist, 78; racial hybridity in work, 78; reaction of reviewers, 82. *See also Kameleon Man*; Stacey Schmidt
Brydon, Diana, 6, 9, 11
The Bush Garden (Frye), 23, 207
Butler, Judith, 98, 192; disidentification, 83; loss, 173

The Cambridge History of Canadian Literature (Howells and Kröller), 3, 33, 36–38, 208; premises, 37. *See also* Coral Ann Howells; Eva-Marie Kröller
camouflage, 90, 99, 103
Canada: Centennial, 202; culture, 9, 14; as unimaginable community, 9;
urban nature of, 12. *See also* post-racial Canada
Canadian literary discourses: changes in, 19–39; lack of historical perspective, 12; reshaping of, 20; restructuring of tradition, 19. *See also* Margaret Atwood; canonization; Coral Ann Howells; W.H. New
Canadian literature, 1, 3, 26, 45; ambivalence in, 13; changing perceptions of, 26; conditions of production, 10; constant transitioning of, 9; foreign interest in literary history, 33; frame narratives, 21–30; haunting of, 8; institutionalization of, 22, 23; maturation of, 3; nationalist movement of 1960s–1970s, 2, 21–26; Penelopian nature of, 3–5; post-structuralism and, 4; racialization and, 80; radical reappraisal by New, 26; role of, 4; self-consciousness of, 3, 14; twenty-first-century narratives, 30–38. *See also* Canadian literary discourses; canonization; hauntology, Corall Ann Howell; Smaro Kamboreli; W.H. New; *Survival*
Canadian Literature in English: Texts and Contexts (Sugars and Moss), 32, 33
"Canadian? Literary? Theory?" (Godard), 28
Cane, Langston, the Fifth, 80–84, 87–91, 100; ancestors, 87–89, 93–95; gender codes, 97; mixed race, 82, 97; personal history, 88–89; self-definition, 89, 98. *See also Any Known Blood*; Lawrence Hill; zebra
canon formation. *See* canonization
canonical reformation, 47, 48
canonization, 10, 45, 46–52; nationalist paradigm of, 62; process of, 45, 62, 68. *See also* area studies; cultural nationalism; curriculum

development; discipline; Donald Goellnicht; literary histories; pedagogy
Caron, David, 169, 170
Cavell, Richard, 9, 13, 22
censuses, 102
"The Centennial" (Kröller), 23
Centennial Poetry Competition, 23. *See also* Margaret Atwood
Chafe, Paul, 184
Chariandy, David, 158. *See also Soucouyant*, 158
Chinatown, 135, 140, 141
Cho, Lily, 44, 57, 69, 71n7
Chorus of Mushrooms (Goto), 43
Choy, Wayson, 43. *See also The Jade Peony*
chronicling, 190
citizenship, 147
City of Glass (Coupland), 132, 135–37
Clarke, Austin, 23, 25
Clarke, George Elliott, 78, 97, 100, 101n1; archival cultural nationalism of, 101
Clayton, Barbara, 5
close reading, 45, 46, 69, 70; misreading and, 46
cognitive imperialism, 221
Coleman, Daniel, 10, 23, 80
collective memory, 160
colonialism, 52, 160; frameworks, 14; guilt for, 13; negative effects of, 211. *See also* Otherness
colour-blindness, 77–79, 81, 100, 102n5; dangers and contradictions of, 84; multiculturalism and, 82, 84; politics of, 78. *See also Any Known Blood*; Kim Barry Brunhuber; *Kameleon Man*; multiculturalism; post-racial Canada
commodity fetishism, 51
communal identity, 1
community, 163, 164, 167–70, 173, 174; difference from family, 170;

disidentification, 171; memory, 160; relations, 167, 169; service, 159; West Coast Asian Canadian, 137. *See also* imagined community
confession, 184–86, 188; as aversion to history, 188, 196; in narrative, 191; private and public, 184; res publica and, 169; testimony and, 187
confession narratives, 13, 184, 185, 188; interpretation of, 186
conflicting site, 136
Contract with the World (Rule), 158, 167–71, 172; as satire, 172. *See also* loss
counter-memory, 166
Coupland, Douglas, 132, 136–38. *See also City of Glass*
critical fallacy, 64
critical intimacy, 199
critique of commodity capitalism, 214
Crummey, Michael, 13, 183, 193, 195. *See also River Thieves*
cultural capital, 48, 91
cultural contexts, 2
cultural memory, 9, 12, 20, 148, 158, 176n7; affective memory and, 166; Canadian, 158, 159; constructions of, 20; ecological memory and, 147; embodied, 162; emotion in, 6; formation of, 5; gender, sexuality, identity and, 161; Newfoundland, 195; sexualized, 161, 162, 177n8; in Vancouver, 145. *See also* queer cultural memory; Jane Rule
cultural memory, queer. *See* queer cultural memory. *See also* cultural memory
cultural nationalism, 77, 133; in 1970s, 134; archival, 101; ideology of, 3, 25; mixed-race and, 11; official policies of, 24; utopian nationscape of, 8. *See also* canonization
cultural studies, 50

culture of celebrity, 52
curriculum development, 44, 47, 50, 53, 54. *See also* Asian Canadian literary studies; Guy Beauregard; canonization; Donald Goellnicht
Cvetkovich, Ann, 166, 169. *See also* affective memory; *An Archive of Feelings*
cyborgs, 114, 115, 123, 124; cyborgian, 109; in *Salt Fish Girl*, 113, 114; as "signifiers," 123

Darias-Beautell, Eva, 12
dark humour, 218
The Dark Side of the Nation: Essays on Multiculturalism, Nationalism and Gender, 30
Davey, Frank, 24, 29. *See also Reading Canadian Reading*
Davis, Colin, 6, 7
The Deepening Darkness (Richards), 164
Delany, Paul, 132, 133, 135
Derksen, Jeff, 136
Derrida, Jacques, 13, 15n6, 58, 161, 199; Freud and, 172, 173; hospitality, 220; *mémoire*, 161. *See also* apostrophe; hauntology
Desert of the Heart (Rule), 172
Diamond Grill (Wah), 43
diaspora, 11, 33, 43, 44, 70n3; African, 89, 90, 98, 101; Asian, 44; black, 87, 99. *See also* Rinaldo Walcott
diasporic: approaches, 141; citizenship, 140; displacement, 139; space and black Canada, 78; text, 140; writers, 10, 34
Dikeakos, Chris, 137
Disappearing Moon Café (Lee), 43, 153
disciplinary unconscious, 54
discipline: formation, 50, 56; politics, 54, 63; structures, 50, 54, 60. *See also* canonization
discourse, 116, 121; institutional, 11, 79; liberal, 80; official policy, 24, 71, 116, 119; policy, 24; rhetoric of, 30; state implementation of, 94. *See also* Multiculturalism Act
discrimination, 100
displacement, 3
disruption, 35
"Dis-unity as Unity: A Canadian Strategy" (Kroetsch), 25
diversity, 164; management by nation-state, 47; multiculturalism and, 80, 91, 121; Native cultural, 220
diversity in Canadian literature, 20, 24, 25, 27, 35; *Cambridge History of Canadian Literture*, 36, 37; impact of, 36; John Ralston Saul and, 32; transcultural, 34. *See also* canonization; Otherness
"Dogs in Winter" (Robinson), 201, 216, 218
domesticity, demands of, 183
Downtown Canada (Ivison and Edwards, eds.), 133
Downtown East Side, 143

Edwards, Justin D., and Douglas Ivison, 133
Encyclopedia of Literature in Canada, 32
Engdahl, Horace, 187; Shoshana Felman and, 186
Episkenew, Jo-Ann, 211–12
Espiritu, Yen Le, 61. *See also* pan-ethnicity
estrangement, 98
ethics of embodiment, 145
ethnic minority writing, 22
evil deed, 187, 196
excitable utterance, 192
Expo 67, 202
Eyland, Cliff, 12

Fagan, Christina, 201
Fagan, Kristina, and Sam McKegney, 209
A Fair Country: Telling Truths about Canada (Saul), 32

Fall on Your Knees (MacDonald), 158
False Creek (B.C.), 145
family, 160, 161, 163, 164, 165; narrative line of, 171
Family Frames: Photography, Narrative and Postmemory (Hirsch), 177
Fanon, Frantz, 90, 95
Felman, Shoshana, 195; Horace Engdahl and, 186
feminist gothic. *See* gothic
feminist science fiction, 112
Findley, Timothy, 165. *See also The Wars*
Fish, Stanley, 80
Five-Part Invention: A History of Literary History in Canada, 31
forgetting, 160
Foster, Denis A., 185–88
foundational narratives, ambivalence in, 13
Fraile, Ana María, 10, 11, 77
Freud, Sigmund, 172, 173. *See also* Jacques Derrida
Frye, Northrop, 3, 4, 6, 171, 210; conclusion to Klinck's *History*, 23; framing narrative, 22–24; land-based metaphors, 14; on national culture, 1. *See also An Anatomy of Criticism; The Bush Garden; Literary History of Canada*; wilderness
Fuss, Diana, 88
Future Indicative: Literary Theory and Canadian Literature (Moss, ed.), 25

Gates, Henry Louis, 92
gay community, 159
geometrical space, 144
Gibert, Teresa, 8, 202
gift, 220
Gilligan, Carol, 164
Gilroy, Paul, 80; *Against Race: Imagining Political Culture beyond the Color Line*, 79

global discourses, 147
globalization, 20, 31–33, 36, 109, 121; age of, 120; Asian-Canadian communities, 137; borders and, 8; cultural, 160; diaspora and, 11; economic, 120, 160; national literary history and, 33; trends, 132; ultra-capitalist, 114
Godard, Barbara, 1, 2, 14, 28, 29
Goellnicht, Donald, 45, 46, 53, 57–64, 64–67; call for formation of Asian Canadian Studies, 68, 69; canonization, 67; close reading of, 70; institutionaliation of Asian Canadian literature, 62, 70. *See also* Asian Canadian literature; "Asian Kanadian, eh?"; canonization; "A Long Labour"
Goldchain, Rafael, 162, 163
The Golden Ass (Apuleius), 164, 165, 172, 178
Goldman, Marlene, 7
"Goodbye, Snauq" (Maracle), 132, 145–48, 149; colonial appropriation in, 146
gothic, 109, 110, 118; feminist, 116; post-colonial and post-feminist, 116, 117, 125; postmodern, 123. *See also* grotesque
Goto, Hiromi, 12, 43, 110–17, 122, 123; bodies in, 109, 111; family/community in, 114; myth in, 112; physical abnormality, 111. *See also Chorus of Mushrooms*; "Hopeful Monsters"; *The Kappa Child*; speculative fiction
grassroots education, 203
Gross, Conrad, 34. *See also Kanadische Literaturgeschichte*
grotesque, 117, 119, 121, 123, 124; grotesque gothic, 117. *See also* gothic; *Venous Hum*
"The Group of Sixty-Seven" (Yoon), 132–34

Gynocritics/Gynocritiques: Feminist Approaches to Canadian and Quebec Women's Writing (Godard), 25

Halbwachs, Maurice, 160, 161
hauntology, 6–8, 15n6. *See also* Canadian literature; Jacques Derrida
Highway, Tomson: *Kiss of the Fur Queen*, 158
Hill, Lawrence, 11, 77, 78, 81. *See also Any Known Blood; The Book of Negroes*
Hirsch, Marianne, 177; Valerie Smith and, 162. *See also Family Frames: Photography, Narrative and Postmemory*
historical fiction, 186; family and, 160, 161, 163, 164, 165; narrative line of, 171
history, 186, 187, 189, 194, 195; denormalizing accounts, 185; dynamics of, 185; historiography, 30, 36; local, 141; progress of, 185; purpose of, 187; rupture of meaning, 13; of slavery and diaspora, 98; truth and, 183; uses of in *River Thieves*, 184, 186, 188, 194–96. *See also River Thieves*
A History of Canadian Literature (New), 26
History of Forgetting (Adderson), 158
History of Literature in Canada: English-Canadian and French-Canadian (Nischik, ed.), 33
(homo)sexuali-ties function in, 166
"Hopeful Monsters" (Goto), 110, 111
Hopkinson, Nalo, 12, 109, 114–16, 123. *See also Midnight Robber; Skin Folk*
hospitality, 220
"How Corporal Colin Sterling Saved Blossom, Alberta, and Most of the Rest of the World as Well" (King), 201, 216, 217

Howells, Coral Ann, 3, 9, 15n3, 19–39. *See also The Cambridge History of Canadian Literature*; Eva-Marie Kröller
Hughes, Langston, 81
Hulan, Renée, 14
Hutcheon, Linda, 33; *The Canadian Postmodern: A Study of Contemporary English Canadian Fiction*, 25
hybridity: diasporic, 11; morphological, 113, 114; racial, 78, 86; theories of, 4; threatening, 122
hypercity, 135, 137, 141, 152
hyperreal, 135, 136

I Am My Family (Goldchain), 162, 163
identification with blackness, 98
identity, 158, 166
identity politics, attacking, 168
imagined community, 167, 170. *See also* community
immigrants, 23, 110, 122, 138, 175n2; arrival, 24; dreams, 138; first generation, 110, 133; illegal, 103n8; loss of dignity, 139; nation of, 147; in *Venous Hum*, 119; writers, 29. *See also* alienation; "A Map of the City"; Jane Rule
immigrant urban fictions, 23
In Another Place, Not Here (Brand), 158
Indigeneity, 206
Indigenous: challenges to the Canadian state, 201–3; contemporary culture, 219; literary nationalism, 208; spirituality, 220. *See also* Aboriginal; Native; Bryan Palmer
Indigenous literary criticism, 13, 199, 200, 204–12, 220; history of, 205; literary theorists, 204, 220; literary theory, 219; post-colonial studies, 220; recurring approaches, 205. *See also* Aboriginal literary history;

Aboriginal literature; Thomas King; Indigenous literature; Native literary criticism
Indigenous literature, 13, 199, 200, 212; commodification of stories, 210; nationalism, 205, 208; ways of reading, 206; writing, 199. *See also* Aboriginal writing; Thomas King
inequalities, 147
interdisciplinarity, 8
interracial sex, 93–97; in Canada, 93. *See also* miscegenation; race and sexuality
intertextuality, 200
intimacy, 191, 193, 194. *See also* critical intimacy, 194
Ivison, Douglas, and Justin D. Edwards, 133

The Jade Peony (Choy), 43
Japanese Canadian redress, 43, 107
journal writing, 184, 192–94; confession and, 189; unstable nature of, 193
Justice, Daniel Heath, 208

Kamboureli, Smaro, 4, 9, 10, 11, 43–70; Aboriginal writing, 24; multiculturalism, 80, 108; "scandalous body" as form of dissent, 12; TransCanada Institute, 32. *See also* Asian Canadian literature; Asian Canadian studies; canonization; *Making a Difference: Canadian Multi-cultural Literature*; Roy Miki; *Scandalous Bodies: Diasporic Literature in English Canada*; *Trans.Can.Lit: Resituating the Study of Canadian Literature*
Kameleon Man (Brunhuber), 11, 77–101; history of racialization in, 89; mixed race in, 84–87; social construction of race in, 81, 82. *See also* Kim Barry Brunhuber; mixed race
The Kappa Child (Goto), 111, 112, 113; Tiptree award, 113
Keith, W.J.: *Canadian Literature in English*, 25
Kelly, Jennifer, 199
Keon, Wayne, 26
Kertzer, Jonathan, 29
King, Thomas, 26, 207, 209, 219, 221; commitment to social justice, 211; commodity capitalism critique, 214; essay parodies, 210; four categories of Indigenous literature, 210; literary critiques, 207, 209–11; Native literature and, 209; post-colonial theory, 209, 211; satirizing stereotypical notions of "the Indian," 201; subversive use of magic realism, 212. *See also* "Borders"; "How Corporal Colin Sterling Saved Blossom, Alberta, and Most of the Rest of the World as Well"; *One Good Story, That One*; postcolonial; "Trap Lines"; *The Truth about Stories*
Kiss of the Fur Queen (Highway), 158
Kiyooka, Roy, 64–67, 69
Klanak Press, 167
Klinck, Carl F., 26, 28, 35, 40n3; framing narratives, 22–23; thematic criticism of, 24; treatment of Aboriginal cultures, 22. *See also Literary History of Canada*
Kloos, Wolfgang, 34. *See also Kanadische Literaturgeschichte*
Kogawa, Joy, 25, 43, 53, 59, 153n5. *See also* Guy Beauregard; *Obasan*
Kroetsch, Robert, 25, 35. *See also* "Disunity as Unity: A Canadian Strategy"
Kröller, Eva-Marie, 3, 23, 36. *See also The Cambridge History of Canadian Literature*; Coral Ann Howells

Kuokkanen, Rauna, 199, 200, 220. *See also Reshaping the University: Responsibility, Indigenous Epistemes, and the Logic of the Gift*

LaCapra, Dominick, 195
Lacombe, Michèle, 13, 14
Lai, Larissa, 12, 43, 44, 69, 107, 108, 109, 123; criticism of late capitalism, 114; mythical characters, 112, 113; use of speculative fiction, 110. *See also Salt Fish Girl; When Fox Is a Thousand*
land-based national identity, 12, 14. *See also* Northrop Frye
LaRocque, Emma, 206–7, 220
Lecker, Robert, 2, 12
Lee, Chris, 44, 57, 69
Lee, SKY, 43, 153n5. *See also Disappearing Moon Café*
"Legally Single" (Rule), 173
Lerena, María Jesús Hernáez, 13, 183
Lesbian Images (Rule), 158
lieux de mémoire model, 161, 163. *See also* memory
literary community, 167
literary contexts, 2
literary histories, 4, 20–39; boundary shifts, 39; challenge of diversity, 20, 25, 26; cultural memory and, 20; fractured nature, 36; genre of, 27; Indigenous, 9; national literary history, 33, 39; paradigm crisis, 28, 29; pluralist constructions of, 32; production of, 9; questions around, 20–21; radical reappraisal, 26; revisionist impulse, 20, 32. *See also* Margaret Atwood; canonization; cultural memory; Northrop Fry; Coral Ann Howells; W.H. New
Literary History of Canada: Canadian Literature in English (Klinck), 22, 26, 207, 208; 4th edition, 27, 208;

Native literature issues, 208. *See also* W.H. New
locality, 135, 140, 146; representation of, 148; simulation of, 136, 137. *See also* locality, production of
locality, production of, 132, 137, 138, 141–45, 147, 152; normative production of, 148; processes of, 134, 148
"A Long Labour: The Protracted Birth of Asian Canadian Literature" (Goellnicht), 10, 45, 57–64. *See also* canonization
loss, 160, 164, 166, 169, 173; as agency, 174; Beothuk and, 184, 185; of country, 140; of dignity, 139; discovery of, 163; globalization and, 120; guilt and, 13, 185; mourning and, 172; permanent, 13; in *Survival*, 24; traumatic, 163. *See also* mourning; queer mourning
Loss: The Politics of Mourning, 173
Loving the Difficult (Rule), 173

MacDonald, Anne Marie: *Fall on Your Knees*, 158
Making a Difference: Canadian Multicultural Literature (Kamboureli), 30
"A Map of the City" (Thien), 132, 138–41, 147; emotional map in, 138, 141
Maracle, Lee, 132, 145–49; critique of citizenship inequality, 147; cultural memory in, 148. *See also* "Goodbye, Snauq"
The Marais and the Queerness of Community (Caron), 169
marginalization, 25, 31
Marlatt, Daphne, 137
Martín-Lucas, Belén, 10, 11
master narratives, dismantling of, 10
Mayr, Suzette, 12, 109, 116, 117, 123. *See also Moon Honey; Venous Hum*
McCallum, Pamela, 6

McConnell, William, 167
McMaster, Gerald, 144
mémoire, 161. *See also* Jacques Derrida
memory, 157, 159–62, 166; affective, 163, 166; ecological, 147; embodied, 6, 13; identity politics, 176; *lieux de mémoire* model, 161, 163; Lee Maracle and, 148; mediation and, 160; monolithic, 158; multiculturalism, 176; questions of, 160; Romantic inheritance, 163; studies, 160. *See also* cultural memory; national memory; queer cultural memory
Memory Board (Rule), 158, 172
memory, community. *See* community memory, cultural. *See* cultural memory
metamorphosis, 11, 99, 116, 122. *See also Moon Honey*; mutation; shape-shifting; skin-stripping; transmutation; transnational feminist fiction
Midnight Robber (Hopkinson), 115
Miki, Roy, 9, 44, 58, 59, 65, 68. *See also* "Asiancy: Making Space for Asian Canadian Writing"; Smaro Kamboureli; *Trans.Can.Lit: Resituating the Study of Canadian Literature*
Miller, Bernie, and Alan Tregebov, 12, 132. *See also Street Light*
mimetic fallacy, 55, 56
minoritized communities, 43, 47, 60, 64
minoritized literatures, 48, 63, 67, 69
minority writers, 25, 29
miscegenation, 93, 94, 97; history of, 93, 98. *See also* interracial sex; mixed race; race and sexuality
misreading, 46. *See also* close reading
misrecognitions, 164, 176
Mistry, Rohinton, 25, 29
mixed race, 11, 77–101; aesthetics, 11; ambiguous position, 82; black nationalism and, 11; Canadian identity and, 11, 77; cultural refraction, 80; diasporic hybridity and, 11; exclusion, 81; male body, 78, 97; mulatto, 83, 84, 86; multiracialism and, 86; subject, 81; subjectivities, 77, 78, 99; as transnational, 11; unease, 85. *See also Any Known Blood*; colour-blindness; *Kameleon Man*; miscegenation; multiracialism; post-racial; Stacey Schmidt; zebra
model blackness, 91, 98
Monkey Beach (Robinson), 158
monstrosity, 120, 122; female, 122. *See also* gothic; grotesque
Moon Honey (Mayr), 116, 117. *See also* metamorphosis
Mosionier, Beatrice Culleton, 25
Moss, John, 25
Moss, Laura, 32. *See also Canadian Literature in English: Texts and Contexts*; Cynthia Sugars
mourning, 171–73; Aborigines, 185; Derrida and, 172–73; Freud and, 172–73; loss and, 172; post-colonial, 185; Rule and, 176. *See also* loss
Mukherjee, Arun: *Postcolonialism: My Living*, 29
mulatto. *See* mixed race
multiculturalism, 20, 21, 80, 82–84, 88, 108–10; in *Any Known Blood*, 89; boutique multiculturalism, 80, 84; colour-blindness, 82–84; context, 32; discourse of, 121; diversity and, 80, 91, 121; first policy, 24; fractures in, 82; institutional, 12, 79; in *Kameleon Man*, 91; language of, 109; memory and, 176; official policies, 10, 71n8, 79, 82, 102n5, 116, 119; racialized space, 78; rhetoric of, 30; state implementation, 93; understood through minority writing, 29; writing, 37
Multiculturalism Act, 25, 40n8, 78, 107, 108

multiracialism, 86, 87, 100; anti-blackness of, 87; exceptionalism and, 102. *See also* mixed race; multiculturalism
Munro, Alice, 151. *See also* "Royal Beatings"
mutation, 115, 116, 122. *See also* metamorphosis; shape-shifting; skin-stripping; transmutation

narrative of failure, 139
narrative tradition, nature of, 2
narratives, public and transcendent, 189
national culture, 1, 2, 6, 10, 132; articulations of, 1, 6; Canadian literature and, 24; literary tradition and, 31; metanarrative and, 31. *See also* Canadian literature; Northrop Frye; national identity
national identity, 2, 14; anxieties about, 29; decentralization of, 3; deconstruction of, 4, 6; myths of, 6; nationalism, 24, 29; paradigms of, 2, 3. *See also* Penelopian metaphor
nationalism, Canadian, 201, 202, 208, 210. *See also* Canadian literature; canonization
national literature, 14, 21, 49, 67; boundaries, 39; conditions of production, distribution, reception, 14; literary traditions and, 46; what constitutes, 29
national memory, 160. *See also* memory
nationhood, multicultural post-colonial, 28
nation-state, 33, 49, 52, 60, 121; abstract, 132; borders of, 50; globalization and, 132; hegemonic, 47; locality and, 148; multiculturalism and, 108; normative view of, 59; strategies of containment, 52
nation-state and literature, 12, 43, 55, 59, 65; Asian Canadian literature and, 68; national imaginary, 59; Jane Rule, 13, *Tish* work, 66, 134. *See also* Donald Goellnicht; Roy Kiyooka
Native issues, 202
Native literary criticism, 201, 204, 206. *See also* Aboriginal literature; Indigenous literary criticism
Native literature, relation of Western genres and traditions to, 208
Native stereotypes, 207
New, W.H., 26–29, 32–34. *See also* Canadian literature; canonization; *A History of Canadian Literature*
new historicism, 56
The New Oxford Book of Canadian Short Stories in English (1995), 26
Nischik, Reingard M., 32–36. *See also* Conrad Gross; *History of Literature in Canada: English-Canadian and French-Canadian*; *Kanadische Literaturgeschichte*; Wolfgang Kloos
No Fixed Address (van Herk), 5, 6
Nora, Pierre, 160, 161
nostalgia, 139
Nyong'o, Tavia, 93. *See also The Amalgamation Waltz: Race, Performance, and the Ruses of Memory*

Obasan (Kogawa), 43, 56, 59, 72n16, 153n5; centrality in Asian Canadian canon, 54, 69
The Odyssey, 5
Olympics, 136, 137, 146
Ondaatje, Michael, 25
One Good Story, That One (King), 200
one-drop rule, 81, 102
Otherness, 31, 47, 69, 112, 141; Belmore's ethics of, 144; Canadian culture and, 8; colonial frameworks and, 14; monstrous Other, 120, 122; sexual otherness, 165
The Oxford Book of Canadian Short Stories in English (Atwood and Weaver), 25, 26

palimpsest, 147, 148
Palmer, Bryan, 202
pan-ethnicity, 61. *See also* Yen Le Espiritu
pan-Indian nationalism, 201, 203
paradigms, 5, 9, 63, 220; Asian Canadian literature and, 10, 45, 58; Canadian history, 23; centrality, 59; crisis, 28; global, 14; literary, 4; locality, 136; national, 2, 3, 11, 62; old, 28; post-colonial, 120; post-structuralist, 4; shifting, 1, 10, 11, 45; understanding, 184; use/abuse, 63
paradox, 187
Patterson, Orlando, 79
pedagogy, 44, 56. *See also* canonization
Penelope, 5
The Penelopiad (Atwood), 5, 15
Penelopian: formation of cultural memory and, 5; metaphor, 4, 5, 6; mode of criticism, 14; process, 3–6. *See also* cultural memory; paradigm
Phelan, Peggy, 173
place: absence of, 147; social construction of, 12
plurality and inclusiveness, 100
politics of representation, 43, 51
post-colonial, 109, 110, 116, 136, 206, 209; critical circles, 211; national ethos, 147; studies, 208, 220; theory, 208, 211, 221. *See also* gothic
post-colonialism, 2, 20, 21, 30, 33; post-coloniality, 43, 47
post-Indian, 205, 216–19
postmodern city, 135
postmodernism, 21
post-national identifications, 158
post-racial Canada, 77, 79, 86. *See also* colour-blindness
post-racial discourse: fallacy of, 11
production of locality. *See* locality, production of
production of meaning, 142
public testimony. *See* testimony writing

queer, 13, 159, 162, 164–66, 173; Canadians, 167–74; community, 168–69, 171; identification and identity, 166; queerness, 13. *See also* community; queer cultural memory; Jane Rule
queer cultural memory, 13, 158, 162–64, 169; trauma of, 166. *See also* cultural memory
queer mourning, 174. *See also* Jane Rule. *See also* mourning
queer sexuality, 165, 166; the state and, 159

race: as aesthetic, 85; social construction of, 81. *See also* entries following *and* mixed race
race and gender, 77, 80, 93–97
race and sexuality, 93–97; black male as sexual threat, 93, 96; masculinity, 81; stereotypes, 96. *See also* interracial sex; miscegenation
racial hybridity, 78. *See also* mixed race
racialization, 10, 70n3, 86, 120, 121; Asian Canadian literature and, 55; of Canadian society, 81; denial of, 78; evolution of, 86; historical dimensions of, 87–93; increasing, 80; Otherness, 47; persistent, 108; race and, 82; and Stacey Schmidt, 80–87. *See also Any Known Blood*; Langston Cane the Fifth; colour-blindness; *Kameleon Man*; Otherness; racism, 77; Stacey Schmidt; zebra poetics
racial self-identification, 102. *See also* blackness; mixed race
racism, 77, 79, 82, 85, 91; consumer culture and, 85–86; dehumanization and, 92. *See also* racialization
Reading Canadian Reading (Davey), 24
representation of locality. *See* locality, representation of

Reshaping the University: Responsibility, Indigenous Epistemes, and the Logic of the Gift (Kuokkanen), 199
Rethinking Literary History: A Dialogue on Theory (Hutcheon and Valdés), 36
Ricci, Nino, 29
Richards, David A.J., 164. *See also The Deepening Darkness*
River Thieves (Crummey), 13, 183–97; confession in, 196; core historical events in, 189; diary, 193; journal writing, 184; last Beothuk, 183, 184; narrative communication, 184; plot summary, 189; testimony writing in, 185. *See also* Beothuk; confession; history; testimony writing; witnessing
The Robber Bride (Atwood), 10, 19, 20, 30, 39
Robinson, Eden, 158, 209, 218, 219; satirizing stereotypical notions of "the Indian," 201. *See also* "Dogs in Winter"; *Monkey Beach*; "Traplines"
rootlessness, 141. *See also Kameleon Man*
"Royal Beatings" (Munro), 151
Ruffo, Armand, 203–4, 207, 209
Rule, Jane, 13, 157, 167–74; books, 172; cultural memory, 158; lesbian identity, 158; mourning and, 171. *See also Contract with the World; Desert of the Heart; Lesbian Images; Loving the Difficult; Memory Board; The Young in One Another's Arms*

Salt Fish Girl (Lai), 111, 113, 114. *See also* cyborgs
same-sex marriage, 177
Saul, Joanne, 7
Saul, John Ralston, 32. *See also A Fair Country: Telling Truths about Canada*
Scandalous Bodies: Diasporic Literature in English Canada (Kamboureli), 30
"scandalous body" as dissent, 12

Schmidt, Stacey, 80–87, 89, 90–93, 96; authenticity, 84; black identity, 98–100; camouflage, 90; commodification of, 82, 95; desire for self-definition, 90; experience as mixed race, 81, 84–87, 97; racialized world of, 97. *See also* Kim Barry Brunhuber; *Kameleon Man*; racialization
science fiction, feminist. *See* feminist science fiction
sculpture, 149; as cancellation device, 151. *See also Street Light*
self-consciousness, 14
Senna, Danzy, 86
sexuality, 158, 163. *See also* racialization
sexual politics of comic structure, 171
shape-shifting, 109, 113, 116, 120, 123; shape-shifter, 109, 115. *See also* hybridity; mixed race; skin-stripping
Shuster, Marilyn, 168
signifying monkey, 92, 96
silence, meaning of, 13
simulacra, 135
simulation of locality. *See* locality, simulation of
Skin Folk (Hopkinson), 115–16. *See also* shape-shifting
skin-stripping, 110, 120. *See also* shape-shifting
Smith, Les W., 186, 188
Soucouyant (Chariandy), 158
space, 141, 144, 138; social production of, 134
speculative fantasy, 111
speculative fiction, 11, 107, 109, 110, 123; metamorphosis in, 12
spirituality, 209, 216
Spivak, Gayatri, 8
Springgay, Stephanie, 144
"Standing on Richards" (Bowering), 132, 141–43
statist community, 169

statist ideology of family, 167
stereotypes, 177, 201; of Native people, 207; racial and sexual, 92, 96
The Stone Carvers (Urquhart), 157
storytelling, 22, 91, 140, 147, 148, 201; emotional conditions and, 187
strategic essentialisms, 80
Street Light (Miller and Tregebov), 132, 148–51, 153
Sugars, Cynthia, 7, 8, 32, 184, 194. *See also* Canadian Literature in English: Texts and Contexts; haunting; Laura Moss
Survival: A Thematic Guide to Canadian Literature (Atwood), 2–4, 21–24, 62
Surviving the Paraphrase (Davey), 24
symbolic dimensions of locality building, 152
synthesis, 205
Szeman, Imre, 14

Taylor, Charles, 164
termination views, 12
testimony: failed, 194; literature, 186; narratives, 188; private confession and, 195
testimony writing, 184–87, 189, 191, 195, 197; public, 194. *See also River Thieves*
Teuton, Christopher, 204, 205
therapeutic narrative, 194
Thien, Madeleine, 44, 132. *See also* "A Map of the City"
Tish group, 66; 134. *See also* literature and the nation-state; nation-state tradition, deconstructive approach to, 6. *See also* loss
Trans.Can.Lit: Resituating the Study of Canadian Literature (Kamboureli and Miki), 9
transformational stories, 212
transmutation, 122. *See also* metamorphosis; mutation; shape-shifting; skin-stripping

transnational feminist fiction, 11; strategies of dissent, 11, 107–24
transnationalism, 29, 32, 33, 39, 166; trans-nationality, 100
transraciality, 100
"Trap Lines" (King), 201, 212, 213, 215; counter-narratives in, 201; education in, 215; love and loss in, 214; marginalization, 201; modernity in, 201; point of view in, 212; "realist" humour of, 212
"Traplines" (Robinson), 200, 201, 214–16; counter-narratives in, 201; education in, 213, 215; marginalization, 201; modernity in, 201; synopsis, 213–14; youth's point of view, 212
Trasco, Mike, 167
trauma, 164, 166, 169, 172; belatedness, 51; celebrated, 169; Canadian foundational, 185; of loss, 163
Tregebov, Alan, and Bernie Miller, 132. *See also Street Light*
trickster, 201, 206, 217, 218, 222; motifs in "Sterling" and "Dogs," 201
trickster studies, 201, 205
The Truth about Stories: A Native Narrative (King), 209–11

unhomely, 120
urban belonging: special modes of, as produced by literature and art, 12
urbanization, 146. *See also* Vancouver
urban life, perception of, 133
Urquhart, Jane. 157. *See also The Stone Carvers*

vampire, 115, 117–19, 123. *See also Venous Hum*
Vancouver, 131, 134–36, 138, 140, 141, 167; Aboriginal place, 148; archival city, 145–48; in art, 137, 152; artists, 134; Asian Canadian nature of, 152; collapsing space, 138; colonial past,

141; conflicting representations of, 152; contested zones, 151; development of, 152; discordant views of, 12; economic structure, 135, 136; in fiction, 137, 152; growth of, 132, 146; historical vision of, 148; idealized views of, 12, 132, 145; representation of, 12, 131, 134; social cohesiveness of, 12; stage or simulacrum, 137; transformation of, 149; urban experience of, 134; writers, 134
van Herk, Aritha, 5, 6
Vassanji, M.G., 25, 29. *See also The Assassin's Song*
Venous Hum (Mayr), 117, 118. *See also* grotesque; vampires
"Vigil" (Belmore), 132, 143–45
Vizenor, Gerald, 205, 206, 218

Wacquant, Pierre, 79
Wah, Fred, 43, 44, 64–67, 69. *See also Diamond Grill*
Walcott, Rinaldo, 78; diasporic sensibility and, 78, 101. *See also* diaspora
The Wars (Findlay), 165–66
Weaver, Robert, 26. *See also The Oxford Book of Canadian Short Stories in English*

web of relationships, 219, 220
Weeks, Jeffrey, 163, 164
When Fox Is a Thousand (Lai), 43, 112, 113. *See also* shape-shifting
white civility, 10, 11, 23
Whitehead, Anne, 161, 162
White Paper, 203
wilderness, 21, 23, 62, 133, 134; national identity and, 3, 8, 21. *See also* Northrop Frye
Wilderness Tips (Atwood), 30
Willis, Susan, 86, 102
witnessing, 189–94. *See also River Thieves*
Worrying the Nation, 29
writing, Aboriginal. *See* Aboriginal writing, 19

Yoon, Jin-me, 133, 152. *See also* "Group of Sixty-Seven"
The Young in One Another's Arms (Rule), 172, 174

zebra, 82, 83, 101; zebra incorporated, 84, 98; zebra poetics, 77. *See also Any Known Blood*; Langston Cane; *Kameleon Man*; mixed race; Stacey Schmidt